**Banish those words "If only I had known!" from your vocabulary forever with this smart, savvy compendium to daily living.**

**Bet you didn't know . . .**

   o Salt, lemon juice, white vinegar, and baking soda can be used as environment-friendly household cleaners.

   o You can prevent stove spills from burning by pouring salt over the spill while cooking. When cool, wipe up.

   o To cut the risk of prostate cancer by a whopping 34 percent, think "red," as in two to four servings of tomato sauce a week.

   o You can use a clean soft-bristle paintbrush to dust pleats on a lamp shade.

   o When applying to colleges for scholarships and financial aid, you should look beyond the brand-name colleges and also apply to a variety of public and private schools for a wider range of offers.

   o Apples lose flavor and firmness about ten times faster at room temperature, so store them in the refrigerator.

Plus, *Bet You Didn't Know* features cooking substitutions when you're in a pinch, decorating do's and don'ts, catering the perfect party, pulling together a profitable yard sale, handling legal matters, preventing heart disease, selling or buying a house, and *much, much more!*

# Bet You Didn't Know

Smart Answers for Every

Aspect of Your Life

**ROBYN FREEDMAN SPIZMAN**

Ballantine Books
New York

A Ballantine Book
Published by The Ballantine Publishing Group

Copyright © 2000 by Robyn Freedman Spizman Literary Works, L.L.C.

All rights reserved under International
and Pan-American Copyright Conventions. Published
in the United States by Ballantine Books, a division of Random
House, Inc., New York, and simultaneously in Canada
by Random House of Canada Limited, Toronto.

Ballantine and colophon are trademarks of Random House, Inc.

www.randomhouse.com/BB/

LIBRARY OF CONGRESS CATALOGING-IN-PUBLICATION DATA
Spizman, Robyn Freedman.
Bet you didn't know : smart answers for every aspect of your everyday life /
Robyn Freedman Spizman.—1st ed.
p.   cm.
ISBN 0-449-00337-X (alk. paper)
1. Life skills—United States—Handbooks, manuals, etc. 2. Consumer
education—United States—Handbooks, manuals, etc.  I. Title.
HQ2039.U6   S65   2000
646.7—dc21                                              99-047557

Text design by Holly Johnson
Cover design by Ruth Ross
Cover photo of author by Keiko Guest

Manufactured in the United States of America

First Edition: January 2000

10   9   8   7   6   5   4   3   2

To you, the reader, I dedicate this book.
For no matter where you roam
Don't fall into the age-old trap . . .
If I had only known.

DISCLAIMER

This book is designed to provide general information in regard to the subject matters covered. At the time of initial publication, all of the information is believed to be accurate; however, some or all of the information is subject to change from time to time. No warranties or representations with respect to the information provided are made and neither the publisher nor the author is engaged in rendering expert advice or professional services or shall be liable for any loss or damage to persons or property arising from the use of this book. The reader should obtain the services of a competent professional to discuss his or her specific situation when using the general information published in this book, since each reader's individual needs may be different.

# Contents

# Acknowledgments

My appreciation goes first and foremost to my wonderful husband, Willy, for his invaluable assistance and support. To our children, Justin and Ali, whom we learn from daily and who continue to be our very best teachers. To my parents, Phyllis and Jack Freedman, who still give the best advice of all, and to Doug, Genie, Sam, and Gus, who are the best cheerleaders anyone could ever have. To Bettye Storne and Mary Billingsley for their endless help and guidance, and to my wonderful family and group of friends who encourage and inspire me daily.

Writing a book of this magnitude couldn't have been done without the help of an endless team of tireless researchers and experts who cared enough to share what they knew and believed would be helpful to others. My warmest thanks goes to the following individuals, who through their commitment to doing uncompromising work are the best and brightest at what they do in life. First, my unending thanks goes to my literary agent, Meredith Bernstein, who continues to listen to my every idea and thought. Her encouragement and friendship continue to be the steadfast reasons I am so prolific. Second, to my dedicated editors, Elizabeth Zack, who bravely stepped in and valiantly took this project to completion, and Elisa Wares, who gave me the inspiration to write this book and uncover every imaginable tip on earth. Their wonderful assistance will always be appreciated.

My unending thanks also goes to my outstanding group of writers and researchers, who strove to leave no stone unturned: Sandy Amann John, Linda Frysh, Laura Raines, Lisa K. Mowry, Ashley Sparks, Rebeca Racofzy, Leslie Brice, Paige Trager Janco, and Anna Hemphill. And to the following experts who contributed information, opinions, and helpful tips that I hope will guide you down the path of "bet you didn't knows!" My thanks to: Alane Mackay, The Association of Home Appliance Manufacturers, Jack Morton,

Indulgence Salon, Kelly Carney, The Spizman Agency, Joni Alpert, Mary Ann Snider, Car Care Council, Peggy Glazener, Marty Benton, Jarosz Associates Inc., Don Hutcheson, Bob McDonald, the Highlands Program, Karin Koser, Egleston Children's Healthcare System, Leone Ackerly Hinzman, Mini Maids, Diane Cardinale, Toy Manufacturers of America, Janice Gams, the College Board, Patrick L. Bellantoni, Bellantoni Financial Advisory Inc, Dr. Mark L. Fisher, Kevin Crossman, *The Princeton Review*, Jadwiga Sebrechts, Women's College Coalition, Jean P. Hague, Carol R. Delucca, Linda B. Schulz, Galloway School, Missy Sanchez, Woodward Academy, Eileen Tropauer, M.A., Edward Smith, the Better Business Bureau of Metro Atlanta, Barbara Roos, Event Design Group, David Galusha, Marla Shavin, Brian Molinet, Barbecues Galore, Dr. Don Schaffner, Rutgers University, Walter Reeves, Dekalb Co., Cooperative Extension Service, Dr. Michael Randell, Northside OB/GYN, P.C., UGA, Dr. Irving Miller, Dr. Ronald Goldstein, Dr. David Garber, Goldstein, Garber, Salama & Gribble, D.D.S., P.A., Dr. Winston Gandy, the Atlanta Cardiology Group, P.C., Dianne Knapp, World Inspection Network, Ken Austin, Tony Conway, CMP, Legendary Events, Earl D. Tillman, State Mutual Insurance Company, Bob Bradshaw, Cecil D. Dorsey, American Insurance Association, Insurance Information Institute, David J. Comans, Georgia Insurance Information Service, National Association of Life Underwriters, Richard Coorsh, Health Insurance Association of America, Julie Senzig, National Kitchen & Bath Association, Michael Weinstock, Esq., Steven M. Winter, Esq., Weinstock & Scavo, P.C., Steve F. Freedman, Kay R. Shirley, Ph.D., CFP, Ten Speed Press, Titan Value Equities Group Inc., Drs. Stephen and Marianne Garber, Adrian Grant, Aarons, Grant & Habif, P.C., Bruce Weinstein, CLU, George M. Fox, P.C., George E. Bennett, James M. Peters, Georgia Power Company, the American Cancer Society, Dr. Alan Sunshine, Dr. Peter Gordon, Dr. Winkler G. Weinberg, Dr. Arthur Simon, Dr. Mitchell J. Ghen, Dr. Dennis L. Spangler, Dr. Richard Sturm, Kimberly Segale, American Moving and Storage Association, Carla Lovell, Jill Rubino, the American Academy of Pediatrics, Nell Tillis, DVM, Michael Walters, American Veterinary Medical Association, Robert B. Wilensky, Wilensky & Co., P.C., Betsy Wilkowsky, Lorie Lewis,

Patty Brown, the Organized Executive, Stephanie Denton, Denton & Company, Judy Udwin, Susan Lurie, the Sophisticated Traveler, Sue Winner, Bruce Morris, Esq., Morris & Finestone, P.C., Andy Siegel, Jerry Siegel, Siegel Insurance Inc., Christopher Owens, CIC, Jeff McCart, CPCU, ARM, McCart Insurance and Risk Management, Theodore Hersh, M.D., Thione International, Lisa Carlson, Executive Director, FAMSA, Elizabeth Kloss, Memorial Society of Georgia, Alex Rodgers, Arlington Memorial Park, Hospice, Arlington Memorial Cemetery, Phil Faulkner, H. M. Patterson & Son, Arlington Chapel, Geraldine Askenazie, Rosy McGillan, National Safe Kids Campaign, Tracy Green, Marla Shavin, Genie Freedman, R. S. Owen & Co. Realtors, Elliott Farmer, Wayne Freedman, Ed Hansen, MindSpring, Deloria Howard, Terri Zieve, Ava Wilensky, Betty Sunshine, Carla Lovell, Shirley Retter, Helen Cauley, Lori Simon, Norma Gordon, Gail Heyman, Donna Weinstock, Cheryl Isaacs, Nancy Freedman, Suzi Brozman, Kristine Bernhard, Micheall Bonilla, Joan Alexander, Rick Doble, $avvy Discount$ Newsletter, Arlene Hoffman, Lois and Jerry Blonder, Ramona and Ely Freedman, Laurie Selzer, and Keiko Guest.

# Introduction

*If only I had known!* Familiar words repeated by many of us who have made a costly error or discovered a vital bit of information when it was simply too late. The fact is, *what we don't know can hurt us.*

We all want to manage our money wisely, feel protected, simplify our lives, make smart purchases and good decisions, and avoid life's little and sometimes very big disasters. Yet, when we're twenty years old, who's thinking about life insurance even though the premiums are drastically less expensive? Or, when we're forty and fifty and begin worrying about retirement, why weren't we more concerned about our 401(k)s and saving when we were younger?

But how many of us went to Consumer U. or graduated with a degree in risk management or financial planning? How many of us took Life 101 in college and know all there is to know about being an up-to-date consumer? And how many of us think about the next step before the next step arrives?

Whatever motivated you to pick up this book and read it, keep one thing in mind: If you've been taken advantage of or ripped off, wasted time, money, or energy, you are far from being alone. I decided to write *Bet You Didn't Know* because day after day in my role as a consumer advocate, busy mom, author, and information addict, I discovered hundreds of easier, quicker, and safer ways to go about doing most things. From everyday knowledge about home and family to overwhelming challenges like consumer fraud, I found there was a wealth of information that isn't always readily available to us. To find the life-enhancing answers, I consulted a vast network of experts, from consumer advocates to doctors and lawyers.

It is hoped that this book will save you hundreds of headaches. For the past sixteen years as a network consumer advocate, I have educated hundreds of thousands of viewers on how to find a bargain, save time, avoid losing money, and even get organized! Time and time again, I discovered how many innocent people—including me—fell into bad habits, problems, and the same old traps.

Like anyone out there who has experienced a few of life's lessons, it occurred to me that no one prepares us for the "what-ifs" along the way. We're taught to trust people and do the right thing. While I still believe that people are more often honest than not, what we think we hear isn't always so. Getting a copy of what you're promised in writing is still the best advice on earth, no matter who you are doing business with, including friends and family members. And when in doubt, check it out! There are countless professionals much smarter than you and me who can help us protect ourselves.

Even though I have met my share of charming con artists, the difference now is that I don't have to give up protecting myself just because I like or trust someone. Searching for the things you just might not know, asking questions, and doing your homework are the keys to consumer success. And if you take the time to educate yourself about most situations you are entering, you can prevent costly and emotionally wrenching occurrences in your life.

*Bet You Didn't Know* arms you with knowledge as it addresses a gamut of topics, from the tried-and-true to scams, shams, and consumer nightmares. My single goal in this book is to help you realize that there are smarter, better, brighter answers to everyday living. You don't have to live in fear of the "what-ifs" or be the next victim on the block. You can get up to speed in every area of your life and empower yourself with smarter ways to manage your affairs.

Today there are over 150 Better Business Bureaus in the United States and Canada, receiving more than 14 million consumer contacts nationwide each year. Even with these impressive statistics, there are millions more consumers who are scammed and never know what to do or what they could have done to have prevented their predicament.

According to Edward Smith, president of the Better Business Bureau of Metro Atlanta, "The top complaints nationwide deal with automobile dealers, auto repair shops, and mail-order products. Furthermore, the top ten categories of extensive problems include work-at-home get-rich-quick schemes (i.e., stuffing envelopes for $2,500 a month), home remodeling contractors, roofing and gutter services, miscellaneous [services] from carpet cleaning to air duct cleaning, home construction, auto repair shops, franchised auto dealers, telephone companies (local and long distance), mortgage and escrow companies, and moving and storage companies."

Don't expect people to be smarter than you; it's up to you to get up to speed. While you don't have to get a contractor's license, reading books on the topic of building a house, checking out Web sites on the subject, and talking to experts from A to Z only empowers you to get more for your money and, it is hoped, what you pay for! And remember this—Fooled me once, shame on you . . . fooled me twice . . . shame on me!

While most of the following information in this book was gleaned from a variety of experts in their fields, some of the best tips I discovered were found buried in someone's regret, the kinds of things that cost them the most money, time, and aggravation. When I asked these people where they think they went wrong, more often than not they totally trusted someone (including friends and family members), were too busy and anxious to get a contractor going, felt they hired a professional so they should let him do his job, worried they'd upset someone, or just failed to read and understand a contract. None of these smart individuals ever thought they'd be taken advantage of or have to hire a lawyer to get them out of a problem they didn't deserve in the first place.

Keep in mind that consumer information and laws change regularly, so please use this book as a runway to getting the facts for your individual problem. Every situation is different, and looking before leaping might be an old adage, but it definitely deserves twenty-first-century status. Ask questions, read every word, and get a professional opinion and then a second opinion. Find out the most up-to-date or invasive way to do something. Become your own best advocate and take charge. Listen to your gut if you're ever in doubt. Don't sign until you understand everything, right down to the bottom line!

*"The important thing is not to stop questioning.*
*Curiosity has its own reason for existing."*
—ALBERT EINSTEIN

# Appliances

Has it ever occurred to you that *appliance* rhymes with *science?* There is a science to buying the right appliance. Don't let that thought scare you. This is a science that requires more common sense than rocket science.

As in making any major purchase, do some research before you buy any appliance. Read up on appliances, get to know what's available, then decide what you really need. A good place to start your research is the annual *Consumer Reports Buying Guide*, which usually has chapters dealing with both large and small household appliances. Here you'll find a listing of manufacturers' popular features found in these appliances and results of tests on how the appliances operated in the real world. The Association of Home Appliance Manufacturers maintains a Web page at www.aham.org that also contains lots of useful information.

Your next stop should be at an appliance store—not to buy, but to do further research, such as getting information on various models available. Take this home and study it carefully. You'll quickly discover that most appliances come in a wide range of prices, with those at the low end having few convenience features and those at the high end having a collection of bells and whistles designed to make your life easier. Do you need all those features now? Will you require them in the future? Appliances are expensive to buy and install, so it makes sense to select ones that meet the needs of your family as it grows.

Caring for appliances isn't rocket science, either, but again it may take a little effort on your part. Consider how baffling all those wires and electrical parts will look when the machine is on the blink. Your owner's manual can be your best friend, and you should familiarize yourself with it before you actually use your appliance.

Most of us depend on a wide range of gadgets to help us get through our daily life. You want those appliances to be convenient and worry-free. These tips from experts in the appliance industry and from consumers can guide you in the science of appliance buying.

## Shopping for an Appliance

○ Your appliance dealer has copies of specification sheets from several manufacturers who build the kind of appliance you are look-ing for. Ask for copies you can take home and study, so you can com-pare available features, designs, and capacities before you decide which one to buy.

○ You can ask for a copy of an appliance's user's manual and read it before making your final choice. (The dealer should have manuals available from the display models in the showroom.) Read-ing the manual will help you ask pertinent questions, tell you how the product operates, and inform you of any special care the product needs.

○ If you're buying a room air conditioner, you'll need to know the dimensions of the room you want to cool and the number of windows, which will help determine the cooling capacity required. That's just one example of the kinds of specific information you'll need to have handy when shopping. If you're not sure, ask the dealer what specific data are necessary to determine which appliance best meets your needs.

○ Appliances such as refrigerators can vary widely in height, width, and depth, so you need to know all three measurements for the space where the appliance will go before you select your refrigerator.

○ Dishwashers and many other appliances tend to be standard size. As a smart shopper, however, you should measure the dimen-sions of the space you have allocated for the appliance to make sure it will fit.

○ A large appliance may be too big to fit through the doors in your home or too wide to make a sharp turn into the room in which it will be installed. Get a tape measure and pencil and paper and record all the measurements. It's possible that the door can be re-moved from the refrigerator to get it through a tight spot, or other adjustments can be made. Know exactly how much space you have to work with, then ask the right questions to make sure the appliance can be installed.

o Sound-deadening features can be designed into an appliance to make it run quieter. If you are concerned about the noise an appliance will make when it is operating, check to see how well it is insulated for sound and what other features might be incorporated in the design. Ask the dealer to turn the appliance on, so you can determine how loud it might be when it is running.

o Some kinds of ovens are better insulated to hold in the heat than others. You'll find that ovens with a self-cleaning feature have much better insulation because the self-cleaning cycle operates at much higher temperatures than a regular oven would ever reach. That extra insulation results in an oven that stays cooler on the exterior, with no areas where heat can escape and pose a burn hazard for small, inquiring fingers. If you're concerned about a toddler or pet being safe around a working oven, ask the salesperson to compare the insulation features of various models.

o A service contract on a major appliance—which is often offered to buyers of new appliances—can include limitations that make it difficult for you to take advantage of the benefits you expect to get out of the contract. Before signing any service contract, understand the terms and conditions. While you're reading the document, look for information such as whether you must use a certain service provider to make repairs; whether there is a "deductible," or an amount you must pay to cover repairs before the contract kicks in; whether you must get a second opinion or price estimates before going ahead with the repairs; whether you can renew the contract annually and what it would cost you to do so; whether the repairs will be made in a house call or whether you have to take the appliance to a shop; what is not covered by the contract, such as decorative trim, glass, rust and corrosion, installation, and other exceptions; and whether you will be reimbursed for consequential damage that happens when the appliance fails—such as damage to clothing if a washing machine malfunctions or food loss if your freezer stops working.

## What's Up with Warranties

o Information regarding warranty coverage must be available at the point of purchase for all products that cost $15 or more, according to the Major Appliance Consumer Action Program, an independent group of experts who serve as mediators for consumer complaints against appliance manufacturers. That rule is designed to make it easy for you to read the warranty before making your final decision. When you read the warranty, study it to find out the answers to these questions: Does it cover the entire product or only certain parts? What is the time period of the warranty? If the appliance needs repairs, will the cost of labor be covered under the warranty?

o Manufacturers offer two types of warranties, according to the Major Appliance Consumer Action Program. Full warranties offer the most protection and require the warrantor to remedy a problem within a reasonable amount of time and without charge, as long as the warranty is in effect. The warrantor must conspicuously list any limitations. Under a full warranty, consumers must be given the choice of a replacement or refund if a reasonable number of attempts to correct an in-warranty problem fail. Limited warranties cover only what the manufacturer outlines in the terms. Consumers should study such warranties carefully to determine what the warrantor provides and what costs the consumer will be responsible for. For example, some limited warranties might require the consumer to pay for diagnosis or labor costs, while the manufacturer pays for parts.

o Factory-authorized service may not be readily available in all areas of the country for every brand of appliance. Most warranties require that work done on your appliance during the warranty period be performed by an authorized servicer, someone who has been trained by the manufacturer to fix its appliances. Make sure there is factory-authorized service in your area for the brand you are considering buying, or you may have to ship your appliance to another part of the country or risk voiding your warranty by having it serviced by someone who does not have the proper authorization.

## Insight on Installation

o You may incur additional costs, such as delivery and installation charges, when you order an appliance. And there may be incidental costs for supplies, such as hoses to hook a washer up to the faucet. Be sure to ask about additional fees when you order an item to be delivered and installed, so you won't face sticker shock.

o When you add new appliances to your home, you may overload your electrical system. Make sure your house has adequate electrical service for the appliances you will be adding. Newer-model homes can usually handle the load, but if you have an older home with an electrical system that has not been upgraded, you may need to call in an electrician.

o Many appliances require a grounded three-hole receptacle, so make sure one is located near the spot where the appliance will be installed.

## Caring for Your Appliances

o Rust on appliances is most often a problem in climates where the air is moist or salty, which includes any coastal area and much of the southeastern United States. If you live in such a climate, keep your appliance indoors, in an air-conditioned room, not on a porch or breezeway where it will be constantly exposed to warm, humid air.

o Appliances should be kept clean by wiping frequently with a clean damp cloth and by cleaning with a mild, nonabrasive cleaner. Check your owner's manual for more specific cleaning problems and instructions.

o Touch-up paint that matches your appliance's color is usually available from the manufacturer. Check your owner's manual or call the company's toll-free customer service line for details. It's important to have touch-up paint on hand to cover up scratches on the finish, which can also cause rust.

## The Right Temperature

o As odd as it might sound, most automatic defrost refrigerator/freezer units or freezers may not keep food fresh if they are placed in a room that is cooler than 60 degrees Fahrenheit. The Major Appliance Consumer Action Program explains that refrigerators and freezers with automatic defrost systems are sensitive to the temperature of the air surrounding them. As the air temperature rises, the refrigerator's compressor wastes energy by running more than necessary to maintain the storage temperature. On the other hand, when room air temperatures fall, the compressor may not run often enough to maintain a cold-enough interior to store food safely. Read the owner's manual on your refrigerator to see the lowest surrounding temperatures in which your "fridge" will provide safe storage of food.

o When the air temperature falls below 38 degrees, the refrigerator's compressor may not run at all. The freezer compartment temperature will increase to match the room's air temperature, and the frozen food will thaw.

o Unless specifically designed to operate in low surrounding temperatures, refrigerators and freezers with an automatic defrost feature should not be placed in unheated locations such as garages or porches, where air temperatures are likely to fall below 60 degrees. Manual defrost units generally can be operated in an unheated area without affecting the unit or the frozen food. But before placing it in such a location, check the owner's manual to see if your unit requires any special care.

## What if There's a Problem?

o Most defects in an appliance will show up during the first few uses, according to the Association of Home Appliance Manufacturers. The organization recommends that you try out each feature and control on the appliance as soon as it is delivered and installed at your home. Remember that warranties are based on a time period, not on the amount of use. If you don't try a feature until after the warranty period is up, getting the problem resolved can be much tougher.

o If you discover a problem with your appliance, call your dealer or service agency immediately to report it and arrange for repairs. Do this before the warranty expires.

o Keeping a written record of all your experiences with a problem appliance can be important to ultimately solving the problem to your satisfaction, according to the Major Appliance Consumer Action Program. Make a note of details such as when the problem was discovered, when it was reported, and the servicing history. Include who serviced the appliance, when and what was done, and how often service was required. Keep copies of all correspondence and all of the receipts for service.

o You should get a receipt for all repairs on your appliance, including those that are done at no charge because the appliance is under warranty. Save all the receipts in case you have to file a complaint.

o Any time you call an appliance repair service to come to your home, you are likely to have to pay a trip charge or a diagnostic charge, which is generally a fixed rate that covers the trip to your home. There is also usually a minimum labor charge for a specified amount of time for the technician to diagnose the problem. If it's a complex problem that takes a good deal of time to figure out, additional labor rates are usually set for every 15 minutes the technician is in your home above the time allotted for diagnosis. Any time you need service on a major home appliance, ask the repair service for an estimate before they send out a technician. That will keep you from being stunned by the repair bill. Also ask what other charges are customary.

o If a repair service makes a house call, you'll be billed, even if the technician finds out your problem was simply that the appliance was not plugged in! Before you have a technician come to your home to check out an appliance, make sure you really need a service call. Start by looking for the simple things that could go wrong that you can fix yourself. For example, is the appliance actually plugged in or did it get disconnected? Is it possible the fuse is blown, or that the circuit breaker was tripped and needs to be reset? A few seconds spent checking out possible problems with the power source could end up saving you a lot of money in unnecessary service calls (plus think of the sheer embarrassment of having a technician tell you the only problem with this machine is that the circuit breaker was tripped!).

○ Make sure you always know how the technician or company charges. Is labor included? Is it additional? Are there any other charges that could pop up? Make sure when you are getting an estimate that the technician gives it to you in writing. Check to see if it includes labor. Ask if the new parts are under warranty. What if your refrigerator breaks down again? Sometimes you'll be given an estimate for a specific part your appliance needs and then you are shocked at the amount of labor that you are charged. Get all of the facts in writing and keep a watchful eye on the details.

## If You're Not Satisfied

○ While your appliance is under warranty, you should call the dealer or service agency to report a problem as soon as you discover it. If you're not satisfied by the actions the dealer or service provider takes to repair your appliance, your next step is to report the problem to the manufacturer. The owner's manual should provide details on how to do this. If you've kept detailed records of the problem and your efforts to get it fixed, your case will be much stronger.

○ It's best to register your complaint in writing. Write a letter that clearly describes the current problem or complaint, and exactly what you want the manufacturer or service agency to do to settle the complaint. If at all possible, type your letter. If you must do it by hand, write legibly. Include the date and your daytime phone number, so the agency can contact you if more information is needed. Include copies of related documents, such as purchase and service receipts. Never send the originals of such receipts; send copies and retain the originals in your files.

○ You should let the company know immediately if there are any new developments, such as further repairs or a new problem, after you've already registered a complaint. While your complaint is being processed, provide any additional information that is requested in a prompt manner. You can often help matters along simply by following the directions when you're asked to fill out forms.

o If you have tried getting a problem fixed at both the local level and from the manufacturer and you are still not satisfied, you can turn to the Major Appliance Consumer Action Program, an independent group of equipment, textile, engineering, and legal experts that serve as mediators on consumer complaints against the appliance industry. The program has dealt with more than 50,000 complaints about major home appliances in the last twenty-five years. It handles problems involving refrigerators, freezers, ranges, ovens, microwave ovens, dishwashers, disposals, clothes washers and dryers, room air conditioners, and trash compactors.

o To register a complaint with the MACAP, you must do so in writing. Following the same guidelines you did in dealing with the manufacturer, outline your problem, what you want done about it, and include all relevant material. Mail the material to the Major Appliance Consumer Action Program, 20 North Wacker Drive, Chicago, IL 60606.

## Keep Safety in Mind

o You don't hear much these days about kids getting trapped in abandoned refrigerators, but it is still a concern. If you are discarding your refrigerator, take steps to make sure that no one could get trapped in it, even if it will only be sitting around your home for a day or two before it is taken away. To keep a child from becoming trapped in your refrigerator, remove the door from the unit and take all of the shelves out.

o An oven range can tilt forward when too much pressure is applied to the open oven door. This can result in a tipped range. If the stove top is in use, anyone in the kitchen could suffer scalds and burns as boiling food goes flying. There are several steps you can take to prevent your range from tipping. The most important is to make sure that the antitipping device is properly functioning when the range is installed. Additionally, make sure that the oven door is kept closed at all times, except when you are putting something in the oven or taking it out. Never use the oven door as a step stool, seat, or to support your body or any other object. Putting that much weight on the door could cause the unit to tip.

# Baby Products

Shopping for baby items is a lot of fun. Everything is so tiny, and so pastel and cute. And there are many items that didn't exist when this generation of new parents were children, or maybe even when your last child was born.

This mushrooming number of baby products includes items to make the parents' life easier, to make the infant more comfortable, and even to stimulate young minds from the earliest days of life.

Do you need one of every item for sale at the baby megastore? Probably not. The necessary items are the basics, including a place for the baby to sleep and a car seat. As for the conveniences, to some degree it's a matter of taste or style. For every set of parents who swear they couldn't have made it through the diaper years without a diaper wipe warmer to keep baby's bottom comfy, there's another family who did fine without such a gadget.

Ask your friends who have had children recently what products they found most useful and which they thought were a waste of time and money. That's usually a good clue to how you'll feel, too.

As you're purchasing items that will be used by or for a young child, don't let the cute look of the product color your judgment. Safety should be the first criterion in selecting any product for your baby. Danger can lurk in unexpected spots, from exposed screws to openings that are just large enough to trap your child's head. Heed this advice from experts before you purchase anything that might pose an unexpected danger for a child.

## Look Before You Buy

o The Juvenile Products Manufacturers Association, or JPMA, offers certification for many of the items parents purchase for young children. The association has devised a set of standards that high chairs, play yards, walkers, strollers, gates, cribs, and other items must meet to receive the certification. The standards are designed to make sure that these products will stand up to the heavy use that they undergo with an infant and toddler, and will remain safe in the process. Industry members, consumer groups, and the U.S. Consumer Product Safety Commission help to develop these standards. To receive the JMPA Certified Seal, a product must be tested by an independent testing lab, not just by its manufacturer, to make sure it meets the performance standards. Once a product has passed the necessary tests, the manufacturer can place the certified seal on the product itself or on the product packaging, so that consumers may be assured that what they are buying has undergone testing for safety.

○ Exposed hardware, including screws, bolts, and fasteners, could pose a danger on items your baby uses. When shopping for baby items, make sure the hardware is recessed into the piece or has smooth, rounded edges that can't scratch a child or catch his clothing.

## Choosing a Car Seat

○ Child car seats are required by law in all fifty states. You will need one to take the newborn home from the hospital, and after you get her home, she'll ride in a seat until about her fourth birthday. A child should be strapped into a car seat for every ride, even if you are just going around the corner to the baby-sitter's.

○ The National Highway Traffic Safety Administration, part of the United States Department of Transportation, maintains a safety hot line where you can get information about child safety seats or report a problem with a seat. Call 1-888-327-4236, or visit the agency's Web site at www.nhtsa.dot.gov for more information.

○ The infant car seat is designed to protect your child not just in an accident but also in sudden stops and other jerky motions that could endanger a baby's neck, which is much weaker than an adult's.

○ The infant-only car seat is the best choice for a baby that is less than one year old and weighs less than 20 pounds, according to the National SAFE KIDS Campaign. An infant-only seat is best because it provides a tighter fit around the infant.

○ A car seat that is equipped with a five-point harness restraint system, instead of a T-shield or tray-shield restraint, provides a better fit around infant- and toddler-size children.

○ A child who outgrows the infant-only seat before his first birthday should ride in a convertible seat used in the rear-facing position until he turns one year old. Before buying a convertible seat to use with a child younger than one year old, make sure it has been approved for weights greater than 20 pounds in the rear-facing position. Most infant-only seats and convertible seats are tested up to only 20 or 22 pounds in the rear-facing position, according to the National SAFE KIDS Campaign, which can present a problem when the child reaches 22 pounds before his first birthday. But more manufacturers are engineering their products to accommodate larger infants, and it pays to shop around for the appropriate seat if you have a large child.

## A Safe Place to Sleep

○ Between nighttime sleep and naps, your baby will spend more than half of each day sleeping. That's a lot of time in the crib, and a good reason to choose a safe one for your baby. When you're shopping for a crib, make sure that the slats are no more than 2⅜ inches apart, and that no slats are missing. Choose a style that has no cutouts in the headboard or footboard. Both of these precautions are designed to guard against head entrapment.

○ Corner posts on the crib should be no more than ⅟16 inch high, so that the baby's clothing can't get caught on the post, which could result in strangulation. If your crib has decorative knobs, remove and discard them. The exception is tall posts designed to hold up a canopy. Canopy posts should be at least 16 inches high, to provide plenty of room to get the baby safely in and out of the crib.

○ There's an easy test to see if the crib mattress is a tight enough fit: Try to slip two fingers between the mattress and the side of the crib. If the space is bigger than the width of your two fingers, it's too loose, and there's a danger that the baby could get trapped between the mattress and crib.

○ Screws and other hardware on a crib can loosen up as you get the baby in and out of bed several times each day, so make it a habit to check the hardware periodically and tighten any screws that have loosened with use.

o Cribs are available with a drop-side mechanism on one or both sides of the bed. Those with drop sides on two sides sometimes cost more than a bed with one drop side. If you're planning to use the crib up against a wall or in a similar position where you'll need to have access to it from only one side anyway, you might as well save a little money and get a bed with only one drop side.

o Recent studies have shown that soft, fluffy items left in a crib with a sleeping infant can contribute to suffocation deaths. Most healthy young babies should be laid down to sleep on their back or side on a firm, flat mattress, according to the American Academy of Pediatrics, and all soft items should be removed from the crib. That includes pillows, quilts, comforters, sheepskins, and stuffed animals. Which brings up a good question: Lots of manufacturers sell incredibly cute sets of crib bedding, including matching items such as bumper pads, dust ruffles, quilts, pillows, and comforters. But if you are going to have to remove the quilts, pillows, and comforters from the crib every time you lay your infant down in it, why bother to purchase them? Eventually, remaking the bed every time you put the child in or out of it will get tedious, and you'll pack away the pillows, quilts, and comforters, anyway. Save a little money by not purchasing the items that shouldn't be left in the crib when your child is sleeping.

o A bassinet or cradle should have a sturdy bottom and a wide base, for stability. Make sure the legs of the cradle have a good locking mechanism, too, so it's unlikely the legs will buckle and fold up on your child. Look for smooth surfaces on all exposed areas of the bassinet, with no raised hardware or staples that might scratch the child or catch on her clothing or blankets. It's important that the mattress fit snugly, so that the child can't roll between the mattress and the side of the bassinet or cradle, which could pose a threat of suffocation.

## High Chair Hijinks

o A high chair should have waist and crotch restraining straps that are independent of the tray, so the child stays safely strapped in when the tray is removed. Choose a design that includes a strap buckle that is easy to use, so you won't be tempted to skip that part of getting your child ready for his meals. A good high chair will have a wide base for stability. If it's a folding chair, make sure it locks securely in the open position and there's no possibility of it collapsing while your child is in it.

o Hook-on high chairs should never be used on a glass tabletop, or on a table with a single pedestal, a leaf, or one that has a tablecloth on it. If you choose to use a hook-on chair, make sure it has a restraining strap to keep the child from slipping out. Look for a model that has a clamp that locks onto the table for added security.

## Baby on the Move

o A baby stroller or carriage should have a wide base to prevent it from tipping over. If it has a shopping basket attached to it, the basket should be located low on the back and directly over or in front of the rear wheels to provide more stability for the vehicle.

o The seat belt and crotch strap on a stroller or baby carriage should be attached to the frame of the vehicle. Look for a model that allows you to close the leg openings when you use it in the carriage position, so a sleeping baby can't get caught in the opening.

o The frame of a backpack-style baby carrier should have padded covering near the child's face for comfort and safety, and the folding mechanism should be designed so that it isn't likely to pinch your baby should part of his body come in contact with it. The leg openings should be small enough to prevent the child from slipping out, but large enough to prevent chafing your child's legs.

## Baby at Play

○ The mesh on a mesh-sided playpen or play yard should have a tight weave, with openings that are less than ¼ inch. Check the mesh closely for holes and tears, and make sure it is securely attached to the top rail and the floor of the play yard.

○ On a play yard with wooden slats, the spacing between the slats should be 2⅜ inches or less, and there should be no posts protruding on which a child's clothing could get entangled.

○ The American Academy of Pediatrics advises against baby walkers. The AAP recommends that parents use a push toy or wagon instead of a walker. If you decide you want to use a walker despite the pediatricians' warning, look for one that has a wide wheel base for stability, and be constantly on guard to make sure that your child doesn't use the walker near the top of stairs, where there is a danger he could tumble down before you can stop the accident. Scatter rugs, uneven flooring (such as where carpeting meets vinyl or hardwood flooring), and raised thresholds are other dangerous spots to a child in a walker, and more reasons a parent must be vigilant when her child is in a walker.

○ The National SAFE KIDS Campaign recommends that parents seek an alternative to a baby walker with wheels. Several wheelless, "saucer"-shaped toys are on the market that provide a safer choice. Look for one that is on a stable base, and place it away from stairs, hot appliances, and window-blind or drapery cords.

## Toy Chest Hazards

○ The U.S. Consumer Product Safety Commission has received reports of children being killed or seriously injured by a free-falling lid on a toy chest. If your toy chest has such a lid, remove it immediately so it can't land on your child's head while he's getting a plaything out of the trunk. If you are purchasing a new toy chest, look for one that has a hinged lid with a spring-loaded support that will hold the lid open in any position, so you don't have to worry about it falling suddenly on any part of your child's body.

○ Avoid a lid latch on your toy trunk because your child could crawl into the trunk and become trapped. Select a chest that has some form of ventilation holes or spaces on the sides or lids, so that your child will get some air if he does crawl inside.

## Danger in Familiar Items

o The U.S. Consumer Product Safety Commission recommends against using old accordion-style baby gates or expandable enclosures with large V-shaped openings along the top edge, which pose an entrapment danger. Instead, choose baby gates with small openings, so the child can't trap her head in the gate or manage to find a toehold and attempt to climb over the gate. By the time your baby starts crawling or walking, gates or other enclosures should be installed at the top of the stairs and in other locations to keep the youngster in or out. Gates should have a pressure bar or other fastener that can withstand the force a child might exert pushing or pulling against the gate or shaking it.

o A pacifier should have a large, firm shield around the nipple— a shield that's too big to fit into your child's mouth. The shield should have ventilation holes, too, so that the child can continue to get air if the entire pacifier does get into her mouth.

o The nipple of a pacifier can tear or develop holes in it. Check your child's pacifier regularly, by gently tugging on the nipple. If you discover it is torn or has holes in it, it should be discarded. If the nipple were to break off, it could present a choking hazard for your child.

# Beauty Products

While genes and what you're born with certainly play a vital role in how you look, there are plenty of other factors, too. How you take care of yourself is very important, from eating right and exercising to avoiding sun damage and cigarette smoking. Beauty also comes down to the little things: wearing a shade of lipstick that gives you the confidence to smile more or a new hair color that brings out your eyes.

But perhaps one of the most important principles to looking your best that most of us forget or even ignore is rethinking what's beautiful—accentuating the positive, if you will. For example, embrace your freckles, don't try to hide them. Rather than fight your straight hair with perm after perm, invest in a good cut that makes the most of what you were born with. Forget worrying about making your lips looks bigger with lip liner tricks; play up your eyes instead, and let your lips stay their natural size.

While a totally natural look may be wishful thinking, it's true that most women simply look better with less makeup. Fortunately, the days of complicated contouring and eye makeup involving eight shades of shadow are gone. Today's faces—and hair—are more care-free, less contrived. You can think about cosmetics as serving two purposes: hiding flaws and adding a little color. Use only the minimum you need to achieve these goals.

According to three-time Emmy Award–winning hairstylist and makeup consultant Jack Morton of Indulgence Salon, "The biggest beauty botch both women and men make is with product usage. They think if a little looks good or works, then a lot is better. In the case of hair, it becomes weighted down or can't even move. Avoiding that is simple—less is more! Another beauty goof I constantly see is someone using too many chemical processors, including multiple colors done too often, thus damaging the structure of the hair. Hair must have time to rejuvenate."

When it comes to beauty, the "bet you didn't knows" can also be found at a makeup counter with a complimentary makeup application. One little trick of the trade here and there can brighten your smile and open your eyes. I've learned from being on television for over sixteen years that getting your overall look and makeup updated every six months or seasonally is essential. Feedback from people who are honest with you can also teach you a lot about what looks best on you. Be open to others' opinions and learn from them. You'll be surprised at all the wonderful options you have, from the colors you wear to the makeup you should avoid.

## The Basics: Skin Care

o Get sun-savvy. Dermatologists will tell you that you can't cure wrinkles with a bottle of something, but the closest antiaging serum we've got is sunscreen. Damaging rays from the sun do more to mar beauty than just about anything else. If you doubt it, take a peek at your cheeks (not the ones on your face, your other "cheeks"!) and see how smooth and young-looking they appear. If you want to look like you have a glow, investigate some of the new bronzing gels, which add a little color without the ultraviolet rays.

o Beware of false claims. Did you know that your skin is the largest organ of the body? It's composed of two layers: the epidermis (outer layer) and dermis (inner layer). The epidermis is essentially dead cells, but it's very thick and hard to penetrate, which makes many of the claims by creams hard to believe. It's difficult to reach the dermis layer where living skin is.

o Surprise—makeup can be good for you. Wearing a little foundation, blush, and lipstick can provide some protection from sun, dust, wind, and other elements. Plus, it helps boost your morale!

o Find your own "step program." The four basic steps of skin care are generally thought to be cleansing, exfoliating, toning, and moisturizing. Yet, not everyone needs all of these steps. Some nights you may want to use a light cleansing lotion and moisturizer on your face, other times the full "spa treatment" is in order. Remember that the less you pull and poke your skin, and the fewer harsh chemicals it is exposed to, the better.

○ When in doubt, go mild. Never use a deodorant body soap on your face; it's much too harsh. Stick with a glycerine soap, foaming facial wash, or cleansing cream—something milder formulated for faces.

○ Ask the experts. With all the confusing options in cleansing lotions and moisturizers these days, it's probably wise to ask a dermatologist his or her opinion on what works and what doesn't. But remember that you're the ultimate customer. As long as a "magic cream" isn't hurting you and you like it, keep on using it.

## Saving Money

○ It is actually a law that if you purchase a makeup product and you do not like it for any reason, then you can return it.

○ To save money, purchase makeup brushes at an art supply store. They're often as high in quality, so check out your options and make a proper comparison.

○ Create your own shades of lipstick. Buy a plastic or metal artist's palette and combine different shades of lipstick using a small brush for your own unique color. Mix in some petroleum jelly for a shinier, "wetter" application.

○ Go for drugstore products. Many, many of the top makeup artists regularly shop at your basic neighborhood pharmacy for their cosmetic staples: mascara, eye pencils, pressed powder, lip gloss, and much more. Don't assume that the lower prices necessarily mean lower quality.

○ Just bag it—makeup, that is. There's no need to constantly buy new cosmetic bags, which just get grimy right away. For traveling or in purses, keep makeup and other beauty supplies in sturdy, "zipper-style" freezer bags. Because they're just a few cents a bag, you don't feel bad when you toss them out.

## Quick Makeup Tips from the Pros

○ Remember that, unlike a new haircut, a bad makeup job can be reversed in a second. Just wash your face.

○ The best makeup is well blended and includes blush, eye

shadow, and foundation. Make sure before leaving the house that you check all sides of your face in different mirrors and different lights. It's always smart to take a hand mirror over to a window and check under natural light.

○ Similarly, buy makeup only after it's been "tested" outdoors. Before you purchase any new products, particularly foundation, first apply a sample, then step outside the store for a minute to look at it in natural light.

○ If your skin tans naturally in summer, consider having two sets of makeup, one a little darker for summer months.

○ For a sheer look, mix foundation with moisturizer before applying.

○ Take a powder, so to speak. The pros swear by the power of powder, saying that a light dusting over foundation helps add a matte finish, helps blend tones, provides a good base for blush, and helps stop shine. Use sparingly, however, since an overly powdered face can look dry.

○ For blush, think how your cheeks naturally look after a workout. To choose a color of blush, go for a natural hue such as what you'd see on your own face. (That means no exotic colors in apricot or eggplant shades!) To find where to apply blush, smile. Add some on the apples of your cheeks and blend upward. Make sure there are no streaks.

○ To keep eye shadow from creasing, first apply a matte-finished powder closest to your natural skin color. If you use foundation, your eyeliner and shadow can smear. Always apply lighter colors first, layering darker colors over them and blending.

○ Few women can handle a liquid eyeliner. For a more natural look, stick to a pencil. Shades such as brown or dark gray are often more subtle than black, but it depends on a woman's coloring. To soften the look of eyeliner, go over the line with a small brush of light brown or taupe eye shadow.

○ Create eyelashes worthy of some winking. First, consider using an eyelash curler, particularly if you have short or straight eyelashes (hold for 10 seconds before releasing).

○ To make sure mascara goes on evenly over lashes, Jack Morton advises, "Pull the mascara brush out and gently wipe the bristles along a tissue. This will prevent blobs of color being deposited on your eyelashes. Also avoid pumping the brush because this builds up air in the tube, which encourages bacteria and also makes the mascara dry out and clump. Since bacteria can be high in mascaras, replace yours every three months for good hygiene. If clumping does occur, use a small eyelash brush to separate lashes."

○ Here's how to create the perfect "lip": First outline your lips with a lip pencil similar in color to the lipstick you'll be using. Fill in some lip pencil color right on your lips, also, so that when the lipstick eventually wears off, you won't be left with just lip liner! Always apply lipstick with a brush for the best effect. Blot with a tissue; some makeup artists dab a little powder on, as well.

○ When you apply lipstick, experts recommend that you smile. That way you don't miss any part of your entire lip.

○ To keep makeup bacteria-free, don't ever use saliva when putting on your eyeliner or other products that require water. Also avoid sharing brushes and makeup with others.

○ According to Jack Morton, "Rinsing your hair in cool water makes it shinier. A cool finishing rinse after you shampoo will cause the hair to have a greater luster and shine."

## Recommended Shelf Life for Cosmetics

Be sure to check your products regularly, since the environment you live in could alter the shelf life of your makeup.

| | |
|---|---|
| Mascara | Several months (less if it starts to smell funny) |
| Foundation | 1 year |
| Nail polish | 1 year |
| Lipstick | 2–3 years |
| Eye pencil | 3 years |
| Face powder | 6 months |

○ Some people keep cosmetics in the refrigerator, since bacteria tend to grow in moist, warm places, which is exactly the condition in many bathrooms.

○ Store perfume in a dark, cool place. If it receives constant exposure to light and heat, it could deteriorate.

○ Oily skin holds perfume better than dry skin, so lightly spread a drop of petroleum jelly into your skin before applying perfume.

○ Put eyebrow pencils in the refrigerator for a little while before sharpening them. They'll be less likely to break.

○ To prevent a nail-polish cap from sticking to the bottle and ruining it, rub a drop of petroleum jelly around the top of the bottle before closing it.

○ Some women with dark skin try to lighten their pigment with a foundation lighter than their skin—don't, say the experts. In fact, to even out skin tones, you'll probably have to go with a shade slightly darker than your own skin.

## Hair Tips

○ Get your money's worth at the salon. What's the number-one complaint that women have about their hairstyles? That they can't duplicate what the stylist achieved in the salon. Before you walk out the door, ask lots of questions about how you can copy what he or she did. Have them demonstrate how to blow-dry your hair, for instance, or where to use gels. (But be cautious about having to buy a lot of special products for a certain look.)

○ Get a lesson with a top stylist if you can afford it, or observe the stylist-in-training and see if you like his or her work, for big savings. Some top-name salons bring in apprentice haircutters to get their experience on customers who pay only one-third or so what the salon usually charges. You can also check the Yellow Pages for beauty schools that offer free or reduced-price haircuts as part of the students' training. These sorts of deals work best for women who have simple haircuts. If you require the continuity (and experience) of your current stylist, stick with a sure thing.

○ Go for volume. Experts say the quickest way to add some fluff to flat hair is to spray a bit of volumizer at the roots (on wet or dry hair), then blow-dry hair upside down. To get a little more curl out of your curling iron or hot rollers, spray a small amount of hair spray on tresses before curling. Or, you can also use a diffuser on curly hair.

○ Avoid helmet-head. Another tip for styling products: to keep hair spray use to a minimum, spritz hair spray directly on your hairbrush and run it through your hair.

○ Use a light touch if your hair is oily. Many women with limp, oily hair make matters worse by using a lot of emollient-rich products. Instead, use a conditioner only once or twice a week, not daily. Use any sort of styling product—such as gels or mousse—sparingly, if at all.

○ Shampoos will usually list instructions to wash and repeat, but that's rarely necessary. One lather is usually enough.

○ Even if you're growing hair out, get a trim every six to eight weeks; otherwise, split ends and other ragged tresses develop. Some salons will give you free bang trimmings in between cuts.

○ Choose a hairstyle for your face shape. Round faces benefit from length (hair chin-level or below) or a style with a lot of height. To divert attention away from the roundness, try a side part or layered bangs. For square faces, try to round the edges with curls, wispy layers, and softness.

○ Keep colored hair looking its best by protecting it. Wet hair before and after going in the pool to dilute the chemicals. Protect hair from sun with hats or specially formulated conditioners with a sunscreen. Try to choose hair products that are made for color-treated hair.

○ Raid your kitchen for products. Give dry hair a moisturizing treatment by rubbing hair with olive oil or salad oil, let sit for a half hour, and shampoo out. Oily hair can benefit from a final rinse of lemon juice or diluted vinegar.

○ Let hair accessories be your friend. Experiment with a variety of headbands, barrettes, combs, and other hair "jewelry" (some of which is found inexpensively in the drugstore). Spending a few minutes now and then to come up with some new ways to wear your hair can definitely guard against a "bad-hair day" in the future. Learn how to French-braid hair or make a topknot, for instance.

○ Remember that hair is actually "dead," so therefore many of the claims of shampoos and styling products just don't do the job. The most likely way to have healthier hair is to eat better, say doctors, so that the nutrients go into the hair from the inside.

o A clarifying or purifying shampoo is really important to remove buildup on hair, especially before chemical processing.

o According to Jack Morton, "If you are going to straighten or have your hair professionally straightened, make sure the stylist doesn't leave the neutralizer on too long. It should be left on for only a maximum of five minutes, so beware. Products do differ, but the neutralizer is the one ingredient that can harm your hair."

## Five Ways to Avoid Damaging Hair

1. If your style and hair type allows, never dry hair completely. Allow a little moisture to remain so that it can air-dry. When possible, dry hair on a cool setting.
2. Always choose the least damaging perm or hair color. (Ask your stylist.)
3. Always use a wide-tooth comb on wet hair, never a brush. Be gentle when towel-drying hair; never vigorously rub hair.
4. Shampoo hair after swimming with a clarifying shampoo to remove chemicals.
5. Detangle hair from the ends up. Start with a lower section and comb through, then go up an inch or two and comb down from there.

## Nails

o Regular manicures can help to keep your nails in great shape. Having them buffed at least once every two weeks can even prevent peeling. Buffing will help even out the surface, and polish lasts longer on buffed nails.

## Resources

While there are scores of magazines (*Allure, Glamour*) and books (by supermodels such as Tyra Banks as well as dermatologists and makeup artists) devoted to beauty, the Internet has been providing some access to products and tips, too. Some to try:

## General

www.womenswire.com/beauty
www.salonweb.com
www.hairdos.com

## Magazines

www.cosmomag.com
www.ellemag.com

## Cosmetics Companies

www.avon.com
www.covergirl.com
www.clinique.com
www.the-body-shop.com
www.marykay.com
www.bobbibrowncosmetics.com

# Car Ownership

Whether you look at a car as an extension of your personality or simply as a way to get from here to there, there's no question that even a so-called economy car is a big investment these days. As a smart car shopper, you should start out by reading about the new vehicles, and by talking to friends who own models you are interested in. Information on new cars is easy to find—most newspapers run auto reviews regularly, the newsstands are filled with magazines focusing on cars, and there are hundreds of Web sites devoted to vehicles.

Once you've narrowed down your choice to a few specific kinds of cars, make exploratory visits to new car dealers. Pick up the manufacturer's specifications on the model you are interested in, test-drive each vehicle to see how it handles, and spend some time checking out the car's fit and finish, which can provide clues to the quality of manufacture. Once you've done that, you should have a good idea which car you want.

But buying a car is only part of the work of car ownership. Periodic maintenance is the other part of the equation to long life and higher resale value for your vehicle. (And even if you lease a vehicle, you are required to maintain it.) The best place to learn what regular care your vehicle needs is probably sitting in the glove box or trunk of that vehicle. The owner's manual has a schedule showing when you should perform maintenance activities.

Focusing motorists' attention on the need to maintain and repair their cars is the goal of the Car Care Council, a nonprofit organization whose members are in the automotive aftermarket industry. Through various educational endeavors, including National Car Care Month, the council tries to show motorists that maintenance is less costly than major repairs. It finds that an astounding number of people are shortchanging their vehicles when it comes to basic care.

Overall, 91 percent of cars tested during a recent inspection campaign failed because at least one item needed repair or maintenance. Almost a third of the cars had low or dirty motor oil. Another 24 percent were low on transmission fluid, and the same percentage were low on coolant. Eighteen percent needed new air filters, 26 percent had problems with drive belts, and 14 percent needed new hoses. Nearly a third of the vehicles had low tire pressure.

Most of those items are easy for a motorist to check himself (your owner's manual will help if you aren't sure where everything is located or if you need to know recommended tire pressure), and correcting those minor problems would mean better gas mileage and a safer driving experience. Of course, automobiles are complex machines, and you probably don't want to attempt all the maintenance yourself. But the more you know about your car, problems it can encounter, and how to read the warning signs, the better equipped you will be to help a professional technician diagnose and correct your vehicle's ills.

## Purchasing a Car

○ If you normally get a new car every two to three years, don't put a lot of wear and tear on a vehicle, and drive less than 12,000 to 15,000 miles a year, leasing a vehicle might be a good deal for you. You're exactly the person leasing was designed for, and you will find that the lease payments are lower than the payments to buy a car.

○ If you normally drive a car until it dies, have kids or hobbies that result in muddy car interiors or other kinds of wear and tear, or drive substantially more than 12,000 to 15,000 miles a year, it probably makes more sense for you to buy a car rather than lease one. If you own your own car, you don't have to worry about charges for excessive wear and tear or for extra mileage, and if you keep your car for a long time, you will be able to have years without car payments, when you can be saving money to help purchase your next vehicle.

○ You can find a thorough listing of manufacturer incentives for new cars in *Automotive News*, a weekly trade publication that is available on newsstands or in public libraries. The listing includes both incentives being offered to consumers and incentives being offered to dealers—information that can be useful in negotiating the price of the car.

o Your bank or credit union may offer a better rate on a car loan than the auto dealer is offering. Before car shopping, call at least three lenders to find out what their rates are. When you talk to the dealer about financing, you'll know where the best rate is found. Sometimes manufacturers offer incredibly low financing, but you might not like the limitations that come with it—limits that could include, for example, only 24 months to pay off the loan.

o A fax machine can help you cut the time you spend looking for a car. Once you know the specific make and model you want, including options, fax a letter to several dealers, listing the exact car you want, to see if they have it in stock and what price they are willing to sell it for. Once you know who has the car you want and what the price is, you can go to one or two to negotiate further, or simply to make the deal.

o In many cities, you can hire an auto-buying service that will get several dealers to bid on selling you the car that meets your specifications. The service will charge you a flat fee for this work. You can find such services in the Yellow Pages under "auto brokers." Check out the agency with the Better Business Bureau or your state's consumer protection office before writing a check.

## The Line on Leaks

o Most engine, transmission, and power steering leaks occur because of deterioration of the seals within the systems. As vehicles age, the seals often shrink and harden, which allows the fluids to leak slowly out of the system.

o An estimated 46 percent of all vehicles leak fluids, and more than 50 million gallons of these fluids are leaked annually into the environment, as rainwater washes the leaked fluids off of driveways, streets, and parking lots and into streams, lakes, and rivers.

o The best way to check your car for leaks is to place a clean white cloth or sheet of paper under the vehicle overnight. The color of the fluid that collects on the paper will be a good indicator of which system has a leak.

If the leaking fluid is green, it is antifreeze and indicates a cooling system problem. Reddish spots are a sign of a leaking transmission. If your engine oil is leaking, it's likely to be dark brown. An amber-colored fluid is from the power-steering system.

o A leaking system that goes unrepaired will only become worse. Eventually, the components will malfunction, possibly resulting in expensive repairs or even replacement.

Leak-stopping products could fix your leak and save you some money on a big repair bill. For your engine, transmission, or power-steering system, look for a leak stopper that has synthetic ester plasticizers that will chemically revitalize deteriorated seals. This will expand the seals and keep them soft and pliable, causing many leaks to disappear.

o Cooling system leaks occur when corrosion eats away at the radiator and heater core, resulting in tiny holes. To stop such leaks, use a product that contains helical microfibers that will fill those holes but that will not harm or clog the system. Avoid products that contain metal flakes and solids that can damage a cooling system.

o If a good-quality leak stopper doesn't fix the problem, the seal deterioration or corrosion is probably so advanced that the component must be replaced to solve the problem. It's worth trying a leak stopper first, however, because a good product won't harm your vehicle and it might save you from having to make expensive repairs.

## Keep Your Cool

o The refrigerant most of us are familiar with by the name Freon has been replaced by a product that is safer for the environment in air-conditioning systems of newer model cars. A car that's a 1993 model or older uses Freon, which is technically known as R-12. Newer cars use R-134a as a refrigerant.

o If your vehicle's air-conditioning system is leaking R-12, you are harming the environment, the Car Care Council advises.

○ The two kinds of refrigerants are not interchangeable and should not be mixed. You cannot add R-134a to your older air conditioner without first flushing the system. You may need to retrofit the system before it can handle R-134a. And the Car Care Council warns that some substitutes are volatile mixtures of propane, butane, and flammable hydrocarbons. To be safe, have your air-conditioning serviced only by a reputable, well-trained technician.

○ For maximum freeze protection, the antifreeze mixture in your radiator should be no more than 70 percent antifreeze and 30 percent water. In most climates, a 50-50 solution is adequate because it will protect against freezing at temperatures as low as minus 34 degrees Fahrenheit. Never use pure antifreeze.

○ The radiator cap is designed to keep the cooling system operating at a specified pressure. That's why it's important to install the right one for your vehicle when you replace the original equipment. Pressure recommendations differ for different cars.

○ A broken drive belt can cause overheating, a loss of power steering, and a dead battery. To prevent a broken belt, inspect your drive belts periodically, looking for fraying or excessive wear. Have the belts replaced when they show signs of wear.

○ In the cooling system, the thermostat controls the engine temperature. A thermostat that allows an engine to run too hot or too cold can damage the engine.

○ In many of today's smaller, fuel-efficient vehicles, the cooling systems are equipped with an electric fan on the radiator. The battery-powered fan turns on only as needed, when signaled by a heat sensor, helping the vehicle to achieve some of its efficiency.

## All in the Timing

○ The engine timing belt keeps the valves, pistons, and other internal engine parts properly synchronized. This belt, which is not easily viewed, does not stretch, so there is no need for periodic inspection and adjustment, as there is with the rubber belts that transfer power from the engine to the cooling fan, alternator, power steering pump, and air conditioner.

○ While they don't need to be adjusted, all timing belts eventually weaken and break, and a broken timing belt can cause serious damage to the engine. According to the Car Care Council, many of today's high-tech engines are manufactured to such extremely close tolerances that a broken timing belt will allow the pistons to hit the valves, bending them and possibly destroying the pistons or even the entire engine as a result.

○ Timing belts often fail from the inside out, making visual inspection somewhat unreliable. That's why vehicle manufacturers recommend periodic replacement of timing belts, typically every 60,000 to 90,000 miles, although this varies by manufacturer. The recommended interval for timing-belt replacement can be found in your owner's manual. For most car owners, replacing the timing belt is an investment that needs to be made once every four or five years, and it's well worth the cost, considering that the alternative could be total engine replacement.

## It's a Clean Machine

○ One of the most critical times to wash your vehicle is immediately after a rainfall. Even after a light rain shower, the rain evaporates, but acid remains on your car's finish. The acid rain results when high concentrations of emissions from fossil-fuel-burning engines or manufacturing plants (concentrations found in the atmosphere) come down with the rainwater and react with your car's paint to form sulfuric and nitric acids. You can't prevent acid rain, but you can keep it from ruining your car's finish.

○ Snow and sleet can result in the same damaging effects as acid rain, and the problems can be compounded by chemicals found in road salts. Washing your vehicle in the winter is important to remove these chemicals from the body of the car.

○ The area around the inside of the door and trunk, as well as the area where a power antenna is mounted to the car, should be thoroughly dried with towels after the vehicle is washed. Also make it a practice to open and close all doors, the trunk, and other outside parts of the car that lock several times after you wash the vehicle.

○ Mud can be a problem for a car's finish, and many motorists don't understand the importance of cleaning mud from the undercarriage. Undercarriage treatments, offered by most professional car washes, remove caked-on mud that holds moisture to the metal and causes rust and body rot around wheel wells and door seals.

○ To keep your car's finish in tiptop shape, you should wash your car every ten days and especially after rain or snow.

○ A vehicle should be waxed every six months. If your vehicle is red, black, or white, you need to wax it more frequently because these colors are more susceptible than other hues to acid rain and ultraviolet (UV) rays from the sun.

○ While you can wash your own car, there are advantages to using a professional car wash, both for the benefit of your vehicle's finish and for the environment. According to the International Carwash Association, a member of the Car Care Council, professional car washes use cleaning solutions that are specially formulated for today's new car finishes. Additionally, a professional car wash uses biodegradable cleaning solutions and far less water than a do-it-yourselfer. And professional car washes must dispose of wastewater in a way that meets federal and state environmental regulations, while the water used to wash a car in a home driveway runs directly into storm sewers and then into lakes and streams where contaminants can harm fish and wildlife.

○ If you ever have a cracked windshield, check to see if it can be repaired without replacing the entire piece of glass.

## Brake It Up

○ Brake failure is the leading mechanical cause of highway accidents, according to the Car Care Council.

○ If you spot an emergency situation while you're driving on the interstate highway at a speed of 65 miles per hour, you'd probably travel 70 feet before your foot hit the brake pedal. You'd go another 250 feet before stopping, if you're on a dry road with good tires and brakes. With a minimum of 320 feet from first noticing a situation to being able to stop for it, it's important to keep your brakes in good operating condition.

○ When you feel the brake pedal pulsate as you come to a stop, the reason is probably a warped brake rotor. The wobbling surface of a warped rotor will cause an uneven or pulsating action as you stop.

o If your car steers to the right when you apply the brakes, the reason could be a sticking left front caliper. The faulty action of the brake causes strong braking on the right side. As a result, your car wants to pull in that direction.

o The most common reason for a brake warning light to go on is a leak in the hydraulic system. If the brake warning light does come on, go directly to a technician to find out what's wrong and to have it fixed.

o Two common early warning signs of brake trouble are a harsh scraping or grinding sound when the brakes are applied or a pedal that falls to the floor when the brakes are applied. The harsh noise indicates excessive wear, leading to damaged drums or rotors and eventual brake failure. The falling pedal means a problem in the hydraulic system, and that you're about to lose your brakes.

o An antilock braking system, commonly referred to as ABS, is designed to prevent skidding and help drivers maintain steering control during an emergency stopping situation. If you are driving a rental vehicle and are unsure if it is equipped with antilock brakes, check to see if an ABS light flashes on the dashboard during ignition. If you spend a lot of time driving rental cars, get in the habit of asking whether the vehicle has ABS when you pick up your car.

o You may have to change your driving habits when you are behind the wheel of a vehicle equipped with antilock brakes. Most drivers have been taught to pump their brakes, especially on roads that are wet, icy, or otherwise slippery. But ABS does the pumping for you. As a driver of an ABS-equipped vehicle facing an emergency situation, you need to apply firm, steady pressure to the brake pedal and continue to apply it until the emergency is resolved. ABS reduces the risk of your vehicle skidding out of control and it increases your ability to steer the vehicle.

o ABS uses electronic controls to maintain wheel rotation under hard braking that would otherwise lock the vehicle's wheels. Keeping the wheels rotating increases the vehicle's steering and braking, especially when the tire-roadway friction is reduced, such as when the pavement is wet.

## Clear the Air

○ The catalytic converter on your car plays a leading role in the reduction of harmful exhaust emissions. The exhaust flows through the converter on its way into the atmosphere, and the lethal components of exhaust gas are rendered harmless, according to the Car Care Council.

○ Common causes of problems with your catalytic converter can be discovered and corrected with periodic checks and maintenance of your car's emissions system. Unless it is damaged, the converter should remain effective virtually forever.

○ The emission control system has three critical sensors—oxygen, coolant temperature, and throttle position. If one or more of these sensors sends the wrong information to the computerized fuel, ignition, and/or emission control system, unburned fuel in the exhaust will damage the converter.

○ A leaking fuel injector and ignition misfire, such as one or more worn spark plugs, can also damage your catalytic converter. So can bad gas, a leaking head gasket, or a faulty fuel pressure regulator.

○ Oil burning due to worn engine components and the oily exhaust it can cause is another reason that catalytic converters are ruined.

## Web Sites to Check Out

○ Check www.highwaysafety.org on the Web. You'll find updated information on the safest cars and crash test ratings.

○ Searching for safety tips? Check out the U.S. Department of Transportation at www.nhtsa.dot.gov on the Web.

○ Check out www.edmunds.com to get the rundown on new and used cars.

○ www.kbb.com. Check out the Kelly Blue Book for car value information.

○ www.autopedia.com. Here's an excellent site you won't want to miss. It's the automotive encyclopedia and complete Internet source for automotive-related information.

# Careers

You are about to enter a frontier fraught with more changing climates, challenging obstacles, peaks, valleys, and adventure than Lewis and Clark faced on their trek west. It's called the American marketplace, and it's not the same one your father and grandfather entered. Gone are the days of working forty years for the same company to retire with a gold watch.

If you read the papers or listen to the news, you already know it's a jungle out there. Today's workplace is a lean, mean, fast, global, high-tech engine fueled by mergers, downsizing, streamlining, and layoffs. The flip side, thanks to new technology, is that there is enormous opportunity for entrepreneurship, small business success, working on your own terms, and retiring long before forty years.

Experts predict that today's students can expect to change jobs or directions as many as seven or eight times in their careers. Finding work that is soul-satisfying and economically rewarding is likely to be an expedition for a lifetime.

But it's not mission impossible. Whether you're looking for that first summer job, a step up the ladder, a career change, or a new opportunity in a different location, you can benefit from the advice of those who have gone before and charted the hazards. Here are some tips to get you started down the right path.

## Choosing a Career/Hunting for a Job

o "Knowing yourself is the key to finding a job that will be the best match for you. Nothing is more predictive of career success or personal satisfaction than having a clear sense of who you are and what you want to do," say Bob D. McDonald and Don Hutcheson, who wrote *The Lemming Conspiracy: How to Redirect Your Life from Stress to Balance* (Longstreet Press, Atlanta, Georgia, 1997). The authors ask, "What are your interests, skills, talents, and personal style? What jobs from the past have you enjoyed the most? Why? Do you like to work with others or alone? Are you creative? Good with your hands? Like working with numbers? Can't stand stress? It doesn't matter how much a job pays if you hate the work, so take time first to learn who you are before choosing a career path."

o Don't know what you want to do? You're not alone. We're not all blessed with a calling to be doctors or artists. Personality/type indicator tests are a good way to help you determine a career path. State labor departments, career counselors, temporary employment agencies, and universities offer these and can help you interpret the results.

o Before you start job hunting, have a clear idea of your strengths, your accomplishments, and what you want to do. Establish goals and targets. Unless you do this, people won't be interested or able to help you in your search. Also check want ads to see what particular job skills are in demand in your field.

o You'll be more successful in your search if you know how to answer the question, "Can you tell me about yourself?" Script a one- to two-minute "commercial" that describes your skills, education, experience, volunteer activities, and accomplishments. Practice it until you know the points cold.

o Promote yourself even when not talking to prospective em-ployers. You can speed up your job search by spreading the news that you are job hunting. Begin organizing, expanding, and using your network of friends and acquaintances. Networking, not job ads, ac-counts for most job leads! For every job that makes it into the paper, there are eight to ten jobs that you never read about. Chances are your friends know about some of them, and don't be ashamed or shy to contact people you know in finding and getting a job. Your mom or dad or a relative's reputation may get you in the door, but it's a qualified candidate who ultimately wins.

o Add to your network by attending job fairs, career network-ing groups, and civic organizations and professional associations in your field. Many newspaper want ad and calendar sections list group meetings and contacts.

o Consider joining a nonprofit group. Becoming a volunteer can make a difference in the lives of others, and you'll also find yourself meeting new people in a variety of different careers.

o You can create a business card even before you're in business. List your desired function (i.e., engineer, administrative assistant, sales, accounting), name, address, E-mail, phone, fax, and beeper numbers. Are you a dedicated employee? Hardest worker on the face of the planet? Do you stay late and arrive early? Be creative and consider your strengths and promote them.

o Keep in mind that many individuals are hired on their potential and desire to learn and do a great job! Many employers will take a chance because they believe someone will put forth an outstanding effort. Be sure to communicate your enthusiasm and absolute passion and interest in obtaining that job.

o Know what you're worth and what you can offer a specific job. Articulate what you can do to bring value to that business and don't be afraid to toot your own horn.

o Did you know that many times people don't get all the help they could because they ask too narrow a question? "Do you know of any job openings in my field?" cuts off further communication if the contacts don't know. Instead ask for ideas, opinions, companies, and the names of others who might help or hire you.

o After researching industries or companies that could use your skills, call or write to see if they would be interested in talking to you. Don't call Human Resources. They think in terms of job vacancies with specific requirements; if your skills don't measure up, you won't get any further. Managers have a better grasp of problems, budgets, and goals and might be willing to create a place for you if you can sell yourself. Call the person who would hire you— that is, the national sales manager, the head of engineering, the comptroller, and so on. Get the name and address from the company switchboard.

o Don't overlook the most obvious resources in your job search: the Sunday employment ads, the Internet, the chamber of commerce, and state departments of labor. Many have computerized job banks and will keep your résumé on file for future employers.

o Avoid answering ads that promise you a list of fabulous federal jobs for a fee! Information about federal jobs is available free through the state department of labor, and information on post office jobs can be found at no charge from your local postmaster. Check your telephone book under the state government section.

o Whether you're a nurse or a CPA, your "job" during the search process is to sell yourself. Everything must work toward that goal. No cutesy answering-machine messages; that's not the first impression you want to make with a future employer. Make calls in a quiet place (no screaming children) and coach family members in how to take messages. Answering machines and call waiting are good ideas.

o Did you know that many opportunities get lost in a job hunt because people don't follow up appropriately? They lose the slip of paper with the phone number or forget to send the résumé. Organize your search on a computer database or in a notebook, keeping track of calls, contacts, letters, and résumés sent. Also, rather than just leaving an application at a company where you've applied, ask to see the manager and introduce yourself. Plus don't wait for them to call you, call them back!

o Take your search online. You can use the Internet to locate job leads, research companies that you may want to work for, and compare your résumé with others in your field. Some popular job sites are http://www.careerpath.com and http://www.jobtrak.com. It's now standard practice to fax résumés, and you may be asked to E-mail information. There's even a site for new college grads: http://www.collegegrad.com. (See additional resources at the end of this chapter.)

o Because there is so much telemarketing today, people are wary of unsolicited phone calls. So how do you get past stranger resistance when calling prospective companies, business contacts, and resource people? Know what you want and how you plan to start before you dial. If someone has recommended that you talk to this person, mention his name in the first sentence. Establish a friendly dialogue, but don't waste his time. Practice on your least important prospective employers first, because you'll improve as you go along.

o Avoid job scams that promise to help you find a job or a list of available jobs for a fee up front.

○ If an 800 number leads you to a 900 number, it's a federal law that the cost of the telephone call should be disclosed. Before using one, make sure you know what specific services they are offering you and get reliable references for that company. If it sounds too good to be true, it usually is.

○ Consider an internship (paid or even unpaid) to get your foot in the door. Inquire if there are any internships available at a place you wish to work. Many employees get their first break after showing a prospective employer how talented they are through an internship. This also looks very good on your résumé.

## Avoiding the Trailing Spouse Blues

○ Some companies will pay for a career-relocating consultant for a spouse. If not, they will have useful contacts to aid your search. Just ask!

○ Don't broadcast your intentions to leave your present job until your spouse's move is a done deal, but after that use contacts at work to help open doors in the new city. We're a mobile society. You don't know who may have lived in your future location or has relatives or business contacts there.

○ Update your résumé and compose a list of references before you move. Job titles or licenses may not translate to your new area, but you can always adapt your skills to something new.

○ Research your destination city on the Internet to find information about schools, communities, housing, and employment. You can search for jobs in your new city, even in your zip code, on http://www.careermosaic.com and http://www.careerpath.com. Local chambers of commerce, boards of education, and visitor bureaus also have Web sites. The more you know going in, the easier it will be to get established.

○ Your realtor can be your best first resource. Most large companies have relocation specialists who know not only the housing market but also the community. They have valuable contacts and information to get you started.

○ If you know prospective employers, write to schedule interviews while you're in town house-hunting. Be sure to say that your relocation is already paid for by your spouse's company. They'll like your initiative and the fact that they don't have to pay to move you.

o Get involved in your new community. Visit the welcome wagon. Go to the homeowner's association and PTA meetings. Join professional associations and make it known *everywhere* that you are new in town and looking to continue, change, or start a career. Most people are gracious and helpful to newcomers.

o Check the bookstore to see if your city has a "job bank" book or employment guide where you can find lists of employers, recruiters, career consultants, and the like. Many chambers of commerce have newcomers' kits or lists of industries or companies broken down by categories that they sell for a small fee. Another good source is the business publications, particularly a fabulous listings guide called *The Book of Lists*, published by the *Business Journal* in most major cities, and usually available in the larger bookstores.

o Consider registering with a temporary staffing service. These companies have grown tremendously of late as more corporations outsource functions and hire temporary workers to improve their bottom line. They place workers at all levels in a wide variety of fields. You'll have instant income, flexible hours, and a chance to get to know the city. Because temporary services are now competing for the best workers, you may also have benefits such as health and dental insurance, 401(k)s, and vacation and holiday pay. Assistance in résumé writing, marketing, and business/computer training are other common perks.

o A growing percentage of jobs with temp agencies are temp-to-hire. This means that after a trial period, you could end up with permanent employment if your skills and personality match the company's needs. The "try before you buy" concept works both ways. You'll get to know your employer before you sign on.

o Since many staffing agencies are national, you could get a jump start on the employment search by registering with one in your home city. They'll transfer your records and you could have job leads before you've even unpacked.

o Did you know that many people find jobs through volunteering? It's a great way to pursue a field you love, make useful contacts, and show what you can do. The local United Way lists all funded agencies, their purpose, personnel, and so on—a great resource for nonprofit employment. Some states, such as Georgia, have a monthly publication of open nonprofit jobs.

## Summer/Part-Time Employment for Teens

○ You've got no experience, no sweat . . . if you've got friends. Networking is the best way to find a job. Tell your friends, your friends' parents, your minister, your counselor, teachers, coaches, anyone you know who is working that you are looking for that first job.

○ Did you know that schools and businesses are hooking up on a regular basis to better prepare tomorrow's workforce? If you're interested in a particular field, an internship is a good way to see if it's right for you. Ask your counselor about school-to-work, tech-prep, and other internship programs. Join vocational student organizations such as DECA (for marketing), VICA (for vocational occupations), FTA (for teachers), and FBLA (for business leaders) to make contacts.

○ Start early. If you begin your job search during spring break, you'll beat the college crowd. By May, many employers will already have filled summer positions. Want to make money over Christmas break? Start looking in the early fall.

○ Be sure to also look past the obvious employers of fast-food restaurants, grocery stores, and retail. Call hotels, the YMCA, landscape businesses, parks, hospitals, contractors, and moving companies. Don't leave any stone unturned.

○ Can't find the ideal job? Create your own. You can make good money and learn a lot about running your own business by providing yard work, tutoring, baby-sitting, painting, pet-sitting, party planning, or errand-running services for busy two-career families.

○ Prepare a simple résumé that includes any work experience, community service, grades (if above average), awards, recognitions, and references. It's not required for most summer jobs, but having one will put you heads above other applicants.

○ Before you interview, know how many hours and when you'll be available to work. Transportation is an important issue to most employers, so let them know you've worked that out ahead of time.

o Did you know that good manners don't stand out, but bad manners do? Want people to think you're responsible enough to handle the job? Look the part. Dress neatly and professionally. Greet the interviewer with a firm handshake and a smile. Make eye contact as you talk. Don't mumble. *Never* seem bored or in a hurry.

o Ask questions that show your interest, but don't ask about money and benefits first. Learning about the job should be your first priority.

## The Résumé and Other Necessary Paperwork

o Good résumés are made, not born. It takes time to dig through your past, remember what you did, for whom, where, and when, and to give the best picture of yourself and your accomplishments in two pages. There are numerous books to help, but don't expect award-winning copy with the first draft.

o Writing about yourself is one of the hardest things to do. Try teaming up with a friend or coworker to get another perspective on the subject.

o Be creative, but truthful. You have to be able to defend or support anything on the résumé. The best thing you can do is say as quickly as possible why you are valuable specifically to that company or the area of expertise you are pursuing. Distinguish yourself from other candidates by focusing on your strengths up front.

o A résumé should look like what you want to do. If you're trying to go corporate, you'll want your business expertise to stand out.

o Chronological résumés that list your work history (starting with your present job) are the most common type. To add sizzle to a chronological résumé, use bullets with short statements of accomplishment beneath the job listing—for example: *Landed largest advertising account from XYZ Company in 1996, by creating slogan for national campaign.*

o A functional résumé, which presents similar types of work experience and accomplishments together, not necessarily in the order you did them, works well for people who have a variety of experience, are changing fields, or want to go into something they did early in their career. Job history and dates go at the end of the functional résumé.

○ Did you know that some employers never read past the career summary paragraph that appears right after your name and address? Want to keep them reading? Make it a high-impact statement that captures the essence of your work history, skills, and qualifications. Although it appears first, write it last, after you've completed the rest of your résumé and know what makes you special.

○ Include your education at the bottom of the résumé, listing highest degree first. If you graduated within the last five years, education listed on the top of the resume is appropriate. Only list high school education if you don't have a college degree. Be sure to include business courses or special training that show you are up to speed in your profession.

○ Include professional affiliations, offices held, and selected social affiliations, hobbies, family. This information is more appropriate in some geographic areas than others.

○ Some experts suggest that you do not include references on your résumé or a line that says they are available on request. Other experts recommend including the line depending upon the length and content of your résumé. Regardless of which way you go, a good idea is to have a typed list of references with your name, address, and phone number plus the reference's title, company name, address, and phone number. If possible, also ask your references for letters of recommendation and consider including the best one with your résumé.

○ Be sure to read and reread your résumé. A spelling error immediately tells your prospective employer that you do not pay attention to details.

○ Write a "marketing" letter, not just a cover letter, to go with your résumé. It should include why you're writing, a short description of your present job, bulleted highlights of your accomplishments, and how you plan to follow up with that person.

○ When responding to a job ad, customize your letter to answer the qualifications needed in the order listed, using the same kind of words. You'll be more successful if you "walk the walk and talk the talk."

○ Be sure to have your résumé printed professionally. This can be done at a quick-copy store using desktop services such as a laser printer. Many of these companies have services where they will format your résumé and make you look like a pro.

## Interviewing

○ If you're going to an unfamiliar place, take a test drive before the day of the interview. Arriving late and out of breath doesn't make a good first impression.

○ Arrive ten to fifteen minutes early and use your waiting time to gather information. Read the annual report or product brochures if there are any in the lobby.

○ Research the company before you go in. (Company Web site, books and articles about the company, Dun & Bradstreet, business databases in library, newspaper, etc.) Prepare some questions to show that you've taken the initiative to learn something about their operations.

○ Think about answers to standard questions like, "What strengths would you bring to the job?" or "Where do you want to be in five years?" Books on interviewing skills give examples of common questions asked.

○ Unless it's a human resources manager, the person interviewing you isn't always doing what he normally does for the company. He may be uncomfortable with the process. You'll make a better impression if you help it go smoothly.

○ Reread your résumé the night before. Most interviewers will ask questions from that, so you'll want it fresh in your mind.

○ Have additional copies of your résumé to hand out if you should interview with more than one person.

○ Answer questions directly in several minutes and don't volunteer irrelevant information. You can talk yourself out of a job by going on and on.

○ *Never* criticize your former employer or go into the nitty-gritty of a layoff. It makes you appear petty even if the criticism is valid or the experience was terrible. Have a short, sweet, neutral answer when asked about your last or present job.

○ Don't lie or embellish about your skills. If you're not familiar with a computer program say so, adding that you're willing to learn.

○ When asked about your salary requirements in an initial interview, be vague—words like *flexible* or *negotiable* are useful. If pinned down, give a range, not a figure. Know what your desired salary is in different increments—annually, monthly, weekly, hourly—so that you're not trying to juggle figures in your head if it's mentioned in the interview or in filling out the job application form.

○ Before leaving, reiterate your interest in the job and ask the next step in the process. If you don't hear back by the designated date, give them a few days before calling. It's not uncommon for managers to let deadlines slip, since their first priority is running the company. Indicate your availability and follow through.

○ Write a thank-you letter immediately to thank them for their consideration. Address aspects of the interview that interested you and show enthusiasm for the job.

○ If you don't get the job, part on an upbeat note. Ask to be remembered in the future. Send a thank-you letter and let the contact know that you valued her time and hope that should any opportunity become available in the near future she will continue to think of you. Be specific and tell the company why you still want to pursue it!

○ You may have beaten out hundreds of other candidates, but don't expect every interview to lead to a job offer. Most don't. You can learn a lot from an interview even if you're rejected. Chalk it up to experience and move on with your search.

## Take Your Search Online

To find more information when job searching, surf the Internet. Many companies are highly interested in finding computer-skilled individuals, so use these sites to explore the possibilities. You'll also learn what additional skills you might need, available job openings, services, and other opportunities that are available.

## Resources

America's Job Bank, www.ajb.dni.us
Department of Labor Employment and Training,
   www.doleta.gov
JOBTRAK, www.jobtrak.com
Job Direct, www.jobdirect.com
CareerMart, www.careermart.com
CareerSite, www.careersite.com
Dr. Dane Separing's Job Hunt Page, www.job-hunt.org
Also try: www.monster.com
        www.coolworks.com
        www.careerpath.com

# Child Safety

---

Like most parents, regrettably, we've been there, too: a few trips to the emergency room, calls to the pediatrician's office with alarming concerns, and bumps and bangs and bruises that we wish we could have prevented. In fact, I'll never forget when our son was pretending he was a tornado and spun around so fast he got dizzy and fell and hit an innocent-looking coffee table. While we didn't prevent every accident possible, we certainly took precautions from dozens of others that might have happened and learned quite a few lessons along the way. Our motto: *You can never be too careful when it comes to children.*

One of the saddest facts I learned in researching this book was that unintentional injury is the leading cause of death and disability among children ages fourteen and under in the United States. According to the National SAFE KIDS Campaign, more than 6,600 children ages fourteen and under died from unintentional injuries in 1995, and nearly 120,000 were permanently injured. One out of every four children, or more than 14 million kids, sustains an injury each year that's serious enough to require medical attention, according to the Campaign, which is a coalition of national and local organizations working to prevent unintentional childhood injuries. And every day, nearly 39,000 children are injured seriously enough to require medical treatment.

The biggest threats to children are injuries resulting from motor vehicle accidents, bike accidents, drowning, fire and burns, suffocation, poisoning, choking, unintentional firearm injuries, and falls, the SAFE KIDS Campaign said. And it estimated that 90 percent of unintentional injuries can be prevented! Those sorts of statistics indicate the importance of child safety.

Making your child's world safer is not a one-time job. Yes, there are some things you need do only once—such as putting safety covers on all the electrical outlets in your home—but for the most part, keeping your child safe will require changing habits and remaining vigilant. By changing habits, I mean that buckling up in the car should be as much a part of your routine as putting the key in the ignition. Another example is purchasing medicines only in childproof containers. By remaining vigilant, I mean staying with your child while she takes her bath, even if the phone rings, reading labels to see if a toy might contain a choking hazard, and holding your child's hand when you're in a busy parking lot. If you keep a gun at home, store it in a locked place, out of your child's reach! And be sure the ammunition is stored separately and locked up! You must consider all the "what-ifs" and then do something ahead of time to prevent an accident.

About 40 percent of deaths and 50 percent of nonfatal unintentional injuries occur in or around the child's home, according to the SAFE KIDS Campaign. Obviously, that's the place where a parent has the most control and can do the most good to create a safe environment. Motor vehicle crashes kill 30 percent of kids ages one to four. The car is another place parents can make safer, simply by making sure their children are in the right kind of seat and properly buckled up.

What other steps can you take to keep your children safe? Plenty, according to the experts. Here are some tips to help you play it safe!

## Making Your Home Safe

o You can report product-related injuries and safety concerns about toys or consumer products to the U.S. Consumer Product Safety Commission Hotline. The agency is looking for any information that could help prevent future injuries. Call 1-800-638-CPSC or visit the agency's Web site at www.cpsc.gov for details. Product recall information is also available from those sources.

o Looking at the world from a child's angle is the best way to find items and areas in your home that could be a potential hazard. To do this, you'll actually need to crawl on your hands and knees around rooms where your children will do the same. Only then will you have a child's-eye view of electrical cords that a child could trip over or become entangled in; see electrical outlets that are just at the right height for curious fingers; find sharp edges on coffee tables; and other unexpected dangers lurking in your kitchen, family room, and nursery.

○ Products to make your home safe for babies and children are sold through a variety of outlets, including baby specialty stores, discount stores, and mass merchandisers, and through mail-order catalogs. It's a good idea to study a catalog or visit a store to see what kind of items are available, then inventory your home to decide exactly which items would work best for the problem areas in your home. The obvious things every parent will need to do include putting protective covers over electrical outlets; installing gates at the top and bottom of staircases and other areas where children could fall; using cabinet or drawer locks in the bathroom, kitchen, and workroom where you store cleaning products, knives, scissors, and other sewing equipment; and securing any other item that could be hazardous in the hands of a child.

○ Remember, china and glass are breakable and dangerous to a child, so store those items up high out of reach, or put a locking device on the cupboard doors.

○ Don't assume anything is safe. Be sure to check your home for hidden problems like a door-stopper knob that can easily be pulled off and swallowed or a drawer that's loose. Parents beware!

○ Keep all medicines and vitamins out of your child's reach and locked up. Teach your child the difference between candy and medicine. Be careful giving your child too much praise for taking medicines. He could take extra doses when you're not around in hopes of more praise later on.

○ Removing a dangerous item can be the easiest and most effective way to make a room safe for a child. Store that glass-topped coffee table in the attic until you no longer have to worry about your child bumping his head into it, for example. Breakable knickknacks and other decorative items will be safer on a high shelf or packed into a storage box while your children are very small.

○ Cords for mini-blinds, vertical blinds, and draperies can pose a risk to children, who can become entangled. Keep them out of a child's reach, high enough even to avoid the reach of a youngster who climbs on furniture. Install a cord tie-down device to the floor, wall, or window jamb. When you install window coverings, adjust the cords to their shortest possible length, and when purchasing custom window coverings, specify a short cord.

o The U.S. Consumer Product Safety Commission recommends against knotting or tying together the cords of mini-blinds and other window coverings in an attempt to shorten the cords. All you are doing, the agency said, is creating a new loop in which a child can become entangled.

o The best way to prevent youngsters from falling out of a double-hung window is to open the window from the top instead of from the bottom. Other precautions you can take include moving furniture away from windows so your child won't have an easy place to start climbing. Never think you're safe because there are screens on your windows. Window screens are designed to keep lightweight bugs from coming in through the window, not to keep a much heavier child from falling out.

o The water a child takes a bath in should be below 120 degrees Fahrenheit to prevent scalding. Test the temperature of the water with your fingers spread, running your hand through the water. It's safest to set your water heater at 120 degrees or less, although you can purchase an antiscald device to use in the bathtub where the child will be bathing.

o Those thin plastic bags that dry cleaning, groceries, and newspapers come wrapped in are a suffocation hazard to children. The plastic film can cling to the child's face, hampering breathing. Keep such bags out of children's reach. Do not use such bags in a child's crib or bed as a mattress protector. Safe, crib-sized mattress pads and covers are available at any store that handles children's products.

o Cords and ribbons tied around a child's neck to hold a pacifier can become tightly twisted or they can catch on protrusions, causing strangulation. Never ever tie anything around your child's neck! You can purchase inexpensive, safe pacifier clips at any store carrying baby products. These items allow you to attach the pacifier to your child's clothing, so it won't get lost or fall on the floor and get dirty.

○ Strings used to hang crib toys and other items on the crib, such as the laces you use to tie the bumper pads into place, should be no longer than 7 inches. Cut them off if they are longer than that, so they can't wrap around the infant's neck. If you install a crib gym, be aware that the label warns it should be removed when the infant can push up on his hands and knees, or reaches the age of five months, whichever comes first.

○ Make sure your child's crib is completely safe. This means avoiding quilts or blankets that your child could become entangled in, or toys that your child could climb up on or pull down. Make sure your fitted sheets fit properly and can't be easily pulled up and loosened. A child could become entangled in them and not be able to get loose.

○ Tiny objects can become lodged in a baby's windpipe, ears, or nose, so they must be kept out of reach. Crawling babies are automatically attracted to anything lying on the floor, and once they pick it up, they usually put it in their mouth. As you are working around the home, be careful when you drop items such as pins, paper clips, rubber bands, and buttons, and pick them up immediately so your child can't grab them. Train older children to do the same, and make sure they realize that some of their favorite playthings, such as a small doll's shoes or playing pieces from a board game, can be hazardous to their baby brother or sister.

○ Homes built before 1978 may contain lead paint. Call your local health department for advice if you think your home contains lead.

○ Make sure all hazardous products are labeled so that you know what they are, and keep them high and locked up. Keep poisonous products stored away from food, and all alcoholic drinks should be locked up as well.

○ Products containing lye are extremely dangerous. It's best not to keep these in your home.

○ Flush medicine down the toilet after the expiration date has passed. Do not throw away or keep any medicines within a child's reach.

○ Keep all perfumes, cosmetics, purses, and car keys out of a child's reach.

○ Keep all plants away from your child, and know all plant names in case you need to call Poison Control. In fact, right now, go and write down the Poison Control number for your area and keep it near telephones in the event of an emergency.

○ Teach your children how to handle an emergency and what they should do. Practice role playing. This also is a good tool to help teach children to keep themselves safe from strangers. Consider a secret password and explain to your child that he should tell no one the code. Teach him not to talk to strangers, what he would do if he got lost at a department store, how to call 911 or another emergency number, and how to safely answer the telephone.

○ Have snacks prepared for your child and communicate clearly your kitchen rules. Many children hurt themselves accidentally while preparing their own snacks and using a dangerous knife or utensil.

○ According to the National SAFE KIDS Campaign, "Ninety percent of child fire-related deaths occur in homes without working smoke detectors. Install smoke detectors in your home on every level in every sleeping area. Test them once a month, replace the batteries at least once a year (unless the batteries are designed for longer life), and replace the detectors every ten years. Plan and practice several fire escape routes from your home and identify an outside meeting place. Children need to know what to do in the event of a fire since they often become scared and hide. Also teach your child to 'stop, drop, and roll' if your child is on fire."

○ According to safety experts, all homes (with or without children) should also have a carbon monoxide alarm installed on each level. Carbon monoxide is one of the leading causes of accidental poisoning deaths in the United States. Odorless, tasteless, and colorless, carbon monoxide is a by-product of combustion. It may enter your home from any of these potential sources: gas or oil-burning furnaces, gas-fueled hot water heaters, gas ranges or cooktops, gas dryers, fireplaces, automobiles in attached garages, wood or coal-burning stoves, or a blocked chimney or flue. Check out radon detectors as well. These simple and easy-to-install safety devices can alert you to potential problems.

○ While in the kitchen, make sure you don't leave handles of pots within reach of children. Be aware of all the risks that could occur between the utensils and cooking and be overly cautious.

○ Check the auto-reverse feature on your garage door.

## One "Tip" You Don't Want

○ About 2,000 children a year are treated in hospital emergency rooms because a chest of drawers tipped over on them, according to the U.S. Consumer Product Safety Commission.

○ Even more children, about 2,300 a year, are treated in emergency rooms each year because a television fell on them. Often, the TV was placed on a TV cart, stand, or table, the CPSC said.

○ Another 580 children a year are treated in an emergency room because a bookcase tipped over onto them.

○ To prevent furniture from falling onto children, place televisions on lower furniture, as far back as possible, and use angle braces or anchors to secure furniture to the walls, suggests the U.S. Consumer Product Safety Commission.

○ According to the National SAFE KIDS Campaign, "Each year, an average of 20,400 children ages five and under are treated in hospital emergency rooms for injuries associated with shopping carts, representing 66 percent of all shopping cart–related injuries." Shopping carts have a high center of gravity and a narrow wheel base, making them top-heavy when loaded and therefore easy to tip over, especially when a child is placed in the seat. Falls from shopping carts and entrapped body parts in the mechanisms also contribute to injuries. Never leave a child alone in a cart even for a moment, or let a child stand up or steer a cart. Always use a safety belt to restrain your child in shopping cart seats and supervise them at all times.

## It's Not Bunk!

○ Some bunk beds have a design problem that can lead to the mattress falling through the frame, injuring or killing a child who is on the lower bunk or under the bed. This danger is possible when the mattress rests only on ledges around the frame of the bed. Cross wires or another means of support, such as wood slats or metal straps, need to be installed to add extra support to the mattress and foundation, the Consumer Product Safety Commission advises. Use screws or bolts to securely fasten the supports to the ledges of both the upper and lower bunk bed. The beds need these supports even if they are not used in the stacked configuration, because children often play under regular beds, too.

o Another danger of bunk beds is that a child under the age of six can get his head trapped under the bunk bed guard rails. To prevent that from happening, close the space between the lower edge of the guard rail and the upper edge of the bed frame to 3½ inches or less. Children under six years of age should not be allowed on the upper bunk, according to the Consumer Product Safety Commission. And infants, children under the age of one, can get trapped between the bed and the wall, so the commission recommends that a guard rail be placed next to the wall, even on the lower bunk, to reduce the risk of this kind of accident.

## Safety at Play

o All toys manufactured or imported into the United States require labels to indicate that they have small parts that could be hazardous to a child under the age of three. Those containing balls that are 1.75 inches or less in diameter, marbles, or other small parts are labeled as a choking hazard for children under the age of three. The rule has been in effect since 1995.

o Uninflated or broken balloons can cause a young child to choke or suffocate if she tries to swallow a piece. Quickly remove and discard all the pieces if a balloon bursts, and use Mylar instead when possible. Keep uninflated balloons out of your youngster's reach. They are also dangerous to pets!

o Make sure your child is supervised while playing and that he understands the rules outside—for example, no playing in the street, no leaving the front yard. Establish rules and stick to them. It's also important that you teach your child how to cross the street. Stop, look left, right, left again, and then cross.

o A bike helmet that has met safety standards will carry a

certification sticker on the helmet itself or on the packaging it is sold in. Look for an ASTM (American Society for Testing and Materials), Snell or ANSI (American National Standards Institute), or the New Federal Standard approved sticker inside the helmet or on the box before you purchase it.

○ A bike helmet should sit squarely on the child's head, cover the forehead, and not rock side to side or forward to back. Bring your child with you when you shop for helmets, so he or she can try it on before you purchase one, the National SAFE KIDS Campaign recommends.

○ There may be a discount program for safety devices such as bike helmets in your area, run by state and local SAFE KIDS Coalitions and supported by corporate sponsors. For information about such programs and their locations, call the National SAFE KIDS Campaign office at 1-202-662-0600.

○ Be sure to buy a bike that's not too big or complicated for your child and that has a bell or horn. Bikes need regular checking to make sure the brakes work. When shopping for a bike, take your child with you. A bike must be carefully fitted so that the balls of the child's feet rest on the ground. Don't buy a bike that he'll grow into because it will be too big to control at first.

○ Children who wish to learn how to use skates must have the proper equipment. The International In-Line Skating Association recommends that parents purchase their child a multisport helmet. It can also be used as a bicycle helmet. They also suggest that a child wear knee pads and elbow pads with wrist guards for proper protection when using in-line skates, roller skates, and skateboards.

○ A safe playground should have hardwood fiber, mulch chips, pea gravel, fine sand, or shredded rubber under all the play equipment. The surfacing should be at least 12 inches deep and extend for at least 6 feet in all directions around the play equipment, according to the National SAFE KIDS Campaign. Asphalt, concrete, grass, and soil are not safe surfaces under play equipment.

○ Keep your child away from the gas pump when you are filling your tank. A child could get splashed in the face or eyes if the tank overflows.

○ Never leave a child near water alone. According to Egleston's

Children's Hospital at Emory University, every year 1,000 U.S. children under the age of fourteen drown and another 4,000 are rushed to hospital emergency rooms for care. When your child is underwater, brain damage can happen in just four minutes. Swimming lessons are very important and helpful, but they're not enough; even a good swimmer can panic in the water. A young child can drown in as little as 1 inch of water, so make sure you are always with your child. Learn CPR and keep rescue equipment, a telephone, and emergency numbers poolside.

o Every year 6,300 children age fourteen years and under are treated in hospital emergency rooms for diving injuries, and many of these children are left paralyzed because of injuries to the head or spine. Egleston's experts suggest that home pools aren't safe for diving—the water isn't deep enough. Lakes and rivers are also dangerous. Sliding down a pool slide headfirst can cause serious head injuries. About 4,000 children are injured annually on pool slides.

o Be sure to safety-proof the area around a pool or spa with a childproof fence or wall at least 5 feet high all the way around the pool or spa. Be sure to also have a childproof gate and pool cover. Do not use the house as a side of your fence.

o Beware of pool and spa drains. A child's hair may become caught in the drain and cause drowning. Once again, the main rule should be: Never leave a child unsupervised while in water!

## Safety in the Car

o Babies weighing at least 20 pounds and up to at least one year old should be properly strapped into a rear-facing car seat. Check the manufacturer's instructions on your car seat to see what the age and size recommendations are. It's important to keep a baby facing to the rear, because if the car stops suddenly or is involved in a crash, a baby that is facing toward the front can receive severe neck injuries, according to the National Highway Transportation Safety Administration.

o A passenger-side air bag that deploys and hits a rear-facing child car seat can cause severe injuries or death to the child in the car seat. A rear-facing seat should never be installed in the front seat of a car equipped with a passenger air bag. The backseat is the safest place for kids of any age to ride.

o Children who are over a year old and weigh at least 20 pounds should ride in a car seat that faces the front of the vehicle. Continue to use the car seat for as long as your youngster fits comfortably in it.

o Once a child reaches 40 pounds (about four to eight years), she should ride in a booster seat until she's big enough for the car's lap and shoulder belts to fit properly.

o Usually kids over 80 pounds and eight years old can fit correctly in lap and shoulder belts. Children should be tall enough to sit with their knees bent at the edge of the seat, and the lap and shoulder belts should fit low over the hips and upper thighs and snug over the shoulders.

o Safety organizations recommend that all children ride in the backseat of the car until they are at least twelve years old. The backseat is recommended as the safest part of the car should it be involved in an accident. The backseat rule is especially important in automobiles equipped with passenger-side air bags. While air bags save lives, they are designed for full-sized grown-ups, and the force with which they deploy can cause serious injuries or death to a child, or even to a petite-sized adult. If the child must ride in the front seat for unavoidable reasons, move the seat as far back as possible from the dashboard.

o Send in the car seat registration card so that you will be notified in case your car seat is recalled. If you have any questions, call the United States Department of Transportation's D.O.T. Auto Safety Hotline at 1-800-424-9393.

o Never use a car seat that has been involved in a crash.

o Route the safety belt correctly through the car seat and make sure you have installed it properly.

o Get a tight fit—the seat should not move more than 1 inch from side to side or toward the front of the vehicle.

o Check your vehicle owner's manual to see if you need a locking clip. Not all safety belts will secure your car seat without it.

○ Since not all child safety seats fit all cars, make sure you read the owner's manual and instructions prior to purchasing a specific car seat.

○ To check to see if your child safety seat has been recalled, call the D.O.T. Auto Safety Hotline operated by the United States Department of Transportation at 1-800-424-9393, or check out their Web site at www.nhtsa.dot.gov for a list and helpful information on auto safety recall, child safety seats, vehicle equipment, and more.

# Cleaning

Perhaps you can think of one or more times when you had every good intention of cleaning something and caused more damage or trouble. I'll never forget the time I thought it was a good idea to use nail polish remover on my wooden end table when I spilled some fingernail polish. Within seconds I did remove the stain, but also some of the finish on the wooden surface.

The purpose of this chapter is to guide you to a variety of cleaning solutions recommended by the pros. These tips have worked on many a tough spot or stain; however, experts agree that it's always best to consult with a professional if you are in doubt or an item is valuable. They also suggest that you test an area first and make sure a particular solution is just right for the object you are cleaning. A particular finish or material can be harmed by your efforts to clean it, so do-it-yourselfers beware and take the safe route first by testing a small inconspicuous area so you won't be sorry later on. Less is more when it comes to cleaning things up.

According to Leone Ackerly Hinzman, the founder of Mini Maid, a company that has specialized in home cleaning for over twenty-five years, "People can speed up their cleaning by getting rid of clutter and cleaning as they go. If you are cleaning as you go, what you have left is dirt and dust! If clutter and shoes and toys are scattered everywhere, cleaning takes more time and it's obvious the house is a mess." Leone added, "It's much easier to clean if you do it on a regular basis. Split your home up and that way it's not so daunting. If you have a large home, you shouldn't try and clean it all in one day. Priority tasks begin with the kitchen and the master bathroom, the bigger areas and most used first. Make the beds first and finish one area before you go to the next. As you go down the hall, hit all the bedrooms and continue to vacuum as you go along. Don't leave a room until you finish it."

So, take it from the pros. There are do's and don'ts that will make cleaning your surroundings a lot easier, and the following tips will help you clean up your act. There are also a wide variety of products including environmentally friendly ones, so be sure to check out your choices. But don't forget, every surface and object is different and there are dozens of tricks of the trade, including the ones you know, to keep those floors sparkling and your home clean as a whistle.

## Keep in Mind!

○ It's important to consider that many cleansers are hazardous to the environment, children, and pets, so use great caution in where you store them and how you use them.

○ Cleansers can be dangerous, so be sure to wear rubber gloves and avoid any contact with skin, eyes, and clothes when using bleach or ammonia, as well as other hazardous products.

○ Open windows in the rooms you are cleaning if possible to provide ventilation, and do not combine cleaners, since some can react adversely when mixed.

○ Salt, lemon juice, white vinegar, and baking soda can be used as gentle, environmentally friendly household cleaners. Consider all alternatives when purchasing your household products.

○ Create a cleaning system that you can remember. For example, cleaning from left to right or bottom to top will help you remember what you've already done.

## Cleaners to Have on Hand

(Store all cleaning items out of the reach of children)
    Baking soda
    Bleach
    Borax
    Cornstarch
    Lemon juice
    Vinegar

## Cleaning Tips

### Appliances

○ Ovens can be cleaned while still warm with a damp cloth dipped in baking soda.

○ Wipe out your microwave with each use.

○ Prevent spills from burning by pouring salt over the spill while cooking. When cool, wipe up.

### Artwork

○ Always check with the framer or artist on how to clean a piece of art. Certain household products can be harmful to an artist's finish and even ruin the work of art. A clean paintbrush with soft bristles can be used to remove dust from the surface, but be sure you know what you are dealing with.

○ Avoid spraying glass cleaner on a framed piece of art or a photograph. The glass cleaner could run and seep into the frame, harming what's in it.

### Banisters

○ Put an old sock on your hand and lightly dampen it. This is a great way to quickly dust and clean hard-to-reach areas on your banisters or railings. Use the other clean dry sock to make sure it's completely dry.

### Baseball Caps and Visors

○ Place baseball caps and visors on the top rack of your empty dishwasher. Use a medium heat cycle and wash.

### Bathtub and Shower

○ The best time to clean a bathtub or shower is right after you've bathed. That's because the dirt and scum are loosened and that makes your job easier.

○ Shower doors often have hard-water deposits built up. Wipe the glass door with white vinegar and leave on for up to thirty minutes, and then rinse off. Your glass should be sparkling.

o Enamel and porcelain bathtubs should be cleaned with a nonabrasive cleaner. Rinse thoroughly after cleaning.

o If your drain looks tarnished, try cleaning it with a polish that is suitable for brass or other metal.

## Books

o If you get mildew on books, sprinkle or dust pages with corn-starch. Let stand for seven days. Mildew will brush off with the starch.

## Cabinets

o Use a little baking soda and water to clean cabinets. Dry immediately.

## Candles

o Your candlesticks will clean up a lot quicker if you place them in the freezer for an hour. The wax will harden and be easier to re-move. If your candlesticks are fragile or valuable antiques, it's best to proceed with great care.

## Can Opener

o Don't overlook your can opener, which could be a prime tar-get for harboring germs. Keep it clean after each use. Use a tooth-brush and hot sudsy water to clean it and dry thoroughly.

## Car

o After washing your car, don't let it dry naturally. Most water has chlorine in it, which can damage the finish. Plus, never use household products on your car, since they might be too harsh for a car's surfaces. Use only products designed for car cleaning.

## Carpets

o It's best to vacuum regularly. Don't forget the molding—it collects a lot of dirt. You have to get in the seam with the tools; a whisk broom is perfect for this.

o Check out a vacuum cleaner with a special HEPA (high-efficiency particle absorbent) filter. This filter helps reduce allergens, so if someone you love suffers from extreme allergies, this might be a great investment.

o When I get a stain on the carpet, I like to use cold water on a clean white cloth and blot the stain. When in doubt, try a damp cloth first and blot dry.

o Sprinkle a little baking soda on your carpet to help deodorize it. Let it sit for ten to fifteen minutes and then vacuum it up.

o Use cornstarch to clean your carpets.

## Chandeliers

o Dust them gently. You can get a wand with a long stick and raccoonlike tail that attracts dust, and these work on blinds or ceiling fans.

## Clothing

o If you want to reduce the wrinkles when drying clothes, take the clothing out of the dryer shortly before the dryer stops.

o You should always test a fabric first to make sure it is safe for bleach. Mix 1 teaspoon bleach in ¼ cup water and put a drop on a section of the fabric that won't be seen. Leave it for a minute and then blot with a clean, white cloth. If the color is secure, then it won't change and should be safe to bleach.

o In the event that you have dirty rings around your collars, try mixing a pasty solution of vinegar and baking soda. Let it stand for one hour and then rinse it out and wash. You can also try the solution on a toothbrush and see if a little elbow grease will help.

o Turn all T-shirts inside out to make sure the decals on the T-shirts won't come off or crack during washing. Air-dry if you are concerned.

o Add a dry towel to the dryer when drying a load. The dry towel will heat up quicker and help the entire load dry faster by absorbing some of the moisture from the other items. The same goes for drying a second load right after the first has finished. Once the dryer is hot, it dries quicker.

## Cobwebs

○ Lift cobwebs away from surfaces by using a sock on the end of a broom handle, and check corners of rooms where cobwebs occur.

## Combs and Brushes

○ Soak brushes and combs in a drop of mild shampoo and let soak. Using the comb, scrape the brush until the excess hair and grime is removed. Let soak in fresh water until clean. Rinse and dry thoroughly.

## Counters

○ Every counter is different, from laminates to granite to tile. Match a product that specifically says it is suitable for that surface or you risk harming it.

○ Sprinkle a little baking soda on your laminate counter and use a slightly damp sponge to wipe it up. Dry with a cloth when finished.

## Crystal

○ If you have small crystal pieces and vases you wish to clean, wash with dishwashing detergent to which bluing has been added. Rinse and let air-dry.

○ If you have large crystal flower vases, clean them out by emptying dirty water. Spray inside and out with glass cleaner and wipe dry.

## Cutting Board

○ Avoid a porous surface for a cutting board; clean any cutting board carefully after each use. Use a little bleach and water and rinse and dry thoroughly.

## Dishwasher

○ Clean your plates of food before you put them in the dishwasher. The soap and hot water of the dishwasher keep the appliance clean. Check now and then in your basket that there is no broken glass or seeds, since they affect the way the washer washes.

○ In case you need to clean your dishwasher, sprinkle a little baking soda on the walls of the dishwasher and leave it. Then clean your dishwasher with a damp rag.

## Doormats

○ That's right! Doormats need cleaning, since they are the welcome mat for anyone coming into your home. Why have old dirt tracked in daily? Shake them out regularly and wash if possible.

## Drapes

○ You should dust drapes, and the best way is with vacuum tools. If your vacuum doesn't have attachments, use a cloth as far as you can reach and then put the cloth on the end of a broomstick for the high places.

## Dust

○ Avoid using dusters that just move the dust from one area to another. Use your vacuum attachment to suck up the dust, or a dampened cloth if the area is easy to reach. Purchase the best vacuum you can afford and make sure it has all the necessary attachments that make cleaning a breeze.

○ When you must dust, do it from top to bottom so the dust isn't just spread around.

## Faucets

○ A little toothpaste and water should do the trick when cleaning faucets.

○ Chrome fixtures will sparkle if you spray them with a little white vinegar or window cleaner and polish with a soft cloth.

## Floors

○ Sweep floors with a broom or dust floors first with a terry-cloth dust mop or damp mop.

○ Most floors need a gentle cleaner. A little white distilled vinegar or liquid soap and water will do a good job on no-wax floors or polyurethane-finished wood floors. Never leave water standing, and make sure your mop is slightly damp rather than sopping wet, since too much water can damage a wooden floor.

o Ceramic tile and brick floors can also be cleaned as above.

o Do not use soap when mopping slate or stone floors.

o Keep doormats at all major doors to collect dirt and grime before entering.

### Furniture

o If you dust with a dry cloth, you can actually scratch the surface of your furniture. Choosing a soft cloth that has been dampened and wrung almost dry can work nicely on some finishes or use a light coat of furniture polish.

### Glassware and Dishes

o Line your sink with a towel to make sure you don't chip your glassware and dishes while cleaning.

### Gum

o Rub an ice cube against the gum, depending on where it is stuck. The gum will harden and be easier to remove when it's not sticky.

### Hardwood Floors

o Hardwood floors are usually sealed. You need a clean mop head that's been dampened to the point that it is just damp and almost dry, and then dust the floor. Your goal is to pick up dust. You don't want any liquid on the floor.

o If you spill something on hardwood, dry it immediately.

### Jacuzzi

o Check with the company you purchased your Jacuzzi from, since it is important to clean it on a regular basis. Get the facts and make sure you pay attention to the jets and the appropriate method of cleaning.

### Jewelry

o Mix equal parts of ammonia and warm water in a dish and let jewelry soak for ten minutes. Do not use this cleanser for pearls or fragile stones, since it will hurt the finish.

o It's always best to remove jewelry when swimming or bathing, since chlorine can damage gold.

## Lamps

o Use a clean, soft-bristle paintbrush to dust pleats on a lamp shade.

o You can dust a pleated lamp shade by using a hair dryer on the cool cycle or the brush attachment of your vacuum cleaner.

## Leather

o Cleaners for leather furniture should always be tested on the back side to make sure you aren't harming the leather. Use a dry-damp cloth to remove anything that is sticky. It is also important to clean leather by dry-damp dusting. Buff dry and use a leather cream recommended by the furniture company. If you want your leather to crack to look aged, then avoid any creams, which moisturize the leather.

o For even very small stains, call the manufacturer or the company you purchased the leather furniture from and get their suggestions for cleaning. Saddle soap is effective in some cases.

## Marble

o Start out with a clean, well-sealed buff floor. All you need to do is damp-mop to remove the dust. Once a year you can have it buffed by an expert.

## Mirrors

o Use only alcohol-based solutions or vinegar water to clean mirrors. Ammonia could damage the back of the mirror. Avoid spraying mirrors, since the solution could seep behind the mirror and cause damage in some way.

## Odors

o Soak cotton balls in deodorizer and place them on windowsills, behind curtains.

o Baking soda mixed with water can help alleviate odors like garlic and onions from cutting boards.

○ Dip a cotton ball in pure vanilla extract and place in the refrigerator in a shallow dish to help eliminate odors.

### Ovens and Stoves

○ Let oven spills cool and then sprinkle with salt. Let stand for at least ½ hour and then scrape off.

### Piano

○ Ivory piano keys are less likely to yellow if you keep them exposed to sunlight. Place a small object to keep the keyboard lid from closing. To clean keys, you can use a soft cloth dipped in lemon juice or alcohol.

### Pots and Pans

○ For copper pots and pans, use a copper cleaner. Coated pots and pans must be cleaned with a gentle cleaner, so check your purchasing instructions before use.

### Refrigerator

○ Crumpled newspaper placed in the refrigerator overnight can help reduce and remove smells and odors after cleaning.

○ Warm water and unscented detergent can help clean a refrigerator. Never use bleach. Or create a mixture by adding a teaspoon of baking soda to a quart of warm water.

### Shoes

○ If you get a black mark on patent leather, you can usually use fingernail polish remover to take it off instantly. Put a little on a cloth and watch it disappear. Test an area before doing this to make sure it's safe.

### Shower

○ The shower should air-dry, so avoid leaving the door or shower curtain closed all the time. Mildew breeds in moist areas, so open it up after cleaning or a shower.

## Silver

○ Wash silver immediately, since many foods that contain ingredients like salt and other acids can lead to tarnishing.

## Sinks

○ Clean your porcelain sink by filling the sink with hot water and adding a few drops of household bleach. You can also line the sink with paper towels and saturate with diluted household bleach. Let stand for five minutes and then remove towels. Rinse well before use.

○ To keep stainless steel beautiful, put baby oil on a soft cloth or an old diaper and, after you clean the appliance, gently buff it for a shiny appearance.

○ If you have a black sink, never use a cleanser or detergent. Use a degreaser and no water at all. Wipe thoroughly and shine it with a glass cleaner.

## Sponges

○ Put your sponge in the dishwasher to clean it. The hot water should kill the bacteria.

## Stains

○ Whenever possible, try to get a stain of any kind out of clothing as soon as possible. If you are in doubt about how to remove it, take it immediately to a dry cleaner and identify the stain.

○ Coffee stains usually will come right out if you rub a little baking soda and water into the stain. Soak and rinse and blot dry.

○ To remove bloodstains, soak or rinse in cold water as soon as the stain occurs. Hot water sets the bloodstain, but cold will get it out!

○ Wine stains can be removed by sprinkling a little salt right onto the stain. Then pour seltzer water right on top. This mixture should sit for five to ten minutes and then come right out. Do not rub the area.

○ Items with grass stains should be washed in hot suds.

○ Ink stains can be treated with hair spray put directly on the spot and then blotted with a clean cloth. For polyesters, use alcohol and blot dry.

o Perspiration stains on articles that must be dry cleaned should be discussed with your dry cleaner. For other items you wash, try sponging the area with a weak solution of white vinegar and water or lemon juice.

### Stickers

o Car stickers stuck to glass are a definite pain. Remove them with a little vinegar and water. They should come right off.

o Remove label stickers from objects you purchase with vinegar and water, or soak the sticker for five minutes in a little dishwashing detergent and then use a sponge to see if you can pry it loose.

### Smoke

o Burn candles in a room that has the smell of cigarette smoke. This will help remove the smoky odor.

o Put small bowls of vinegar in a room where smokers are congregated. This helps control the smell of smoke.

### Sterling Silver and Flatware

o To clean sterling silver or silver-plated flatware, unless otherwise noted, wash it in the dishwasher, provided that the detergent does not have any lemon scent, which might hurt the surface.

o Silver-treated cloths that protect silver from tarnishing really work. Store silver in a cabinet or closet to slow down the process.

### Telephones

o Clean telephones lightly with rubbing alcohol. Clean the ear- and mouthpieces with antiseptic fluid, applied on a cotton ball.

### Tiles

o Remove all soap scum, then apply three coats of cream furniture polish. Buff well between each application, then water and soap scum will bead off.

**Toilets**

o While the surface is wet, use a toothbrush to clean around all the rubber bumpers and hinges in your toilet tank.

**Tub**

o An all-purpose tub cleaner can go to work for you! Check out how long you can safely leave it once sprayed on. The guck and grime will be ready to wash off. If you're using too much muscle, you might scratch the finish, so let the product do the work.

**Upholstery**

o Rub on cornstarch to clean upholstery. Let stand for twenty-four hours and then vacuum.

**Vacuum Odor**

o On a regular basis, spray a small cotton ball or piece of tissue with a preferred room deodorizer. Allow the vacuum to suck item in bag. This will disseminate a fresh odor as you vacuum. Keep your vacuum cleaner clean and don't let odor build up.

**Vinyl and Linoleum**

o To remove crayon marks on vinyl wall covering, use silver polish paste applied with a clean cloth. Always test a small area first.

**Wallpaper**

o Dust nonwashable wallpaper regularly to prevent dirt from building up; do not use water, because it will loosen the paper from the wall. Make sure you know if your wallpaper is washable before trying to clean it.

o Most wallpapers can be washed with water; however, you should test an area first. Whenever possible, check with the store you purchased the wallpaper from and let them know what the spot is before cleaning it.

**Walls**

&#9675; Each wall is obviously different, and while you can test a small area that's inconspicuous, water often works best. Simply blot with a clean, damp soft cloth on the spot and let dry. I always suggest calling the manufacturer or the paint store where you purchased your paint to ask them how best to clean a spot. Depending on exactly what the spot is, you'll have to adjust your approach.

&#9675; An artgum eraser that's very gentle is good to have around to remove fingerprints. Gently rub without pressure to try to remove the mark. If you rub too hard, you might dull the finish and it would look worse than the original mark.

**Wicker**

&#9675; Wash wicker with a solution of warm salt water and blot dry. To keep it from drying out, apply lemon oil occasionally.

**Windows**

&#9675; Mix vinegar and water to clean windows.

&#9675; Lightly spray window cleaner on the window and use a squeegee to remove it. The squeegee helps you avoid streaks and is perfect for larger windows that don't have panes.

Please note: Surfaces and cleaning products can vary. Test an area that is out of sight to make sure a cleaning procedure is safe for each individual surface.

# College

If one size fit all, choosing a college wouldn't be such a dilemma for parents and teens. But colleges, like the students who attend them, come in all shapes and sizes and have different personalities and strengths.

According to the *Chronicle of Higher Education*, there are 3,706 colleges and universities in the United States, so the road to the school of your dreams may be long and winding. Start early, certainly no later than the junior year of high school, and expect to have some surprises, disappointments, time-consuming paperwork, and hard decisions during your exploration.

"Unfortunately, too many families put more time and effort into a car purchase than they do the college-planning process. Students may choose colleges based on what sounds good or where their friends are going," said Dr. Mark L. Fisher, president of Fisher Educational Consultants. "Make sure your selections are based on sound reasoning. Ask questions like, What are the advantages of a large or small school? Does this college fit academically? Is it too far away? Active research makes for better college choices and experiences," he added.

The better you understand the selection, application, and financial-aid processes, the better your chances of finding the school that meets your personality, plans, and pocketbook. There are resources available at libraries, bookstores, and on the Internet. Don't overlook close-to-home experts—guidance counselors, teachers, and alumni whom you know.

College, as a life milestone, is too important to be taken lightly, but lots of families have survived, even grown closer from the adventure. You can, too, especially if you follow these tips from those who know the game best.

## Making a Match: The College Selection Process

○ Self-assessment is an important first step in selecting colleges. Many students thrive on large university campuses; others love the nurturing atmosphere and the individual attention of a small college. "Know your personality, talents, interests, and what you expect from a college education before you begin," said Dr. Carol E. DeLucca, of Carol E. Delucca & Associates, an educational consultant.

○ Start your search wide and narrow it by considering these basic options: enrollment size, campus setting, type of school (university, liberal arts college, conservatory), geographic location, academic needs, extracurricular activities, campus life, cost.

○ Don't eliminate schools based on sticker price. You don't know what financial-aid package you may receive.

○ If you feel you need additional help with your search, consider the services of a qualified independent educational counselor. Ask for references from other people they have helped, and get a clear picture of how they might assist you. Check out www.nacac.com, the national certifying association for public, private, and independent counselors.

○ Comparative college guides put facts and figures at your fingertips quickly, but that information changes, so make sure you have the latest edition.

○ The best place to get accurate data is from the college itself. Write to the college admissions office to request information, then start a college file, with a folder for each school.

○ Explore colleges using the Internet. Most colleges have Web sites; some even have organization and/or individual student pages that tell you about activities or dorm life.

○ Want to college-shop in one spot? Try a college fair, where many colleges set up information booths. It's a great place to gather information, especially about schools too far away to visit. Also check with your high-school college counselor, as well as nearby private and public schools.

○ Don't overlook the unique benefits of women's colleges. There are about eighty women's colleges in the United States; some are among the most highly ranked institutions in the nation. Studies show that students at female colleges have more opportunities for leadership, feel satisfied with their college experience, and are more likely to graduate and go on to higher education, according to the Women's College Coalition, an organization that documents and promotes the value of women's colleges.

o Religion is not mentioned in many college brochures. Ask about religious opportunities when you visit. If you're Jewish, the *Hillel Guide to Jewish Life on Campus* (13th edition, Princeton Review, 1997) is a valuable resource.

o Don't choose a college based solely on your major. More than half of college students change their major at least once. Also, check out the required courses in your major and get the facts.

o Did you know that 80 percent of the jobs in the United States don't require a college education? They do require skills and training beyond high school. Technical institutes offer a range of healthcare and other career programs, from certificates to associate degrees, at a lower cost than most colleges. Because their programs are market-driven, they offer graduates a very high job-placement rate.

## Checking It Out: The College Visit

o According to Missy Alford Sanchez, high school counselor at Woodward Academy, "After doing serious soul-searching about what you (not your friends) want in the college experience, the best thing you can do for yourself is to visit the colleges to determine what you like and what you don't. Until you have sat in large classes and small classes, seen what urban vs. rural vs. suburban campuses are like—in other words, compared the actual with the perceived— most students don't really know what they want."

o Sanchez adds, "Ideally, a student would go visit his top three picks, but until you have seen the choices, how do you know those top three are good matches for you? Waiting to visit until a student has been accepted in his senior year is too late and a major mistake. At the latest, begin visiting colleges the summer before your junior year. You don't need to spend days to obtain the essence of a college; three or four hours works just fine. Start with your local colleges as you investigate types, then based on what you like, find those types in the part of the United States you think you'd like to live for four years."

o "Go visit this second group over spring break, on school holidays, and even during summer vacations. Many colleges have summer schools, so you still have a pretty good idea of facilities, programs, courses offered, dorms, and surrounding area. Visiting during the summer is not as grim as it is often portrayed. Just make certain you can visit your top three choices during the fall of your senior year if needed," suggests Sanchez.

o College brochures make all schools look exciting and wonderful. That's their job—to entice students to come. But they can't tell you how the campus looks and smells, whether the students are friendly, the library small, or the surrounding neighborhood questionable. Get past the hype and do your own research. Don't pick a college sight unseen.

o Call in advance for information sessions and tour reservations. If you'd like to sit in on classes, meet a coach, or tour the fine arts facilities, ask ahead of time.

o Read all the materials sent, so that you don't waste everyone's time by asking questions that have already been answered. If the tour is led by a student, talk as you walk. Here's your chance to get a view of campus life from the best source of all.

o Concerned about safety issues? Crime statistics must be kept by colleges. That's the law. If you have questions about safety, be sure to ask.

o After the "official" information session and campus tour, check out the bookstore and student center. Eat in the cafeteria. Talk to students. Pick up a college newspaper. See how the campus feels to you.

o Before you leave, gather admission/application materials, brochures on special programs, and financial-aid forms. It will save time later.

o While thoughts are fresh, make notes on your reaction to the campus, students, academic programs, housing, athletics, social environment, and opportunities. Writing down your pros and cons will make it easier to make good decisions.

o Beginning in your freshman or sophomore year of high school, start a résumé that reflects your honors, achievements, community involvement, and so on, and keep a running list of all activities you participate in while in high school. Be specific about what each item was and how many hours you spent doing it, and prepare your résumé over time. Avoid waiting until your senior year to do this, since it's too late then to do anything about your achievements. Colleges look at what you've accomplished during your entire career in high school, not just the last year. Type your résumé and make sure that it is accurate and honestly reflects you.

## Doing the Paperwork: College Applications

o To avoid messy mistakes, make a photocopy of your application to use for your first draft. When it's letter-perfect, transfer the information and essays to the real document. Typing the application makes for a better presentation, say most experts.

o Create a file for each school and keep up with all of the details. Keep notes about when you applied for applications, telephone numbers, Web and mailing addresses, and the like. You'll appreciate being organized later on when you need this information.

o Compile and type an accurate list of each college admissions office and key numbers and contacts. This list will be helpful when you prepare labels and address your application packet.

o Want to make the process even easier? Apply electronically. Some schools have applications on the Internet. You submit a cleaner, neater application and only have to fill in your personal data once. If you are unsure of how to apply, or which application to use, call the college admissions office and ask their preference.

o There is also a Common Application, good for about 150 colleges. Make sure that when schools ask for additional information, however, that you provide it. If you are in doubt, call each college you are applying to and make sure the college accepts this application.

o Know what college admission staffs look at first? In many

cases, your high school record. Good grades and steady progress at increasingly complex courses are the best indicator for success in college.

○ College admission staffs like students who face challenges. They are often more impressed by a B in an Advanced Placement or honors course than an A in a less rigorous course. Get the facts.

○ Have your counselor include an academic school profile with your application. That way you won't be penalized for not taking an AP course or a fourth year of language if it isn't offered.

○ Writing the essay is the hardest part of filling out a college application, but don't leave it to the last minute. This is where you get to present yourself as a personality with hobbies, values, and dreams, not just a statistic. A winning essay can make a difference, especially in a borderline application. A helpful idea for some students is to gather a selection of college essay questions from seniors or actual online applications and give them a try in your junior year. Questions usually probe personal challenges or accomplishments. Fill out a sample application just for practice and see what you are in for.

○ Eileen Tropauer, an English teacher and tutor for over thirty years, guides students in the writing of college essays. She advises, "Reveal your feelings and thoughts to maintain the reader's interest and empathy. Your transcript shows the facts, so you must disclose deeper responses. Also, remember that less is more, and exclude any extraneous material unrelated to the thesis."

○ Avoid clichés and generalizations. Don't say you want to be a nurse because you want to help people . . . you were inspired to be a nurse by a person or experience. Tell about it. Concrete details will make your essay memorable.

○ Tailor your essay to the college; they're looking for a good match, too. If it's an urban university, write why you're attracted to city life, not the joys of the country.

○ Don't be a shrinking violet. You're up against tough, national competition. If you were voted most improved player in your first soccer season, say so.

○ It's difficult writing about yourself, so ask teachers or parents to read your draft and make suggestions.

o If you need a reference from your counselor and she doesn't know you well, have a favorite teacher fill her in on your sterling qualities or give the teacher a list of your achievements.

o Check to see if recommendation letters from people who know you or alumnae are accepted.

o Applications cost money, so only apply to schools that truly interest you. Apply to one "safe" or "fallback" school—one you know you can get into. Get clear which are your reach schools—the ones that will be tough to get into but you are shooting for. Have a realistic understanding of the schools you are applying to.

o Inquire when each college begins sending out acceptance letters and apply as early as possible. You'll be happy you did in the event you get accepted in October.

o It is important to check that your application has been received and your file is complete. Some experts recommend including a stamped postcard with your application submission. On one side of the postcard put your address and on the opposite side type: *The application of [your name, address, etc.] is complete____; is not complete____, missing items____.* This way, when your file is complete, you'll receive the postcard and be reassured or be notified of any missing items. You can also check some colleges online or by calling directly; however, give them enough time to process the application.

## Score Your Best on the SAT and ACT

o Students tend to eliminate colleges if they think they don't have the academic credentials. Remember that average published SAT scores in comparative guides mean that half the students scored higher and half lower than those numbers. Many factors go into accepting prospective students.

o Think you can't study for the SAT? Not so. According to the College Board (creators of the SAT), the best long-term preparation is to take challenging courses and work hard. "Short-term, it helps to know how the test is structured and practice the multiple-choice format, so read the test-taking tips in the registration booklet and take the sample test. Taking the PSAT will give you practice under similar test-taking conditions," said Janice Gams, public affairs officer for the College Board.

○ You can get the following aids from the College Board: *Ten Real SATs, The Official Guide to SAT II Achievement Tests, One-on-One with the SAT* (computer software, IBM compatible), and *Look Inside the SAT* (a video) by calling 1-800-406-4775, or order online at http://www. collegeboard.org. Coaching courses have helped students focus, gain confidence, and improve their scores, but be sure to choose a reputable company, whose results have been audited by an outside source.

○ Take an SAT II (achievement test) exam right after you've completed the course in that subject. You can "hide" your SAT II: Subject Tests by using "score choice." Release the scores to colleges only if you are satisfied with the results. In your senior year, make sure you release the scores in time to meet application deadlines.

○ Linda Schulz, college counselor at the Galloway School, points out, "SAT II: Subject Tests are not required by all universities. Check with each school to which you are applying to determine if SAT II tests are required or recommended for admission or for placement in certain freshman courses. Selective institutions may require three SAT II tests; requested tests typically include writing, math, and one additional test of your choosing." Use "score choice" if you are a junior but not a senior.

○ "Knowing what to expect from any test is always helpful," said Kevin Crossman, executive director of the Princeton Review, a longtime provider of SAT preparation classes and materials (for information, call 1-800-2-REVIEW). "For instance, in every SAT I there is an experimental section, in which ETS is collecting data on new questions. This section does not count toward your score. You won't know which section it is, but it may seem harder than the rest. Knowing that such a section exists can help you work through the test without slowing up or losing confidence."

○ There are two different SAT I options for learning-disabled students. Option A gives students twice as much time per section. Option B gives students unlimited time. "There is no additional cost for this service, but to qualify students must have proof of their disability, including forms signed by approved professionals. Start the process well in advance," advised Crossman. There are also special tests for hearing- and vision-impaired students. For information, write: SAT Services for Students with Disabilities, P.O. Box 6226, Princeton, NJ 08541-6226.

o ACT, another standardized test accepted by colleges, is largely an achievement-based test. Spring of junior year is the best time to take it, because you've completed most of the course work. You can get "The Official Guide to the ACT Assessment" by calling 1-800-543-1918, or register electronically through ACT's home page: (http://www.act.org).

o Both SAT and ACT test a student's readiness for college, but they go about it in slightly different ways. Since some students score better on one or the other, it's a good idea to take both.

o Standardized tests aren't your strong suit? There are selective colleges that do not require SAT I or ACT scores.

o Keep a record of every time a student takes the SAT or any other college admissions test and where he or she requested they be sent. This will be helpful if you must request your scores at a later date.

o While the SAT allows you to choose a select number of colleges they will send your scores to, you might be applying to additional schools. It's critical to make sure you request that they send your scores to every school you are applying. Call the SAT office at 1-800-SAT-SCORE to request that they rush or send scores to the additional schools of your choice. Check with each school to make sure they get them.

## Make the Most of Your College Interviews

o Many colleges no longer grant personal interviews, except to scholarship contenders, but if you're offered one, take it. A good interview can give you an edge, especially if you're in the "maybe" category.

o You'll be more relaxed if you come with some questions to ask. Have a positive, enthusiastic attitude. Don't give one-word answers, whine, or make excuses about teachers, grades, or test scores.

o Don't ask about your chances of being accepted. They won't know until they see the entire applicant pool and it's an awkward question. Instead, ask about their student profile of admitted candidates.

o Scholarship interviewers often ask students about goals,

achievements, values, who inspires them, why they applied, and what they'll add to campus life. Time spent thinking about these things results in more confident interviews.

   o Try to schedule the interview at your favorite college last. The more you interview, the more confidence and skills you develop.

   o Visit college fairs at a variety of schools and meet the representatives. Gather additional information, take the representatives' names, and write a thank-you note for their assistance. It's important to make a good impression, so take these visits seriously.

## "Show Me the Money": College Financial Aid

   o First let's get past the myths. All colleges do *not* cost $30,000 a year. The majority of undergraduate students in this country are enrolled in schools that cost less than $8,000 a year. As a rule of thumb, public schools are better bargains.

   o Second, financial aid is not only for students with financial needs. Over 41 percent of today's college students need help financing their college education, and there is help available—an estimated $52 billion plus, with about 70 percent coming from the federal government. Many factors other than income determine how much your family is expected to contribute toward your college education. Don't miss out by not applying. You can't win money if you don't apply.

   o To find out about federal financial aid, call 1-800-4-FEDAID to request the free booklet, "Financial Aid from the U.S. Department of Education," or check out the Web site, http://www.ed.gov.

   o Another invaluable Web site is www.finaid.org. It has links to free scholarship searches. Under "tools" you can estimate your need-based financial-aid prospects. Also check out www.fastweb.com.

   o The FAFSA (Free Application for Federal Student Aid) is the linchpin for all federal aid and many college scholarships. You can't send the form in until January of your high-school senior year, but you'll save yourself aggravation if you start organizing the requested information ahead of time.

   o Much of the FAFSA is based on your federal income taxes, so plan to complete (or estimate) them early.

o "Aim for mailing the FAFSA as soon after January 1 as possible, because aid is given out on a first-come, first-served basis. Grants and scholarships go fast. If you file online (http://www.fafsa.ed.gov), make sure you print, sign, and mail in the certification page within twenty-one days of transmitting your data to avoid delays in receiving your Student Aid Report," said Pat Bellantoni, author of *College Financial Aid Made Easy* (4th edition, Ten Speed Press).

o Tax accountants aren't necessarily experts on college financial aid. It's a different ball game. The timing of stock sales, charitable gifts, and IRA withdrawals can affect your financial aid, as can your understanding of the forms. A financial-aid consultant might save you money, but you must choose someone experienced in the process. Check out reputation and credentials very carefully.

o There are numerous reference books and Web sites to help you with your scholarship and financial-aid search, including those that will take you step-by-step through the forms. The Taxpayer Relief Act of 1997 created some new opportunities and changes, so make sure your references are up-to-date.

o "According to the Higher Education Act, college financial-aid officers can use their professional judgment in adjusting the federally determined Expected Family Contribution toward college costs. If you feel that your family has a special circumstance that would affect their ability to pay (i.e., divorce, death, loss of job, medical bills, etc.), communicate that immediately to the college financial-aid officers where you have applied," said Bellantoni.

o It's better to put college savings in the parents' rather than the student's name for financial-aid purposes. According to federal law, 35 percent of a student's assets are considered eligible to pay for college, versus about 5.65 percent of parents' assets. Get the facts for your specific situation.

o Financial-aid offers aren't always set in stone. Schools may up the ante from their own funds if they truly want your child and you can show that a rival school is willing to pay more. Negotiate before you accept the admission offer. It's a delicate process, so get some advice from seasoned counselors first.

o Colleges today want diverse student populations, so apply to some schools outside your geographic region. A southern university may offer more money to lure a good student from the West Coast than someone close by.

o Don't mistake applying for college with applying for financial aid. They are separate applications with separate deadlines.

o Keep a calendar of financial-aid deadlines for every college application. One of the biggest reasons families don't receive aid is that they miss deadlines!

o Verification is an important step in the process. Don't ignore letters from schools requesting additional information or copies of your tax forms. Your aid award depends on their getting all the information they need to make a determination.

o Your tuition doesn't always have to be paid before you register. Some colleges have programs where you can pay monthly for a nominal fee.

o Some colleges have guaranteed tuition plans, where the cost remains the same for all four years.

o Cut college costs by taking Advanced Placement courses in high school. By scoring a 4 or 5 on the AP exams, you'll get college credit for those courses. Some students shave a semester or a full year off their college tuition that way.

o Some students stretch their college budget by taking the first two years at a community college close to home, then transferring to their target university to earn their diploma. If this is your plan, check out all your options and get the facts so you know how realistic this goal is when you're ready to transfer.

o Not all college loans are created equal. Ask lenders about interest rates and repayment options such as graduated payments, income-sensitive repayment plans, or interest-only deferment options. Check out a home-equity loan, which has the advantage of tax-deductible interest.

o Pay interest on unsubsidized and private loans while in college. The interest on $20,000 could be as little as $16 to $20 a month, but that would save thousands of interest dollars over the life of the loan. Get the facts for your individual situation.

o You are not required to accept all parts of a financial-aid package. You might choose to take the grants and work-study and turn down the loans. The advantage of work-study is that you pay as you go and graduate with less debt.

o Check out the Scholarship Resource Network at www.srnexpress.com. This Web site is a search engine and database of private scholarships designed to assist students in identifying sources for undergraduate through postgraduate study. SRN contains more than 8,000 programs with a distribution level of over 150,000 awards worth a total of more than $35 million.

## Academic and Athletic Scholarships

o The best way students can help pay for their college education is to get good grades and do their best on the standardized tests. Apply for merit-aid scholarships. Colleges with large endowments award grants from the interest to the students they want.

o Want to receive more scholarships and financial aid? Look beyond the brand-name colleges and also apply to a variety of public and private schools. You'll potentially get a wider range of offers.

o Apply to some schools ranked in the second tier (according to national rankings) or to smaller, regional colleges. When your grades or talents stand out in the applicant pool (you need to be in the top quarter), your chances for scholarships or merit aid increase.

o You have to be as aggressive off as on the field to earn an athletic scholarship. Make sure you start high school in the college prep track. You have to get into college to play, and you have to be a full qualifier according to the National Collegiate Athletic Association to play Division I or Division II athletics. Learn the academic requirements and recruiting rules early. A good source: *Winning Athletic Scholarships*, by Joseph Sponholz (Princeton Review Publishing, 1997).

o By junior year, athletes should create an athletic résumé that includes academic data, extracurricular activities, personal data, athletic history (sports played, position, highlights of seasons, awards), and list of references. Send this with a letter to the coaches of the colleges where you'd like to play. Inquire with your high school athletic or counseling office about the NCAA application process.

○ You have to report outside scholarships that you receive to the college financial-aid office. This will be used to fill a portion (or all) of your financial-aid eligibility; however, you can request that the scholarship replace loan money rather than school grants or any other scholarships, thus lowering your after-college debt.

○ Students often have better luck winning local scholarships sponsored by civic groups or corporations. The awards may be less than some of the national competitions, but so will be the number of applicants. Even small amounts add up.

○ The National Foundation for the Advancement in the Arts sponsors arts scholarships. Check with your counselor for information.

○ Beware of financial-aid and scholarship scams. Companies will "guarantee" you a list of scholarships for a price, but guidance counselors, libraries, books, and the Internet have the same information for free. Buyer beware!

## The College Decision

○ There is no one right school for every student. College is what you make of it. Can't decide between two choices? Review your notes, talk to the schools, then go with your gut choice, knowing that you would probably be happy at either one.

○ Get the facts for the Candidate's Reply Date and make sure you don't miss crucial deadlines.

○ Wait lists are a college's insurance that they will be able to fill their freshman class. It takes time and effort to move up from a wait list, but if this is your first-choice college, tell them immediately. Call them yourself—taking charge of your application shows initiative on your part. Have your counselor call to see what went wrong, how long the list is, and where you stand. Many lists are not ordered. They will look over the entire list to see who has shown interest by calling or sending additional scores, grades, and so on. If you're in the top quarter or half, then ask to send new information, such as an improvement in grades, awards, a new essay, or a reference from an alumnus. Request a personal interview. Then wait and hope, but since you may not hear until summer, send an acceptance letter and deposit to your backup school. Be sure to keep your grades up and work to improve SAT scores. Every achievement counts, especially when you are borderline at a school.

○ If rejected by a college, you may be able to appeal, particularly if there is new information. Realize that not all colleges allow appeals; much depends on their pool. Again, send additional information and try to be flexible. Tell them you're willing to start in the summer, second semester, or at a branch campus. Sometimes schools change their minds.

## Web Sites

www.collegeboard.com
www.finaid.org
www.fastweb.com
www.kaplan.com
www.review.com

# Consumer Tips

Even long before you're born, you are already being thought of as a consumer. And during your entire life, this one title gets you a lot of attention. Thousands of messages, companies, products, and brands are aimed at you daily, and deciding what is best for you and your family can be a big decision.

Most people choose to ignore important facts and delay their decision making when doing a transaction or hiring someone. At some time all of us have acted too fast, made a quick decision without all the facts we need, and ended up with an endless amount of pain and aggravation. How many times have you said those famous last words, "if only I had known."

Thinking ahead, heading off problems before they happen, and asking all the right questions is the best advice. Joni Alpert, producer of *The Clark Howard Show*, a nationally syndicated consumer radio talk show, recommends, "When making a purchase, signing a contract, or making big decisions, it's always easier to get into a situation than to get out of it. Do your homework when dealing with a business, get all of the promises in writing, or you'll discover it's your word against theirs."

## Warning Signs and Red Flags of Fraud

According to the United States Office of Consumer Affairs, toss out the mail or hang up when you hear:

- Sign now or the price will increase.
- You have been specially selected.
- You have won.
- All we need is your credit card (or bank account) number— for identification only.
- All you pay for is postage, handling, taxes.

○ Make money in your spare time—guaranteed income.

○ We really need you to buy magazines (a water purifier, a vacation package, office products) from us because we can earn fifteen extra credits.

○ I just happen to have some leftover paving material from a job down the street.

○ Be your own boss! Never work for anyone else again. Just send in $50 for your supplies and . . .

○ A new car! A trip to Hawaii! $22,500 in cash! Yours, absolutely free!

○ Your special claim number entitles you to join our sweepstakes.

○ We just happen to be in your area and have toner for your copy machine at a reduced price.

## Who Are You Going to Call?

○ Knowing whom to contact is one of the most important details prior to checking out a company or reporting one once you have a problem. Check out a Better Business Bureau (BBB) in your city for free pamphlets on a variety of topics to help you be a smart consumer and aware of the latest consumer warnings. A BBB is a private, nonprofit organization that provides information services and programs to assist consumers and businesses on behalf of an ethical marketplace. The focus of a BBB's activities is to promote an ethical marketplace by encouraging honest advertising and selling practices and fair and prompt resolution of customer complaints. The information services and programs offered by your BBB can help you be a better-informed and more satisfied consumer. Check out their Web site at www.bbb.org.

○ Your state, county, and city government Consumer Affairs Office is another important resource that will help you. State and local consumer protection offices can help you resolve consumer complaints and provide you with information. These agencies might mediate complaints, conduct investigations, prosecute offenders of consumer laws, license and regulate professions, promote strong consumer protection legislation, and advocate in the consumer interest. It is important to report complaints and suspected frauds and misrepresentations to these governmental agencies. Consumer complaints form the basis of most consumer protection law enforcement actions.

o Check with your state department of revenue's unclaimed property division in the event that you have not received information about property that is yours, including important notices, benefits, or stock dividends. Many states also have a Web site where you can go online and check deceased or other family members, etc., to make sure no property has been returned to the state and is now unclaimed. This might include stocks, checking accounts, safety deposits, insurance policies, payrolls, and matured policies that couldn't be returned to their appropriate owner. Be sure to check with this department regularly! You might be one of the deserving individuals who discovers an unexpected windfall that's rightfully yours!

o A fabulous free *Consumer's Resource Handbook* is published by the United States Office of Consumer Affairs. Single copies of this publication are available by writing:

Handbook
U.S. Office of Consumer Affairs
750 17th Street NW
Washington, DC 20006-4607

## Protecting Your Privacy

o If you have an unlisted telephone number, but you include it on applications or warranties or any form you fill out, your telephone number could easily become public knowledge to companies who sell their lists. Put your work number if you want to keep your home number unlisted for much longer, and avoid listing any number if you want to steer clear of unsolicited calls and junk mail.

o To protect yourself even further, make sure you stop receiving credit cards you didn't apply for. Be sure to cut any cards you do receive into tiny pieces prior to discarding them. Call any of the following companies to opt out of and have your name excluded and removed from "preapproved" credit card offers and marketing lists:

Experian: 1-888-567-8688
Equifax: 1-888-567-8688
Trans Union: 1-888-567-8688

○ When filling out credit applications, make sure you request that your information is not given out to anyone under any circumstances. Sometimes there is a box on the form, but you can also give those instructions in writing. Add: *This information is private and this company* [state name] *does not have any right to give my name out.*

○ Think twice before giving your home telephone number and address to those "enter to win" opportunities. Your information could be sold to other companies and you never know how many lists you'll be added to.

○ Beware of calls from people who claim they are telephone technicians or repairmen running a check on your telephone line and asking you to press certain numbers to assist them. Certain codes you press could actually give the caller access to your telephone line and long-distance capabilities! A legitimate repair person would come on a scheduled call and/or be able to show you proper credentials. Do not cooperate with these unsolicited requests, and report the call immediately to your telephone company and also to the police.

○ To avoid problems with 900-type numbers, you can request "blocking" from your local phone company. Blocking prevents 900 numbers from being dialed from your phone.

○ Talk to your bank about having a security password required to access your bank information.

○ Handle your credit cards and other important pieces of information you carry around daily carefully. Limit what you carry to what you use and store the other cards in a safe place. Whenever you write a check, by law a store's employee cannot write your credit card number on the check. Once you use your card, also make sure you are given back the correct card.

○ The United States Office of Consumer Affairs states that federal law gives you the right to ask telemarketers to take your name off their lists and not to call you again. Keep records of their names and addresses, and the dates of your requests. File a complaint with the Federal Communications Commission if they don't remove your name from their marketing lists once you have made your request. Call 1-888-322-8255 or visit their Web site at www.fcc.gov for more information.

○ Telephone Preference Service (TPS) enables people to receive fewer telephone sales calls in their homes by removing their names from many national telephone sales lists. State that you do not want to receive any telemarketing or telephone solicitations from any organization that *encourages the purchase or rental of, or investment in, property, goods, or services.* To properly make your request, provide your complete name, including all variations of spelling, your home address, including apartment number and ZIP code, and your telephone number with area code. It can take up to three months for TPS to take effect. Note that local telephone marketers, as a rule, do not participate in TPS. You must speak to them directly. Address the letter to:

> The Telephone Preference Service
> Direct Marketing Association
> P.O. Box 9014
> Farmingdale, NY 11735-9014

○ The Direct Marketing Association Mail Preference Service (MPS) is available to individuals who prefer to substantially reduce the amount of national advertising mail they receive in their homes. Simply register with MPS and your name will be removed from many national mailing lists. Of course, you will still get catalogs from companies with which you do business. Provide your complete name, including all variations of spelling, as well as your home address, including apartment number and ZIP code. Allow up to three months for MPS to take effect and note that some small local organizations do not participate and you will need to contact them directly.

Mail Preference Service
Direct Marketing Association
P.O. Box 9008
Farmingdale, NY 11735-9008

For more detailed information about MPS or TPS or any other services provided by the Direct Marketing Association, go to the DMA's Web site at www.dma.org.

o To screen unfamiliar companies for reports of fraudulent activity, call the following groups: National Fraud Information Center (1-800-876-7060); Better Business Bureau (check your local phone directory).

## Credit Problems

The United States Office of Consumer Affairs suggests the following tips in regard to credit reporting:

o The Fair Credit Reporting Act controls how your credit history is kept, used, and shared among lenders. The three biggest credit reporting agencies—Experian (Formerly TRW), Equifax, and Trans Union—have millions of credit files on consumers nationwide. Their toll-free numbers are:

Experian (Formerly TRW): 1-800-392-1122
P.O. Box 1017
Allen, TX 75013
To report fraud, call 1-800-301-7195 and write to address
above
To order credit report, call 1-800-682-7654 or
1-888-397-3742
Their Web site is www.experian.com

Equifax: 1-800-685-1111
P.O. Box 740241
Atlanta, GA 30374-0241

To report fraud, call 1-800-525-6285 and write to the address
   above
To order credit report, call 1-800-685-1111
To discuss a credit report, call 1-888-909-7304
Their Web site is www.equifax.com

Trans Union: 1-800-888-4213
P.O. Box 390
Springfield, PA 19064
To report fraud, call 1-800-680-7289 and write to
   Fraud Victim Assistance Division, P.O. Box 6790,
   Fullerton, CA 92634
To order credit report, call 1-800-916-8800
To opt out of preapproved offers of credit and marketing lists,
   call 1-800-888-5-opt-out or 1-888-567-8688
Their Web site is www.transunion.com

○ Ask the credit bureaus for a copy of your credit report, which
gives an itemized statement of the companies that have asked for
your credit information. Be sure to get the information from all
three sources, since they do not share any information.

○ You can find other credit bureaus in your area by looking in
the Yellow Pages under "Credit Bureaus" or "Credit Reporting."

○ If you apply for credit, insurance, a job, or to rent an apartment, your credit record might be examined. You can make sure
yours is accurate. Get a copy once a year or before major purchases.
Your report is generally free if you've been denied credit in the past
sixty days. Otherwise, the credit bureau can impose a reasonable
charge.

○ Read the report carefully. The credit bureau must provide
trained personnel to explain information in the report.

○ Dispute any incorrect information in your credit record.
Write to the credit bureau and be specific about what is wrong with
your report. Send copies of any documents that support your dispute. In response to your complaint, the credit bureau must investigate your dispute and respond to you, usually within thirty to
thirty-five days; information that is inaccurate or cannot be verified

must be corrected or taken off your report. The credit bureau cannot be required to remove accurate, verifiable information that is less than seven years old (ten years for bankruptcies).

o If you are dissatisfied with the results of the reinvestigation, you can have the credit bureau include a 100-word consumer statement giving your version of the disputed information. You also can contact the source of the disputed information and try to resolve the matter.

o If there is an error on a report from one credit bureau, the same mistake might be on others as well. You might want to contact the three major bureaus, as well as any local bureau listed in the Yellow Pages of your telephone book.

o Credit bureaus sometimes sell your name to banks or others who want to offer you credit cards or other forms of credit. If you don't want your name included on such lists, write or call the three major credit bureaus and tell them not to release your name.

o You can rebuild your good credit by handling credit responsibly. You might want to contact a Consumer Credit Counseling Service (CCCS) office. This is a nonprofit organization that will provide help at little or no cost to you. For a CCCS office in your area, call 1-800-388-CCCS.

## Consumer Problems at the Dry Cleaners

o Using a dry cleaner regularly and being a repeat customer doesn't protect you from problems; however, establishing a positive relationship with your dry cleaner gives you a better chance of resolving a dispute if there is one. Find out before you patronize a dry cleaner how he handles problems. What are his policies?

o If you have a disagreement with the dry cleaner over whose fault a ruined or damaged garment was, the dry cleaner can submit the garment to the International Fabricare Institute, an independent testing laboratory, if he or she is a member. Their address is IFI Garment Analysis Laboratory, 12251 Tech Road, Silver Spring, MD 20904. Choose a dry cleaner who is a member of this organization, which has standards that must be upheld.

o According to David Galusha, owner of Professional Cleaners of Sandy Springs, and a member of the American Institute of Conservation of Historic and Artistic Works and the International Fabricare Institute, "You shouldn't smell any chemicals in your clothing when picking it up from the dry cleaners. [If so,] this means they didn't do it properly and that chemicals have been left in the clothing which can irritate sensitive skin."

## Tips for Shopping by Mail, Phone, or Fax

The Direct Marketing Association, founded in 1917 and the largest trade association for companies interested in database marketing, suggests the following tips:

○ Before ordering from a catalog, read the customer service section of the catalog. Usually located near the order form, this section is a gold mine of information for the shopper. You'll find satisfaction and return/exchange policies, phone numbers for inquiries and ordering merchandise, sizing charts, shipping and handling information, insurance fee options, special services such as monogramming, personal shoppers, and registry.

○ Most catalogs have liberal return and exchange policies, but some products that can be duplicated, like computer software and recorded music, are sometimes not returnable.

○ Before you order something from a catalog, you can request to see the product warranty by calling or writing to the catalog company.

○ Use common sense when making a purchase. If an offer sounds too good to be true, it probably is!

○ When ordering by phone, fax, or mail, keep a record of what you ordered and when. Record the method of payment you chose, delivery date, and all other information. You'll be glad you did this if there's any problem later on and you don't receive what you ordered.

○ Check the delivery schedule and shipping options. Many companies now offer overnight or two-day delivery of their products. Check out how much it costs so you won't be surprised when the bill comes.

○ Hold on to your receipts and product packaging and literature until you are sure you are satisfied with your purchase.

○ Instructions for returns are usually on the reverse side of the packing slip. Some companies provide a return form and shipping label for convenience. When ordering, request one if you are concerned. You can also fill out all of your information on a piece of paper if a return form is not available.

○ Some companies provide free pickup and shipping for returns. It is not unreasonable to request this, especially if the item is broken or damaged.

○ If you request a refund, you will be reimbursed in the manner in which you paid for the order. If you paid by credit card, your account will be credited within one billing cycle. If you paid by check or money order, the company will issue you a check within seven business days. Be sure to keep up on whether or not you received the money.

○ Not satisfied? The DMA's Mail Order Action Line (MOAL) is a free service for consumers who have not had success in resolving disputes with particular mail-order companies. MOAL works directly with the mail-order company to solve the problem, and the majority of complaints are resolved within thirty days. Provide details about your order, the company from which you ordered, and an explanation of the problem. Include photocopies of any documentation that substantiates the complaint, such as a canceled check or credit card invoice, or correspondence attempting to rectify the situation. You can request assistance by writing to:

Mail Order Action Line
Direct Marketing Association
1111 19th Street NW, Suite 1100
Washington, DC 20036-3603

○ For a free booklet of tips for consumers who shop by mail or phone, request a copy of *Make Knowledge Your Partner in Mail or Telephone Order Shopping*. Send your name and address to:

Consumer Services Department
Direct Marketing Association
P.O. Box 33033
Washington, DC 20033-0033

## Shopping Online

○ It is generally safe to use a credit card when you shop online as long as the Web site provides you with a secure, encrypted online ordering system. An encrypted connection encodes sensitive data while it's in transit, and then decodes it once it has successfully reached its destination. This will ensure that your private credit card information will remain private as it travels from your computer to the online store. You can check to see if a site is safe for credit card transactions by looking at the checkout area. Often, a notice will pop up on your computer screen, indicating that you are entering a secure area. Look at the URL (the Web address) of the checkout page. Frequently it will start with https://, which means that the document is coming from a secure server. If you are using the Netscape Navigator browser, you will see that the picture of a broken key on the lower left corner of your computer screen transforms into an unbroken key on a blue background. If you are using the Microsoft Internet Explorer browsers, an icon of a lock will appear. Once you have submitted your order, be sure to print out a copy for your letters and note the order confirmation number and the URL of the site.

○ Using a credit card is the best way to pay, since you will be covered under the Fair Credit Billing Act in the event of non-delivery or other types of fraud. The Fair Credit Billing Act ensures that the bank issuing your credit card will help resolve disputes between customers and merchants. Additionally, you will be responsible for only up to $50 in the unlikely event that your credit card is misused.

○ Do not do business with a company online that does not have a phone number or street address available. Find out the satisfaction guarantee and return policy before you place your order.

## Consumer Identity Fraud

Consumer identity theft is on the rise. Criminals, using a variety of methods, steal credit card numbers, driver's license numbers, ATM cards, Social Security numbers, telephone calling cards, and other key pieces of individuals' identities. Often, this information is even sold to criminals by dishonest employees. Criminals then use the information to impersonate the victims, spending as much money as they can in as short a period as possible. To avoid being a victim, the Better Business Bureau, along with other consumer agencies, recommends that consumers exercise extreme care with their vital data. To minimize your losses due to identity theft, the BBB suggests the following tips:

○ Don't carry extra credit cards, your Social Security card, birth certificate, or passport unless absolutely necessary.

○ When using an ATM or public telephone, shield the screen or keypad so "shoulder surfers" cannot read your personal identification number (PIN) or other data.

○ Take ATM, credit, and other receipts with you, and either save them in a safe place or destroy them in such a way that they cannot be read. Also, shred preapproved credit card offers. "Dumpster divers" can get them from the trash.

○ Cancel all unused credit card accounts. Even though you don't use them, their account numbers are recorded in your credit report, which is full of data that can be used by identity thieves.

○ Keep in a safe place a list of all credit cards, account numbers, and telephone numbers of the customer service departments.

○ Protect your Social Security number (SSN). The SSN is the key to your credit and banking accounts and is the prime target of criminals. Don't give your SSN or any credit card number over the phone to anyone you don't know or a company you are not familiar with. One ploy criminals use is to call and pose as your bank or landlord and ask to "confirm" your SSN or other data.

○ If you become the victim of identity theft, it is extremely important that you act immediately to stop the thief's further use of your identity. Immediately report the crime to the police and get a copy of the report in case you ever need proof of the crime. Report a missing driver's license to the department of motor vehicles. Get a new number that's not your Social Security number. Change locks if your keys were stolen. Call your credit card issuers (the call can save you from any liability from any fraudulent charges). Call the fraud unit of the three credit reporting agencies—Equifax, Experian (formerly TRW), and Trans Union—and order copies of your credit report. Only then may you discover the full extent of the damage to your credit card. Have your file flagged and add a "victim's statement." Also, notify your bank(s) of the theft. Cancel all bank accounts and obtain new account numbers. The Federal Trade Commission, Postal Service, and National Fraud Information Center can also be of help.

## Where to Turn for Help

Equifax: To report fraud, call 1-800-525-6285
Experian: To report fraud, call 1-800-301-7195
Trans Union: To report fraud, call 1-800-680-7289

### Federal Agencies

o Federal Trade Commission: To report fraud and to request more information and brochures on a variety of educational consumer topics, call 1-202-FTC-HELP or check their Web site at www.ftc.gov.

o U.S. Postal Service, Postal Inspector: To report mail fraud, call the mail fraud complaint center at 1-800-372-8347. The public information office can also assist you and can be reached by calling 1-202-268-5400.

o Social Security Administration: To report a lost card or get a new one, call 1-800-772-1213.

o To report check fraud: Call any of the following companies to determine if there is any activity on your account as a result of fraud:

CheckRite—1-800-766-2748
Chexsystems—1-800-428-9623

Equifax—1-800-437-5120
National Processing Co.—1-800-526-5380
SCAN—1-800-262-7771
Telecheck—1-800-710-9898

## Avoiding Scams and Deals

o Avoid door-to-door sales that promise amazing savings! A common pitch you'll hear is that a contractor or company is doing work in your area and they can offer you an unbelievable deal since they are already nearby. My best advice is simply don't answer the door. Also, if they are a reliable company, then you can have them leave their information or card in your mailbox and check them out.

o When hiring a company to do work for you, always get a second opinion and written estimates on work you're doing to compare quotes. Make sure the company is insured; request that their insurance company send you a certificate of insurance. Since insurance can easily be canceled, don't just rely on a copy of the insurance. Check out the company's liability insurance and workers' compensation. They must be insured for injury or damage both to you and your home, as well as their workers while on the job.

o When hiring a company to do work, ask to see their business license. Many companies and individuals work without a license to do business in that field.

o Don't jump into a deal that promises a discount today only. This is often a sales tactic. Only take advantage of today-only deals when you know that the company is reliable and you have checked them out.

o The grass is not always greener! Often people hire a person because a neighbor was happy. I can promise you that one person's happiness is another's aggravation. This is often how a con artist does his job. He completely pleases one neighbor and then gets the recommendation of their best friends, family, the entire neighborhood. He puts a sign out front and everyone thinks he hung the moon. That's until he arrives at the next person's house and they pay up front, and he leaves with all the money! This scenario really happened and could happen to you, so do your homework and check people out far past their last few jobs next door. Get recent recommendations as well as checking back further. Remember—references, references, references.

o No matter who is doing work in your house, never run errands for them or leave them alone. I even heard of someone leaving a contractor with their children while she ran to get him some extra paint samples! What in the world could she have been thinking? Anyone who works in your home should be monitored. Make sure all your valuables are put away and don't assume anything.

o Watch where you store your checks, keys, and any other items that are important. Workmen should not be exposed to these or any other personal belongings. Even a charge card receipt has your charge card number, so be aware!

## Memberships

o There are many buying clubs available. It often pays to join these clubs in the very beginning if you plan to become a member, since they usually offer special rates and discount fees. Never be afraid to ask what incentives for membership they are offering and ask for a trial offer to test that it's worth the price you must pay and that you will really use it.

o When buying a health club or any other club membership, check out all your options before signing a contract. Experts recommend month-to-month memberships even though they might cost a drop more. Whatever you choose, make sure you won't suffer any consequences if you should cancel your policy.

## Multilevel Marketing

The Better Business Bureau advises:

o Be wary if the startup cost for an investment is substantial. Legitimate multilevel marketing companies usually require a small startup cost. Pyramid schemes, on the other hand, pressure you to pay a large amount to become a "distributor." The promoters behind the scheme make most of their profit by signing up new recruits.

○ Find out if the company will buy back inventory. If not, watch out—you could be saddled with unsold inventory. Keep in mind that legitimate companies that require you to purchase an inventory should offer and stick to inventory buy-backs for at least 80 percent of what you paid. Some state laws require 90 percent buy-backs.

○ To check on a company, contact your local Better Business Bureau, district attorney, or state attorney general's office. You may want to also contact the Direct Selling Association (1666 K Street, NW, Suite 1010, Washington, DC 20006), a national trade association representing legitimate in-home sales companies, many of which engage in multilevel marketing.

## Tips on Choosing a Modeling or Talent Agency

○ Choose a company that has a solid reputation in the community.

○ Check with the Better Business Bureau to obtain a reliability report on the firm. Make sure the company actually has jobs available and is not just trying to sell you photography. Talk to other people who have actually gotten legitimate jobs with this agency.

○ Do not sign any written agreement or contract until you have read and fully understand all terms of any agreement. Any verbal promises should be included in the agreement before signing, and determine if the company has a refund policy and what the requirements are in order to obtain a refund.

○ The Better Business Bureau takes the position that no modeling or talent agency should advertise under "help wanted" unless they are actually hiring people to work for them. They also urge consumers to be wary of any modeling or talent agency requiring a purchase or investment when responding to an advertisement for employment.

## Recommended Reading

*Clark Howard's Consumer Survival Kit: It's Your Money. Get the Most for It* by Clark Howard and Mark Meltzer (revised and expanded edition, Longstreet Press, 1995). Or check out www.ClarkHoward.com.

# Cooking Tips

For many of us, food is a passion. It's one of those rare aspects of life that involve all senses: taste, smell, sight, touch, and even sound (crunch!). Who doesn't get excited over a sublime dessert, a succulent piece of fruit, or a hot-from-the-oven muffin? As an added bonus, when we eat well we're nourishing our bodies and can feel good about ourselves.

Dining is also emotionally tied to many aspects of life. After all, it's often over a meal that we've made marriage plans, toasted a new graduate's future, spilled the beans about a baby, wished a best friend a happy birthday, or just enjoyed a leisurely chat with a favorite person. Going to a fancy restaurant is often a rite of passage, as is the newlyweds' creating the first home-cooked meal.

Today, the world of food is more exciting than it's ever been. Restaurants are flourishing, with all sorts of creative concoctions and a host of international influences. Grocery stores and specialty farmers' markets allow us to buy exotic items from all over the world. With our constant battle to save time but eat well, quality take-out places (and even gourmet delivery services) are popping up everywhere. Of course, with all these choices, everyday meals are more confusing than ever. How do we get the best value at the store or in restaurants? While fresh foods are best, how do we keep them at their peak? How can we save time in the kitchen? Can you eat out and still eat healthy?

Even if you're not a "foodie," you've got to eat, after all! It's one common denominator we all share three times a day. Getting smart in and out of the kitchen is the goal. Here are some tips to help you along the way.

## Be a Smart Shopper

o Shop around. Consider additional food sources other than your local supermarket, such as day-old bakeries, farmers' markets, food co-op programs, produce stands, pick-your-own farms, and wholesale butchers. Factor in the cost of gas (and your time) to determine true savings. If you've got the land, sun, and talent, grow your own vegetables.

o Use supermarkets for their specials. Almost all grocery stores have weekly "loss leaders," those real bargains you see advertised in flyers, such as "Buy one, get one free" crackers, or "This week only, strawberries at 50 cents a pint." Similarly, some supermarkets have certain days of the week when they double if not triple manufacturers' coupons.

o Buy in bulk. Consider buying a used freezer so that you can purchase items in larger quantities and freeze them. Often turkeys are less expensive right after Thanksgiving, for instance, so you could buy a couple to have over the next few months. Buying larger cuts of meat (such as whole turkeys or chickens) and cutting them up yourself is always a way to save money.

o Go vegetarian occasionally (if you're not already). Since meats are an expensive part of any grocery budget, plan for vegetarian meals at least twice a week, such as spinach quiche, three-bean chili, or pasta primavera. Similarly, learn to think of meat as a side dish rather than the star of your plate. Make side dishes such as rice, potatoes, and vegetables the larger portions. Experiment with salads, perhaps adding small amounts of grilled chicken as your protein.

o Take time to compare the real prices at supermarkets. To cut down on cost confusion in the grocery aisle, look closely at the printed prices for items. In a smaller print than the whole-unit cost is a "per unit" breakdown to allow you to compare different-sized items.

o Sometimes a smaller quantity item is actually less expensive than the jumbo size. Almost always, the supermarket brand is cheaper.

o Don't fall victim to the "eye-level" syndrome. Grocery stores often put their most expensive (or most heavily advertised) products at eye level, where hurried shoppers will grab the merchandise quickly. Look at the top and bottom shelves to find more interesting, possibly less expensive, items.

o Children can be budget-wreckers at most stores, with supermarkets being among the worst. To avoid having to buy excess cookies, cereals, and the like, either arrange to leave the kids with a sitter or make sure they have a snack before leaving the house so they're not famished in the store. Some experts recommend shopping right after lunch or dinner (good advice for adults, too).

o Purchase items in the baby-food aisle sparingly. Many mothers find that making their own baby food (cooking or microwaving vegetables with a little water, pureeing in the food processor, then storing in ice-cube trays for easy thawing) makes good economic sense. Consider that a large bag of frozen peas that yields twenty or so servings may cost 79 cents, yet a single-serving jar of baby-food peas costs the same!

o Go stove top. Did you know that cooking on the range top costs less than using the oven? (It's also less hot, which can be awfully important in summer months.)

o Learn to cook! Some of the best cooks around became that way out of economic necessity. Rather than trying to whip up gourmet meals, novices should train themselves to make some basics, such as homemade vinaigrettes, from-scratch gravies, and some standard desserts.

## Quick Tips for Saving Time When Cooking

o Make do in the marinade department. Almost any oil-based salad dressing makes an easy marinade for meats and vegetables. For best results, marinate food at least an hour before cooking.

o Substitute time-consuming sauces and condiments with store-bought ones. Many of today's trendy recipes feature gourmet specialties such as pesto, roasted red pepper sauce, or tapenade (black olive spread). Stock up on these when in specialty cooking stores and you'll be ahead of the game for many recipes.

o Go for the vino. A splash of wine can add a quick-and-easy seasoning to many stews, chicken dishes, and pasta. The trick is to use a good wine, one that you would enjoy drinking.

○ Cook extra rice when making a side dish for dinner. Freeze the extra, and thaw it for recipes such as stuffed green peppers or rice-vegetable salad.

○ Create a "soup starter." Rather than throwing away tiny amounts of leftover vegetables and meats, toss them into a freezer-safe container for future use in a soup. When your container is full, mix with a can of seasoned tomatoes and chicken broth, plus anything else you want to add, and voilà . . . soup.

○ Invest in a cookbook for making quick meals. Keep it in your car when not using it and even take it with you into the supermarket.

○ Coffee and tea are perishable in that they lose their flavor over time. Coffee should be stored in an airtight, moisture-proof container. The container should always be placed in your refrigerator or freezer—the colder the better.

○ Spray with a nonstick cooking spray the cutting surface of tools that usually stick to your food, such as cheese graters and cutters.

## Tips about Fruit

○ When choosing citrus such as oranges and lemons, select by weight. The heaviest fruit will contain the most juice.

○ Apples can last up to a month when stored in the refrigerator.

○ Keep pears at room temperature until they ripen. If you store them in your refrigerator, they will not get soft. (If you prefer hard pears, then storing them in the refrigerator is fine.)

○ Before refrigerating grapes, remove all of the grapes that have spoiled. This will help keep the other grapes fresher longer.

○ Grapes should be stored in the refrigerator in a plastic bag. This saves them from spoiling too soon.

○ Do not take the stems off of berries or wash them until you are ready to eat them.

○ Strawberries are a highly perishable fruit. Store unwashed strawberries for one or two days in the refrigerator.

○ A pineapple is fresh and ready to eat if its leaves pull easily away from the stem. The bottom of the pineapple should yield slightly to gentle pressure, but make sure it is not too soft, which could mean the pineapple has spoiled.

○ Separate bruised and spoiled berries from ones that are good, since mold can spread from berry to berry.

○ You can get more juice from a lemon if you roll it on the counter or between your hands gently to soften it. You'll also get more juice if the lemon is at room temperature.

○ A peeled banana or a pear will not turn brown as quickly if you sprinkle it with citrus juice.

○ Peaches will peel easily if you add them to boiling water for 1 minute.

○ The color of an orange is no indication of its quality or taste, because oranges are sometimes dyed to improve the way they look.

○ Make sure you cover all cut fruits and vegetables very tightly with plastic wrap to prevent bacteria from sticking to their surfaces.

○ In order to avoid contamination, wash all vegetables and fruits in clean water before cutting, eating, or peeling. Dry thoroughly.

## Tips about Vegetables

○ If you store tomatoes in the refrigerator, they will become soft and mushy.

○ Put tomatoes in a brown bag to ripen them quickly.

○ Tomatoes and cucumbers taste best when stored at room temperature rather than in the refrigerator. If a tomato does not smell like a tomato, it won't taste like one, either.

○ When cooking vegetables in water, keep them whole instead of cutting them up. This way, they will retain more vitamins and minerals.

○ A pinch of baking soda added to broccoli while steaming will help it retain the bright green color.

○ To lessen the odor while cooking cabbage or cauliflower, add a few small pieces of bread to the pot while cooking. The bread will absorb the smell.

○ Reduce the tears when slicing an onion by cutting off the

root end of the onion last. You can also peel it under cold, running water; to reduce inhaling the smell, breathe through your mouth instead of your nose.

○ Never add salad dressing to lettuce until just before serving. The lettuce will become soggy and limp.

○ It's true! Lettuce should be torn rather than cut with a knife. The cut edge will brown while the torn edge won't.

○ To prevent raw potatoes from turning dark before cooking, submerge them in cold water until ready to cook.

○ Never chop fresh vegetables or salad ingredients on a surface that was also used for raw meat; properly clean the cutting surface first.

○ Avoid broccoli that is discolored or has yellow florets on it. Choose broccoli that is tight with a fresh green color and leaves that aren't wilted.

○ The deeper the color green is in celery, the stronger the flavor is.

○ Beets and carrots have the highest sugar content among vegetables.

○ Do not refrigerate potatoes, but do store them in a cool, dark area with good air circulation.

○ Avoid cauliflower that has dark spots or mold on it. Mold can spread into food beyond the surface and shouldn't just be cut away.

○ Do not store mushrooms in a plastic bag, or they will darken and become very soft.

## Staples to Keep on Hand in Your Pantry, Refrigerator, or Freezer for These Last-Minute Meals

○ Sun-dried tomatoes, Parmesan cheese, and angelhair pasta (easy pasta dish when mixed with olive oil)

○ A can of tuna, white navy beans, and balsamic vinegar salad dressing (Tuscan-style salad)

○ Eggs, Swiss cheese, and broccoli (omelet or quiche)

○ Chicken breasts, chunky salsa, and rice (Mexican-style chicken)

○ Orzo (rice-shaped pasta), chopped zucchini, and pine nuts (vegetarian fare)

○ Baked pizza shell, pesto sauce, fontina cheese (gourmet pizza—add fresh herbs, if you've got 'em)

○ Chili-seasoned canned tomatoes, kidney beans (or garbanzo beans, northern beans, any type of beans), and canned corn (easy chili)

○ Deli-department roast beef, crumbled bleu cheese, and mixed greens (gourmet salad with favorite dressing)

○ Tortillas, black beans, and Monterey jack cheese (quesadillas)

○ Spinach fettuccine, broccoli florets, and ricotta cheese

## Keeping It Fresh

○ Apples lose flavor and firmness about ten times faster at room temperature. For your best apples, store in the refrigerator.

○ Use berries at once. Mold travels quickly within berry containers, so always check the bottom of containers in the store to make sure no berries are moldy.

○ Bananas ripen faster in a brown paper sack.

○ Refrigerated kiwis stay ripe in the refrigerator for weeks, making them a popular food for fruit junkies. They're also healthy; one kiwi contains fiber content similar to a half-cup of bran flakes.

○ Peaches ripen faster if left in a box covered with newspaper.

○ Store asparagus wrapped in a wet paper towel. Cut bottoms of stems off first. Similarly, cut the green tops of carrots off before refrigerating. They tend to get moldy.

○ Iceberg lettuce lasts the longest in the refrigerator, but it is the least nutritious. Romaine lettuce has about six times the vitamins of iceberg.

○ Tomatoes keep better at room temperature. To avoid mushy bottoms, store stem sides down. Green tomatoes ripen faster if stored with apples.

○ Spices will dry out and lose their flavor around heat, so keep them away from ovens.

○ Not all items freeze well. Never freeze sour cream, yogurt, cream cheese, omelets or soufflés, mayonnaise, uncooked vegetables such as lettuce and cucumbers, raw tomatoes, and potatoes.

## Hot Off the Grill

o Put safety first. According to Brian Molinet of Barbecues Galore in Atlanta, it's wise to check for gas leaks before using any gas grill.

o Spray gas hoses with soapy water to see if any leaks show up.

o To avoid damaging porcelain-coated cooking grids, Molinet adds, always use a brass brush to clean them. Other brushes, such as plastic ones with metal scrapers, can damage the rack.

o Change is good. Check with your manufacturer or retail store to find out how often to change the lava rocks or briquets.

o Here's a new way to use herbs: place them directly on coals to enhance the flavors of meats and vegetables. Try stalks of rosemary or basil, for instance.

o Make sure the grill is really ready. Allow at least 20 minutes for charcoal to heat up and get the coals coated with white ash. Never squirt lighter fluid directly on a hot fire, no matter how much of a hurry you're in.

o To avoid burning meat, remove during flame flare-ups (caused by dripping fat). You can spray the coals with a plant water mister to reduce the flame, if it needs it.

o For meats and vegetables to be properly flavored for grilling, allow up to 24 hours' marinating time in the refrigerator (less time for fish).

o Contrary to most people's actions, barbecue sauce should be put on only in the last few minutes of cooking; otherwise it might turn hard and become caramelized or burn.

o Give vegetables a head start. Thick vegetables, such as potatoes, benefit from a quick cooking indoors (boiled or in the microwave), then coat them with oil and placed on the grill. (Otherwise they might become too charred before they're actually cooked on the inside.)

o Don't forget the corn outside, too. Corn is tasty cooked on the grill, right in its own husk! Carefully peel back the husk to remove the silk threads, then put the husks back around the corn (some people tie it together with flame-safe string) and grill for about 15 minutes.

o Expand your barbecue repertoire. Almost anything can be grilled as either kabobs or on its own. A few more unusual foods to try are Belgian endive, cucumber chunks, and peach and grapefruit slices.

o Need additional help? Call 1-800 GRILL OUT (1-800-474-5568) and reach the Weber Grill-Line, America's only toll-free consumer barbecue information hot line, which is sponsored by Weber-Stephen Products Co. The line is open from April 1 through Labor Day. A team of home economists have been trained in a wide variety of grilling subjects, including cooking advice and food and product safety. All callers receive a free booklet with recipes, basic grilling instructions for cooking with direct and indirect heat, and safety guidelines. A new and different booklet is available each year.

## Cooking Substitutions— When You're Really in a Pinch

| Instead of | Use |
|---|---|
| 1 teaspoon lemon juice | ½ teaspoon vinegar |
| 1 tablespoon cornstarch | 2 tablespoons flour |
| 1½ cups corn syrup | 1 cup sugar, ½ cup water |
| 1 cup bread crumbs | ¾ cup crumbled crackers |
| 1 cup buttermilk | 1 cup whole milk (or yogurt) and 1 tablespoon lemon juice or vinegar |
| 1 square unsweetened chocolate | 3 tablespoons cocoa and 1 tablespoon butter |
| 1 cup self-rising flour | 1 cup flour and 1¼ tablespoons baking powder and a pinch of salt |
| 1 garlic clove | ¼ teaspoon garlic powder |
| 1 cup honey | 1¼ cups sugar and ⅓ cup water |
| 1 tablespoon tomato paste | 1 tablespoon ketchup |

| | |
|---|---|
| 1 cup tomato sauce | 6 tablespoons tomato paste and ⅔ cup water |
| 1 teaspoon vinegar | 2 teaspoons lemon juice |

## Just in Case

o Make sure your refrigerator or freezer hasn't defrosted and re-frozen while you are out of town. Put two ice cubes in a sealed-tight plastic bag in the freezer and upon your return, check to make sure they haven't melted and changed shape.

o When you cook something ahead of time, divide large portions of food into small, shallow containers for refrigeration. This ensures safe, rapid cooling.

o If you cook food on the grill, do not use the same platter to carry cooked food that you used to carry uncooked food to the grill. Always use a clean platter to serve cooked food.

o A cooler does not always keep things cold enough, so don't leave food sitting out. Many coolers still need ice or ice packs, so be sure to read the instructions when purchasing one and check to see that the food is staying cold enough.

## Eating Out and Getting the Most for Your Money

o Skip the dinner crowd. At many trendy restaurants (particularly if the atmosphere is the thing), savvy eaters go for lunch, brunch, or even breakfast, when prices are significantly lower. This is always a good idea in large cities, such as New York.

o Go early. You don't have to live in Florida (or be a senior citizen) to take advantage of the early-bird specials. Many restaurants offer special deals to those who eat fashionably early, usually at times such as 5:30 to 7 P.M.

o When in doubt, pick the nightly special. Restaurants' specials are usually fresher and cheaper than other items on the menu, which makes them a good bet.

o Eat beforehand. It may sound like odd advice, but to avoid filling up on bread because you're starving, eat a light snack before heading off to the restaurant.

○ Learn the health-wise lingo. When perusing the menu, look for entrees that are grilled or broiled, which will usually be the leanest dishes. Watch out for words such as *fried* and *parmigiano*, or anything in cream.

○ Don't be afraid to ask restaurants to lighten up. More and more eateries have learned to accommodate patrons' requests, so don't hesitate to request such things as dressings on the side, food that is broiled instead of fried, and well-done (not seared) meats.

○ Most restaurants these days understand the concept of grazing and are happy to even serve appetizer portions for entrees.

○ Better safe than sorry . . . always take a glance at the restaurant's latest inspection report before putting a morsel in your mouth!

## Recommended Reading

Rosemary Brown's *Big Kitchen Instruction Book* (Andrews McMeel, 1998).

## Web Sites

www.GourmetSpot.com. Check out this food lovers' Web spot and you'll find recipes and lots of helpful information.

www.caloriecontrol.com. If you are searching for information on cutting calories and fat in your diet, as well as achieving and maintaining a healthy weight, this is the site for you!

# Death

While this entire book deals with an enormous number of life issues, a friend of mine suggested over dinner one night, "But what about a chapter on death?" The second Terri brought it up, I knew she was absolutely right. I also knew it'd be the toughest topic to write. That's because the most common response to this subject is usually "Let's not talk about it" or "I'd rather think about that later."

The overwhelming number of details we must deal with in regard to death make it a topic far too important to overlook. As I researched what you should do when someone dies, I found myself getting comfortable with the fact that, once again, knowledge is empowerment and, in the case of death, can provide an enormous amount of comfort and guidance.

You might be someone who has avoided this area of your life entirely, or perhaps you're one of the small but increasing percentage of individuals who are proactive and have already bought burial plots. Prepurchasing funeral arrangements is as personal as whether you wish to be buried or cremated. What's right for one person is not right for another. The purpose of this chapter is not to have you either rush to purchase a plot or delay the decision. Rather, my single goal is to encourage you to think about what would happen if there were a death in your family.

Some people believe planning ahead lessens the overall emotional burden. Others feel that being involved in a loved one's funeral plans is therapeutic. Still others I interviewed feel that by identifying their wishes and making their plans ahead, they have the luxury of time to comparison shop, check out all their options, and get the facts about their death arrangements. For example, my parents purchased their plot next to my in-laws so the family would be kept together. But my mother, the smartest shopper of all time, purchased the burial plot with a credit card and got frequent-flier miles!

While this topic is easy for some and difficult for others, death is usually a subject avoided until the choice is no longer ours. It's no wonder death arrangements continue to be a final frontier filled with unknowns and costly surprises. According to Alex Rodgers, general manager of Arlington Memorial Park, "The average cost of a funeral service is approximately $6,500 and the cemetery expenses average $2,500 to $3,500 if there have not been any prearrangements made. However, if you are prepared for the experience and have some understanding of how it works, you'll be better prepared and can avoid costly mistakes."

When someone dies, not only are you emotionally drained but you also have a very short time frame to take care of endless details. With that type of pressure, death arrangements can be quite worrisome, especially if you don't have a family member or friend who is knowledgeable and can assist you. When someone dies, it's hard enough to deal with your own grief. Add dealing with the onslaught of details and many people feel entirely overwhelmed.

So what can you do ahead of time? What do you need to know if someone is terminally ill or death is imminent? By getting the facts you can actually make the entire experience less draining on you and your loved ones, offering yourself or the deceased a final farewell that everyone will find meaningful. Keep in mind that, while cultures and religions differ in customs that relate to death, there are some things that are common to the entire experience. Check with your clergy about particular customs and ceremonies that relate to your beliefs and make sure you are educated about what to do. The following tips will be enormously helpful in planning your funeral or making the arrangements for a loved one.

## The Inevitable

When death is imminent, a hospice is a special way of caring both for people with terminal illnesses and their families. To find out more information and locate the hospice organization nearest you, write or call:

National Hospice Organization
1901 North Moore Street, Suite 901
Arlington, VA 22209
1-800-658-8898

## Preneed

o Prepurchasing a burial plot can often save you a lot of money.

o There are many packages available and they vary from location to location. Comparison shop for the best buy.

o When you buy a burial plot, consider buying everything you can afford. It's clearly a better deal if you buy all your plots at once, but get the facts and make sure you understand all of your options. If you change your mind, it is not easy to sell an unwanted interment space, so understand your contract and all of the details.

o Make sure perpetual care—which is caring for the gravesite, cutting the grass, and keeping it clean—is included in the price.

## Planning Ahead

o According to Alex Rodgers, "There are many details that must be handled in regard to death, with approximately forty-nine separate decisions ranging from what type of service to the clergy's role, selecting what the deceased will wear, the location, and more. While some decisions are small, when you are confronted with a death with little or no preparation, small things feel huge. A family that does not make and discuss these decisions in advance will wind up facing these important decisions on the worst day of their lives."

o Rodgers adds, "The cost also may increase when people don't make these decisions in advance; they find themselves caught up in emotional overspending. Statements like 'nothing's too good for my husband' are commonly heard, and later on when these individuals are confronted with very large bills, they realize they could have buried their loved one in a respectable way without spending more than necessary."

o "Preplanning allows a person or a couple to avoid putting the decision on the children or survivors, and the survivors have peace of mind that the decisions are what their loved one wanted. They also don't have to second-guess what ought to be done. Sometimes you'll find disagreement among the children, but if decisions have been made in advance, everyone is spared having to decide what Dad might have wanted."

o When preplanning your choices for the inevitable, there are many forms that a funeral home can provide to assist you in identifying your wishes. It's a good idea to fill them out ahead of time. This information will be very helpful to your loved ones.

o Expressing your likes and dislikes is important for the well-being of your family. Find out what they want, too. If you go to a funeral that you thought was particularly meaningful, discuss why. Don't avoid the subject. Make it a meaningful part of life.

o Record your wishes in writing and make sure the document is in a safe place where it can be easily reached. Do you want everyone to go in a limousine or ride in their own cars? How do you want to be buried? Do you want flowers or prefer donations that will go to a specific worthwhile cause? Be specific.

o There are many different kinds of caskets, from wood to metal. There are three varieties of outer burial containers (vaults), which are metal, concrete, and polypropylene. Get the facts and understand what's what. Compare your final resting place to buying a car. You can have a luxury sedan with all the bells and whistles or have a car that gets the job done and is a fine mode of transportation.

o Make a list of all of your insurance policies, assets, location of policies, and contracts and store that list with your wishes for how you desire to be buried. This information will save everyone time and energy when dealing with your death.

o Local affiliates of a national organization called the Funeral and Memorial Societies of America (FAMSA) (1-800-765-0107) are dedicated to simplicity, dignity, and economy in funeral arrangements. Since many people prefer to have a simple and inexpensive funeral, you can do this by joining the Memorial Society in your area. It is a nonprofit, nonsectarian organization, and many societies have agreements with licensed funeral directors to provide cremation or burial at a discount. An individual joins the society through application and payment of a nominal lifetime membership fee. The fee includes dependent children under age 18. The member receives copies of a prearrangement form on which to record the funeral director selected and the type of service desired. Upon death of a member, the family or representative notifies the cooperating funeral director of choice and all necessary steps follow automatically. This arrangement does not include the funeral plot and other services, so it's important to understand exactly what you are getting and how this organization functions. Their arrangements with the funeral directors cover only one aspect of the obligations ensuing from death—the disposition of the remains. The Web address is http://www.funerals.org/famsa.

o According to Lisa Carlson, executive director of FAMSA and author of *Caring for the Dead: Your Final Act of Love* (Upper Access, 1998), "Given the lack of completely consumer-oriented preneed laws in most states, another option for your money is a pay-on-death account (Totten trust) at a bank, with next-of-kin (not the funeral home) as the beneficiary. Be sure to go to the 'trust' department of your bank, not just one of the tellers at a counter, and get the facts on how this works and if it's appropriate for you."

o Carlson also gave the following guidelines for when it might make sense to pay ahead: (1) When your funeral plans will cost more than $2,500 or so (states differ) and you need to legitimately shelter assets to pay for your funeral before applying for Medicaid; (2) when you're sure you're not likely to move or travel, perhaps because you're going into a nursing home; (3) when you're sure of the funeral options you and your family want or there's no penalty for changing your mind; (4) when it is unlikely that the ownership of the funeral home and staff will change.

## What to Do When Someone Dies

o According to Alex Rodgers, "The first thing you must understand when someone dies is that there are two separate contacts that need to be made. One is with the funeral home and the other is with a cemetery. The funeral home includes professional services such as the memorial service (on location or off), as well as preparation of the body or embalming, viewing or a wake of the deceased, and picking up the deceased at the hospital, nursing home, or wherever. It is the funeral home's responsibility then to transfer the body to their facility. The funeral home also assists you in the preparation and gathering of all pertinent papers such as data for the government, Social Security, and information for the Veterans Administration. The funeral home applies for the death certificate. Regarding the cemetery, if a family does not have cemetery property, the burial space, mausoleum, or cremation memorialization is selected."

○ According to Lisa Carlson, "There is a third decision you will need to make, which is the kind of memorial marker you will probably purchase. Fortunately, you can take some time and shop around. Price differences can be astonishing."

○ Geraldine Ashkenazie, executive director of the Ahavath Achim Synagogue, has helped coordinate death arrangements for thousands of families over the past twenty years. She suggests you also consider calling someone who is not as emotionally involved to help you handle the basics. She adds, "Refer to your religious institution or friends and family and get all the support you can. Know who the appointed individual is ahead of time who can help you and create a support system for life and death situations."

○ Ashkenazie adds, "Dying wishes shouldn't go with the person to his or her grave. Make sure you know the person's desires, whenever possible, for burial. Don't put your dying wishes in a safety-deposit box in a will that's locked away. If the bank is closed and no one can get to your vault, then no one will know what you want. The best idea is to have everything you want written down, from where you are to be buried to who should be notified. Someone should have access, whether it's your doctor, your lawyer, or someone you can count on."

○ Notifying the community that someone has died can be approached in a variety of ways. There is more than one type of obituary notice and some have a fee associated with them, depending on where they are run. First, there is the death notice, which cites the death, time of the funeral, names the survivors, and place of burial; you pay by the inch or by spatial requirements. Obituaries focus on a person's life and in most cases you can supply a photograph; these do not usually carry a fee.

o According to Phil Faulkner, manager of H. M. Patterson & Son, Arlington Chapel, "Some newspapers will not accept a death notice from a family or individual due to the number of practical jokes people play. Once you contact the funeral home of choice, you should notify them that you would like to place a death notice. Most funeral homes are familiar with what the newspapers in your area will accept, and can advise accordingly. A family who wishes to place the notice directly can do so with proof of a death certificate."

o "The funeral home should ask if you wish to have limousines or have people use their own cars. Other questions include when and where people will arrive, how many cars you expect, where the family will sit during the service, which side of the aisle if it's in a religious institution, and how you want the service to be handled. Other details include your choice of pallbearers, honorary pallbearers, any lodges that need to be notified for fraternal rights, and the choice of flowers or music. The funeral home's job is to help a family be fully informed and know what's about to happen," explains Faulkner.

o All funeral homes should be flexible and help achieve a service that reflects the family's wishes. Don't compromise your desires for a final farewell. These memories and the time you take become a crucial part of your life. "I encourage the family to write something to be read at the service and also be placed in the obituary. These words become a memory that lives on, and it's important to remember that the funeral is for the living," adds Faulkner.

o At the time of death, the funeral home is immediately called to pick up and receive the deceased. A time is arranged for the family to go to the funeral home to make the decisions, purchase the casket, and handle all necessary details. The cemetery is contacted after the family visits the funeral home, and the family must select the cemetery property. It's important to see what you are buying to make sure you like the location.

o Phil Faulkner adds, "It's the funeral home's responsibility to coordinate everything from the moment they receive the remains. They will contact the family and request specific things such as when and where the service will be, who the minister or clergy will be, whether it is a visitation or wake; the funeral home also assists with placing funeral notices or obituaries (even worldwide). It's important to discuss if there are any other cities to be considered for the death notice. The family will be asked to bring vital records such as insurance policies for making claims, Social Security information, veteran information if applicable (form DD/214, which is the service record and military discharge and might warrant an individual being presented with an American flag). They will also be asked what the deceased will wear, including full undergarments, hose, shoes, belts, and any accessories."

o Phil Faulkner also suggests, "For a death certificate, the funeral home will request the following information: the deceased's full given name, maiden name, and race. Many states ask about origin of descent, date of birth, county and state of birth, marital status, and if married, the spouse's full name, Social Security number, and the kind of work done during the working life and specific industry. They will also be asked for the deceased's full address, county, state, whether that address is inside or outside the city limits, and his or her father and mother's full names."

## Planning the Funeral

o When you go to a funeral home, be sure to take the deceased's Social Security number, because it must be included on the death certificate.

o It's a good idea before you go to the funeral home to tell the director how many certified copies of the death certificate you need. You will need copies to change the names on titles or to remove a name on a title of a home or automobile, for the executor of the will, to close bank accounts or remove a name from an account, and to transfer stocks, bonds, certificates, and so on. Believe it or not, a death certificate is even necessary to get a spouse's frequent flier miles.

o If you want someone buried with personal items, take the

items with you when you meet with the funeral home director. Lisa Carlson adds, "Likewise, if there is jewelry such as a wedding ring that you don't want buried, you may need to ask for it."

o If there was long lingering illness, it's a good idea to list the survivors. Often you're emotionally in shock and forget a family member. Plan ahead so you don't leave anyone out and have other members of the family check that you did it correctly.

o Avoid, if possible, planning a funeral during the hottest part of the day, which is often midafternoon. Standing in the heat during such an emotional time is challenging, especially for older individuals. Have water on hand during hot summer months.

o If the deceased was elderly, there will obviously be more elderly individuals attending the funeral. Be considerate and offer additional seating, or consider a service in the institution of your choice.

o The funeral must be paid for before it occurs, so consider how you will do so. Most funeral homes take credit cards, and most will take an assignment for the amount of the funeral upon presentation of a verified insurance policy.

## Resources

*Caring for the Dead: Your Final Act of Love* by Lisa Carlson (Upper Access, 1998). This book is an informative consumer guide concerning funeral laws state by state.

# Decorating

Decorating is one of the most rewarding forms of self-expression, but one of the most intimidating as well. Who hasn't ever stood in a fabric store, overwhelmed by the hundreds of choices and fretting that the blue damask in your hand will clash terribly with the blue-and-white-striped chair you already have? Or felt inferior looking through glossy design magazines? And we've all experienced the blues after paying too much money for furnishings that we loved in the store but disliked when they arrived.

So, what's the solution? Relax, for one thing. Almost all aspects of interior design can be easily changed. Decorating is highly personal, after all, so you can't expect it to happen overnight.

Today, almost anything goes together. We don't have to be so concerned with furnishings matching or having to be from the same style. Mahogany and wicker in the same room? Sure. Silk draperies and sisal rugs? Absolutely. Rooms these days are multipurpose and have a more relaxed feel to them.

Remember, also, that form follows function. What that means is that comfortable and functional pieces are always preferable to those that just look pretty. If you keep that in mind, you might eliminate a good many items you were thinking about. That tall, expensive crystal lamp might not make the best reading lamp after all—and the dog could easily knock it over!

A few other "rules" that designers like to tout: When in doubt, overscale furnishings; a lot of things can look too small for a room, but few look too big. Always take advantage of natural light by keeping window treatments simple. Similarly, make good lighting a priority. Experiment with colors to give your room a fresh look. Use mirrors to make a room look bigger. And last but not least, take your time; the best decors develop over years!

## Decorating Do's:

o Create a picture file. If you don't already have one, start an idea file of decorating looks that appeal to you. It doesn't matter if everything "goes together" yet; at this point, just accumulate pictures of rooms you find attractive. Start with magazines and brochures, or photocopy pictures from library books.

o View rooms in person. Attend designer show houses and walk through as many furniture showrooms as possible to get ideas. A good way to remember what you like at places like that is to take a camera or sketchbook. Another tip: try to visit many of your neighbors' houses; they most likely have similar floor plans and architecture.

o Hold a family conference to enlist everybody's decorating input. Otherwise, you may be in for a lot of complaints down the road! Ask which furniture family members particularly like and dislike (a good thing for you to determine, as well), favorite colors, and any wish lists, such as a game table in the den, a computer desk in the kitchen, or a "napping chair" in the rec room.

o Survey your home. Walk through each room and decide which furnishings are "definite keepers," which might be fine with a paint job or new upholstery, and which get relegated to the yard-sale pile. While you're there, take room measurements so that you know while shopping what kind of dimensions you're dealing with. If you have extra film in the camera, it's nice to take photos of each room that you can carry with you on decorating errands; that way, you won't have to guess about that shade of green on the living room couch.

o Consider the real function of the room you are designing. If it's a television room where most of the activity will be centered around the TV and family activity, make sure everyone has a good view of the TV. Will you eat in this room? Will you entertain? Will the kids play there? Choose fabrics and surfaces that will handle the wear and tear, and kid-proof or pet-proof it accordingly.

o Think and plan ahead! If you are building a house or remodeling and have the luxury to place your lighting and electrical outlets where you'd like, give great thought to where they will be installed. Overhead lighting always makes the job easier, so use it whenever you can. However, consider where lamps, telephones, and televisions will be plugged in so that you can make sure ahead of time that your electricity and lighting are placed correctly and highly functional.

o Create a color scheme. An easy place to start, decorating-wise, is to figure out which colors please you. If you don't know off-hand, look in your closet; most people tend to like the same colors in their home as they have in their wardrobe. If you're a blue-and-yellow person, clotheswise, chances are you'll be happy in a blue-and-yellow bedroom, as well.

o Go neutral. Looking in fabric stores and wallpaper outlets can be intimidating because of all the pattern choices. Here's what many of the pros do: choose a patternless backdrop in rooms by se-lecting sofas, chairs, and window treatments in neutral colors. That way, rugs, artwork, and throw pillows can provide your color and pattern, which are easier—and cheaper—to replace when you get tired of their look. Another way to add interest in, say, an all-white room is to choose different textures and shades of white. It's subtle and sophisticated.

o When in doubt about what to do with an undecorated room, do nothing. Yes, nothing. The pros point out that hastily decorated rooms never have a lasting appeal. It's better to live with a home for a while, gradually adding pieces that you truly love.

o Carry around with you the exact measurements of areas you are wishing to decorate. Everything has to fit the space it's going into, so be prepared.

o In each room, decide where you are going to create interest. If you have a bookcase, think about what other things along with books you might add. From a clock collection to antique plates, you have many options. Kitchens, however, have very few areas that will add excitement, so consider where you will hang art and add ob-jects; use the walls, since they offer an important opportunity to say something about your style.

o Make a budget. When you're out doing your "homework," jot down prices of items that interest you. Before you start any decorat-ing project, determine a budget for each room and whether you can afford to hire a decorator.

○ Buy from sources that allow you the opportunity to see what an item looks like before the final purchase. Even a small installation or delivery and pickup fee is worth it to avoid a costly error you might have to live with!

## Be Creative

○ Look at your furnishings in a new light. Some of the most creative pieces often began life as something else. For instance, an old wrought-iron gate can be painted and used as a twin headboard; a family trunk might make a unique coffee table. More and more outdoor furniture, particularly wrought-iron and wicker, is being used inside; similarly, an easy side table can be made from a large terra-cotta pot with a piece of round glass on top. Got a lot of coffee-table books? Stack them up to make a handy little table.

○ And, of course, what can't benefit from a new coat of paint? Be bold and paint an end table cornflower blue, or a child's dresser fire-engine red, or kitchen stools a sophisticated black. After all, paint is cheap and easy to redo if you don't like the results.

○ Be a clever shopper. Good places to find furniture on the cheap are yard sales and estate sales (the latter usually have more antiques and other fine furniture), unfinished-furniture marts, Penny-saver or newspaper ads that list furniture sales or flea markets, and last but not least, someone's front yard on trash day. Many a resourceful homeowner has driven around a city's "nice" neighborhoods on trash days to pick up discarded treasures! For upscale deals, check out furniture manufacturers' Web sites; some list outlet stores that sell samples (often in North Carolina, but in other areas, too).

○ Call local designers to see what they do with items that don't work. Sometimes you can pick up a fabulous deal. In many markets, interior designers even have stores that sell what they call "designer goofs" (leftovers from decorating projects) at design centers or other locations.

○ Don't forget a decorator's best friend: plants. Large, lush foliage can add instant warmth to a forgotten corner of the room, break up the monotony of books on shelves, and provide green to a stark, all-white kitchen. For best results, use tall, healthy plants in proportionately scaled pots; small plants scattered about aren't as pleasing to the eye. If you do have a lot of smaller plants, group them together in a large basket and cover with Spanish moss. An orchid here or there can add a dramatic touch and enliven a space.

o Artwork doesn't have to be nineteenth-century oil paintings to look great. Real conversation pieces come from unusual mementos that can be framed: a map of a favorite vacation spot (or subway map of your favorite urban getaway), postcards from around the world, or greeting cards that look nice grouped together.

o Be a collector. The power of repetition is always strong; choose a subject that interests you and collect photographs or watercolors. One enterprising art director collects photographs of bicycles—something fun to look for at arts festivals or take pictures of herself on vacation—and displays them in her powder room. Other people hang flea-market finds such as plates, baskets, or miniature chairs on walls.

o Slipcover or reupholster furniture rather than buying new. Consider using inexpensive cotton duck or other durable fabrics to help keep costs down. Sometimes putting new pillowcases on pillows can change the look of a room drastically for only $100 or so.

o Be creative, even a little silly! It's fun to have conversation pieces in your house. Wallpaper a powder room in old magazine covers or, as one stockbroker did, out-of-date stocks and bonds. Let words do the talking; stencil favorite sayings along the ceiling, or maybe nursery rhymes in a baby's room.

o Seek out free or discounted design advice. Some furniture or fabric stores offer free decorating consultation if you buy a certain dollar amount. There are also interior design companies that save you money by using what you have, often looking around in your attic for "treasures" and the like that they can incorporate.

o When making decorative statements, choose objects that can double as storage units. Whether you purchase an armoire that will hold a television set and all your odds and ends or a china cabinet that will store your fine china and other collectibles, consider owning decorative objects that have functional purposes, too.

## Tips on Hiring a Decorator

○ Know the lingo. What's the difference between an interior decorator and an interior designer? Sometimes there's not much difference at all. A decorator, however, tends to focus primarily on the finishing touches of a room: furniture buying and placement, window treatments, accessories, wallpaper, and the like. An interior designer may have more educational training and often helps with safety issues, electrical matters, and structural changes; sometimes he or she can function as a contractor on a remodeling project.

○ Seek the right match. Where to find your designer? Referrals always work best. Ask friends whose homes you admire if they worked with a designer. Or, perhaps a furniture store has room vignettes you are drawn to; ask about an on-site consultation. You can also call the American Society of Interior Designers' toll-free worldwide referral service (1-800-775-ASID) for names of people in your area.

○ Have a face-to-face. Always ask to see a portfolio of a designer's work, and ask about his or her training. Ask for several recent referrals, and do call them. Be sure to determine if the designer has time to work on your project; discuss timetables up front.

○ Talk about costs early on, as well. Many designers charge on an hourly basis, but other options include hourly rate plus commission, flat fee, flat fee plus commission, straight commission, or net cost (the "wholesale" cost to the designer) plus fee. Figure out which means of payment works best for you. Make sure designers know your budget ahead of time.

○ Go with your instincts. If a designer is "all the rage" in your city but doesn't seem interested in your ideas, doesn't ask questions, or appears preoccupied, look elsewhere. With a good designer-client relationship, you become partners—and often friends—so it's important to establish a good rapport.

○ Ask for visual aids. To make sure your designer is focused on your goals, ask him or her to prepare sketches, room renderings, and floor plans, and to gather fabric samples to show you. Don't ever feel bad asking to see what you're buying.

## Common Mistakes to Avoid

○ When purchasing carpet, don't compromise on the quality of the carpet pad underneath. The lowest quality and least expensive pads can disintegrate quickly. Consider how much use a room gets and make sure you buy the best quality you can afford.

○ Dye lots of fabrics, carpet, and wallpaper can vary even from roll to roll or lot to lot, so check out what you've purchased and make sure nothing is hung or used that isn't the correct, matching lot.

○ When you purchase carpet, make sure you know where the seams will run in a room. Carpet is manufactured in specific lengths and widths, and sometimes it's a better investment to buy more so that the seams are not seen and run in unobtrusive places.

○ Make sure you know what direction the pile of the carpet is being laid. It can vary depending on the direction and you should be aware of how your installation will be done.

○ When purchasing fabrics that will be placed in direct sunlight, be certain you know if the fabric can withstand the light. Some fabrics (including really expensive silks) could literally become brittle and fall apart if exposed to too much sunlight, so buyer beware, or completely block out the light.

○ Avoid paying up front. Get everything you contract for in writing and make sure you have references. Know what you're buying and try to avoid ever paying for things ahead of time. Have the contractor specify when your furniture or service will be delivered, and discuss what will happen should it run months later. Get in writing what they will do if there is an unexpected delay on your purchase.

○ Don't dwarf your windows by hanging treatments too low. If you hang curtain rods higher than the actual window, it will accentuate your windows and even make them seem taller. Be sure to measure and order enough fabric if you're going to do this.

○ Not having a common theme or pattern can be a problem.

It's great to mix and match furnishings, but the pros know that there needs to be a sense of continuity. A Chippendale sofa looks fine with a rattan side chair if both are upholstered in coordinating shades of red, for instance. If your Oriental rug has a pink and yellow background, something in the room—from pillows to draperies—should have pink or yellow in it to tie the rug to the furnishings.

o If your emphasis is on the art in a room, avoid using fabrics and patterns on the wall that will fight the art and detract from it. Consider the art as your focus and don't bury it with too many colors or patterns.

o Not working with scale correctly is a huge problem. This can be a tricky area, but it's important to look at a room objectively and make sure size is proportional. An overly large lamp looks funny on a small side table, for example. Or, if your room has all low furniture, consider an armoire, secretary, or other tall piece to add height.

o Hang artwork correctly. Avoid the "floating picture" syndrome, where one sole piece of art hangs in the middle of a large expanse of wall and looks lost. It's best to have an overscaled piece on the wall that makes a larger statement than one that is underscaled. Or, group several pictures together in that situation. To group pictures together on a wall, first practice arranging them on the floor until you've got a pleasing arrangement. One trick is to use a triangle form: One large picture with two smaller ones on either side and a medium-sized one on top. Before you start putting holes in the wall, make sure you've taken the time to get a second opinion and feel comfortable with the placement.

o Don't have too much in a room. Here's a funny but common scenario: often, when people decide to sell their house and remove lots of the little knickknacks and excess "things," they like their house much better. Take a good look at each room and remove the accumulation of stuff that you don't even see anymore. Use baskets, chests, and other storage solutions to keep the clutter out.

o Keep trendy to a minimum. Beware of colors and styles that look cool now, but will look dated in time. If you're going to buy trendy, at least don't spend a lot of money on it.

o Buy enough. Not buying extra fabrics, wallpaper, and carpet can be costly later on. When ordering such staples of decorating, it's always a good idea to get a little extra. That way, you won't have to go through the trouble of reordering if you need to replace something. And you also won't risk the second order's not matching the first, a common occurrence when using slightly different dye lots.

o When using someone else's recommended yardage for a custom upholstery order, be sure to add a clause in your contract with the upholsterer or furniture company that they will be responsible for ordering more matching fabric should they run out. This is a common occurrence and you should be protected in this case and not held at fault.

o The art of decorating on a budget is knowing what to skimp on, yet what's worth paying a little more for. A good-quality sofa covered in a lasting fabric is money well spent, as is a good painter, a well-made rug, and solid case pieces (dressers, secretaries, chests, and other substantial wooden furniture). Nobody is happy with a flimsy coffee table, skimpy fabrics, or poorly hung wallpaper. Be on the lookout for areas where you might be overly frugal.

o Don't forget the "bones" of a room. Good architecture provides the character for a space. Before you redo the sofa for the third time, take a look around and see if some better bone structure is what you need. Consider adding heavier molding around the ceiling or floor, or installing a chair-rail-height molding. Add beaded-board paneling in a country kitchen, or switch out a ho-hum window to a stately Palladian version. After all, just like a Broadway play, the backdrop is just as important as what's going on at the front of the stage!

## Useful Phone Numbers and Web Sites

American Society of Interior Designers: 1-800-775-ASID,
www.interiors.org
American Institute of Architects: 1-800-242-3837,
www.aiaonline.com
www.homefurnish.com: links to furniture manufacturers, plus
tips and discussions on decorating

www.homearts.com: decorating articles from national
   magazines, plus shopping
www.carpet-rug.com: tips and articles from the Carpet &
   Rug Institute
www.pdra.org: Paint & Decorating Retailers Association:
consumer information on paint, wall coverings, floor
   coverings, and window treatments

# Entertaining

Entertaining can be an enjoyable and effortless event for some, but for others it's a major undertaking that requires weeks of planning. Some individuals look forward to the opportunity, while others of us labor over every detail, filled with worry that something might go wrong or our guests won't enjoy themselves.

There is an art to entertaining, but it doesn't require a culinary license. The truly great entertainers understand the dynamics that make a party great, including being relaxed and ready to enjoy yourself, just as your guests do. When it comes to entertaining, the key is preparation. This doesn't mean you stay in the kitchen for days. However, preparing as much as possible ahead of time makes it more enjoyable for you and your guests. It also means you have the know-how and understand the how-to for putting on a party that delights your guests.

The following suggestions reflect ideas from hundreds of parties that I have given or been hired to orchestrate. From events for over five thousand people to evenings for four, I have organized them all. I am neither a gourmet cook nor a magician, but I can tell you one thing: Along the way I have learned that Murphy's Law usually lives at most parties and special events. Just consider all the what-ifs ahead of time, and you can stay ahead of the game. Dot your *i*'s and cross your *t*'s and then try (I repeat, try) to enjoy every minute of the experience!

## Handling Your Guests

o The key to great entertaining is the mix of guests. Most of your guests will be happy to know someone at your party, but everyone enjoys meeting someone new.

o If a guest is arriving late, don't wait to serve dinner.

o Be sure to circulate and speak to every guest. Make sure each guest feels welcomed and attended to. Do not seat your best friend right next to you, because you'll wind up talking only with each other.

○ If a guest spills or breaks something, make as little fuss as possible. No matter what occurs, try to act underwhelmed by the incident to avoid making your guest feel bad.

○ No matter what time of day or night you are entertaining, create a contact list of every vendor's and player's telephone number. Include weekend numbers, pagers—every imaginable contact you can get! If someone runs late or doesn't show up, you'll be glad you have a way to reach that person after hours. Keep an ongoing notebook of recipes you have served that were a big hit. This book will become a long-standing record you can refer to for future parties.

○ When entertaining on a large scale at home, let your neighbors know ahead of time. This is a courtesy they will appreciate, and you'll be less likely to have a problem if you advise them that you'll be entertaining and that there will be increased cars and potential noise.

## Centerpieces

○ Check to see the exact scale of the table you will be placing the centerpiece on. Sometimes you have a great idea, but it might overwhelm the table. Once you add bread baskets, wineglasses, the works, you'll be surprised how much or how little room is left! Be sure to also avoid large, overwhelming centerpieces that cause guests to be unable to see across the table. A single bud vase can often be elegant and very beautiful. Consider an assortment of vases that are different heights to give a festive look.

○ Dress up an ordinary round or oval vase with a lace doily. Set the vase in the center of the wrong side of the doily and bring the doily up around the vase. Tie a ribbon around the neck of the vase for a festive, elegant centerpiece. Add flowers and water and presto!

○ Hollow out the center of an apple and use it as a small decorative vase to hold a few fresh flowers with their stems cut short, as well as your guest's seating card. You can also hollow out any size pumpkin, leaving the walls clean, and use it as a vase. Fill it with a fresh flower arrangement for a spectacular fall centerpiece that will brighten up any table.

○ Combine bright-colored fruit, vegetables, and flowers to make a spectacular statement. Add bright sunflowers together with lemons and other yellow fruit and vegetables, or choose limes and arrange them with an assortment of beautiful green plants.

○ If you don't have a budget for flowers or don't like to waste a dime, a big bowl of fruit makes a spectacular statement, and then the entire centerpiece is edible. Kings and queens of the past adorned their tables with beautiful bowls of fruit overflowing with vines of grapes, so don't feel like you're cutting corners. You can also spray pineapples with gold paint for a festive holiday touch.

○ A festive way to create a centerpiece and enhance a punch bowl is to find a large bowl that sits inside another large bowl with space around the center bowl for flowers or ivy. All you have to do is anchor the center bowl in the middle of the larger one and then fill the outer bowl with flowers, a decorative plant, or even gobs of wrapped candy. A sweet-sixteen party? Use bubble gum. A wedding reception? Fill the outer bowl with roses.

○ The first time I saw this creative centerpiece, I was so impressed. My Aunt Lois purchased a flat of grass that hadn't been cut from a plant store. She placed the flat in the center of her dining room table on a tray and then inserted a variety of single-stemmed flowers in the grass. Each flower had first been cut so that it wasn't too tall and put into a small floral tube that was filled with water. (These are available at a florist's or florist supply center.) The grass looked as if it were growing flowers right in the middle of her dining room. Talk about spectacular!

○ Use leaves as a spectacular way to create a festive centerpiece for flowers. First, wipe the leaves so that they are clean and then dry them thoroughly. Next, use the leaves to completely cover a container of your choice by securing them to the object with a piece of double-sided tape. Finish off the container by wrapping ribbons around the object to hold them in place and add a decorative touch.

○ Core the center of an apple so that the opening is the size of a candlestick. The apple will support the candle, as long as it's not too tall, to make a creative and decorative candlestick holder. Make sure it's steady.

## To Make Flowers Last Longer

o Cut stems on the diagonal with a knife and make a small cut ½ inch up the center.

o Remove all foliage below the waterline when placing flowers in a vase.

o Recut the bottom and change the water every few days.

o Stay away from flowers that have too much fragrance. Some of your guests might have allergies, and the scent could interfere with the smell of your dinner.

o Be creative and consider a variety of vases for your flowers. You might use perfume bottles or miniature vases for a creative touch.

o If your flowers are too short for a particular vase, slip the stems into a straw to hold them upright and make them look taller.

## Creative Presentations

o Presentation and planning ahead are surely part of entertaining success. You don't have to spend a lot of money or time, and it's easy to do. For example, when entertaining kids, make plastic Frisbees your plates. Cover them with paper napkins and use them to serve sandwiches and chips. Later, each guest can try his or her hand at a Frisbee-throwing contest outdoors for tons of fun. Colorful small Slinkies also make super napkin rings and double as fun party favors.

o Use cookie cutters to cut out interesting and fun shapes for sandwiches, pancakes, waffles—you name it. Hearts, stars, flowers, even peanut butter and jelly on bread, can look like festive feasts!

o Cover the table with chocolate kisses or the candy of choice for a fun and creative instant touch. Relate the candy to the theme of your party. Something really sweet like Sweet Tarts for a sweet sixteen party or Lifesavers for a "lifesaving" friend.

o Glad someone tied the knot? Choose licorice strips and tie them in knots, and place them by each plate or use them as napkin rings! You'll be surprised how many different kinds of candy are perfectly suited for entertaining, so check out the candy aisle next time you are at the grocery!

o Gourmet on the go! You don't have to be a pro to make your presentations look fabulous. Fancy garnishes like parsley and radish flowers do the trick. Or, try rolling deli roast beef and turkey together in a spiral. When complete, place a small green olive on top and pierce with a toothpick for a fancy treat. Skewer small vegetables or colorful fruit cubes on a stick. Make your food presentations look almost too good to eat!

o Include the unexpected for a special touch. For a festive flair, add sliced strawberries, dried cranberries, and mandarin oranges to a salad. Or create a sweet sensation by sprinkling sugared nuts or chunks of peanut brittle right on top.

o Give your party a theme and make it festive. My favorite party that was a big hit was a magic party. I hired a top magician to do sleight of hand all evening. While I've also given traditional dinner parties, I love adding festive touches, like personalized chocolate place cards and goody bags of homemade cookies for everyone to take home.

## Hiring a Caterer

o Tony Conway of Legendary Events, a full-service off-premise catering company in Atlanta, Georgia, suggests, "Instead of choosing a different vendor for every service, a full-service caterer can save you money by being a one-stop shop. They can coordinate your rentals, venue, florals, menus, bar, transportation, entertainment, power requirement, lighting, and more."

o Conway also suggests, "Check the references and even the caterer's insurance to make sure they have general liability and workers' compensation coverage. If they are hiring the vendors, make sure you pay the caterer directly, and the caterer is then responsible for everyone and everything. Check to see what industry associations they belong to and what accreditation they have."

o If you find in your initial planning that your telephone call isn't returned in a timely manner, that could be an indication of how you will be handled later. A good caterer listens to the client and then makes suggestions.

o Tony Conway adds, "A big problem with many caterers and contracts is the designated setup time. Make sure you contract for enough time to properly set up and prepare for all the details. If that time is not available, make sure you are working with an experienced caterer who can provide enough staff to set up in a short amount of time."

o While deciding which caterer to use, consider putting a tentative hold on the caterer for your date. This way you'll have time to do some homework, but won't lose the possibility of a particular caterer's availability.

o Interview a few caterers and compare prices. The most important thing you'll learn from doing this is who includes what and which items are additional, like linens, tables, and chairs.

o Ask the caterer for recent references. Try to talk to people who have hosted a similar kind of event as the one you are planning. Word of mouth is key. If you are having an event for a huge group, don't talk to someone who has used this caterer for only fifty people.

o Caterers should carry their own product and food liability insurance, but it's important to discuss these facts. What if a server is hurt at your home? What if a guest gets food poisoning from something you serve?

o Conway suggests, "Make sure you know all the players and the exact services that an outside venue would provide. Are the bartenders in black tie? How are the production people dressed? What about garbage cans? No one wants the Dumpster rolling through their wedding party or tables without skirts at an elegant event."

o Make sure you list in your contract the maximum hours that your party will run. Sometimes a caterer will charge overtime if your party runs later than contracted, so plan for the longest time period up front. Talk about how the party will end and when the caterer will break down.

o If you are being charged on a per-person basis, turn in your head count at the last possible minute. Be sure this is spelled out in your contract. The later you wait, the better, since guests often cancel at the last minute.

○ Check if the caterer will take care of all of your rentals. Often they don't charge a markup and work with rental companies all the time. Not only will they get a good deal, but they oversee everything.

○ Have a no-surprise attitude and make sure you read your contract with your caterer and understand all the fine print. Play out the "what-ifs." What if it snows and the event is canceled? Don't assume anything and get the facts.

○ Discuss tipping ahead of time. What does the caterer suggest and can you tip him one fee and he tip the staff or is that included in your contract? Get the facts!

○ If you're having a large event that requires a staff, make sure you know how they will be dressed. Ask your caterer if you can observe a party they are doing and check out how professional the staff are.

○ Make sure you hire enough staff. No matter how delicious the food is, stacked dirty plates or trays that are empty will detract from your overall goal of having a perfect party.

○ Talk with the caterer ahead of time and make sure her staff understands your expectations. From no smoking to making sure every plate is bused and things are kept clean all night, express your wishes ahead of time.

○ Discuss how leftovers will be packaged at the end of the party. If food that could spoil has been sitting out for hours, make sure it is not combined with food that has been refrigerated. When in doubt, throw it out! Consider food safety first when saving leftovers. Some caterers do not leave leftovers, and donate everything that's still fresh to a food shelter.

○ If you are giving the party at home, clear out the refrigerator for your caterer. Polish your silver or trays if the caterer is using your serving pieces.

○ When giving a large party, it's appropriate to ask for a tasting. Some caterers are happy to provide a sampling of the meal or food that will be served at your event. This is especially common for a wedding or a large event or reception. Be aware of serving sizes and how many portions per guest are included. One piece of tenderloin per person might not cut it. Get all the details and see exactly what you are paying for.

o Find out from your caterer how many pieces of an item he's including. If the filet or shrimp run out early on, you'll be in trouble. Make sure you understand what will happen if you run out of a food item. Sometimes it's best to choose selections that won't be consumed faster than they can be put out.

## Entertaining Do's and Don'ts

o A day or two ahead of your party, take out every serving piece and platter or container and make sure it is ready to be used. This will save you time later on and you'll have more time for presentation details if you consider what is necessary. From pretty paper doilies to lettuce-lined trays, take the necessary time to make each food presentation perfect.

o Unless your guests are dog- or cat-friendly, consider where your beloved pets will be during the party. Not everyone loves animals and some people are even allergic to them, so make sure your pets are safe and sound at a friend's house, overnight at the vet's, or somewhere at home where they will not attack or befriend your guests.

o Make sure everything is turned off when your party has ended. Don't assume this fact until you have checked. See that every door is locked and you are safe and sound.

## Fine China and Silver

o Take care of your fine china. Hand wash each piece that is decorated with gold. Champagne glasses must also be done by hand. Wait until guests leave to tackle the task.

o Count your silver pieces and know what you have. It's also always best to have a special place where the silver is stored. Make sure you don't leave food in or on silver for any period of time.

○ Line your sink with a towel when cleaning your fine china and silver. This will help prevent any casualties.

○ Conway also recommends, "A caterer should ask for the proper soap you use on your china and the storage procedures. On occasion a caterer will ask for a waiver in the event that you are using your finest china and silver. Check out what your insurance covers and theirs does, too. It's important to inventory everything that you entertain with that's of value before and after the event. It's not because of theft; rather, it makes everyone accountable for the items used in entertaining."

○ Read the chapter on wedding tips for additional advice about entertaining and working with vendors and party professionals. Many of the tips that apply to weddings can be helpful when entertaining on a more modest scale.

# Food Safety and Handling

You've heard the old adage, "it's better to be safe than sorry!" That is definitely the theme of this section. When it comes to food safety and food handling, what you don't know could hurt you. In fact, sometimes it's as simple as forgetting to wash your hands. This chapter will help you beef up on your food facts and get the know-how that experts want you to know *now*.

Learning all there is to know about food safety is a huge task, and as soon as this book is printed, there will probably be a new finding regarding food handling and safety. There are, however, tried-and-true facts that will help you protect yourself and your family. With a watchful eye and a proactive attitude, you can prevent many common food-related problems from occurring.

According to Dr. Donald Schaffner, extension specialist in food science at Rutgers University and the expert who contributed many of the tips in this chapter, "Food poisoning is a subject that always concerns us, and it is especially important during the hot summer months. Keeping your family safe depends on you. No matter how carefully a food item is handled before you buy it, if you handle it improperly, spoilage or contamination may occur. Making sure that this does not happen begins in the local supermarket and continues at home."

The following tips are things you may or may not know, but should. From grocery shopping to food storage and handling to food safety, it's crucial that you arm yourself with basic knowledge to avoid preventable problems. You'll also find a hot-line number that will let you call the U.S. Food and Drug Administration with your specific questions. Add the following tips to your grocery list of knowledge and empower yourself to operate a safe kitchen. When it comes to you and your family, nothing is too good or too clean!

## Shopping for Food

According to Dr. Schaffner, the following tips are important to follow when shopping for food safely:

o Fresh meats and poultry may contaminate other grocery items. The best way to prevent this "cross-contamination" is to always keep fresh meats and poultry separate from other items. One way to do this is to put packages of fresh meat or poultry in the plastic bags used for fresh produce. Never place a wet, leaking package of meat in the grocery cart where it might drip on other items. Most important, don't let packages of uncooked meat or poultry touch fresh produce or any other food that you won't cook before eating.

o After you have taken uncooked meat or poultry items from the refrigerated or frozen food case in the supermarket, you should cook, refrigerate, or freeze them within two hours. In warmer weather (from April through October, and especially in July and August), the time limit drops to one hour or less. Meat and poultry should be the last items that you pick up on your way to the cash register.

o Never purchase any packaged or precooked food that has been damaged or has tears, holes, or open corners. Buy ready-to-eat refrigerated foods only if they are actually in a refrigerated case and if they feel cold to the touch when you pick them up.

o Never purchase unpackaged precooked foods from a deli case where other foods are touching meat or poultry items. Always observe the cleanliness of the deli and behavior of the deli worker before purchasing precooked foods. A clean deli will have clean meat slicers, countertops, cutting boards, and floors. Make sure that the employee packaging your deli purchases cleans his or her hands with soap and water between handling different food items. The deli worker should not lay your food on the bare counter before putting it into your package.

o Purchase food products labeled "keep refrigerated" only if they are being stored in a refrigerated case. Purchase dated packages only if the label sell-by, use-by, or pull-by (removal date) has not expired.

o Buy frozen products only if they seem to be completely frozen to the touch. Do not purchase more refrigerated or frozen food than you have room to store at home.

o In hot weather it is best to pack all refrigerated, frozen, or raw foods in an ice chest for the trip home. This is especially true if the time between leaving the store and arriving at home will be more than one hour. Remember that even short stops during hot weather may let your groceries warm up to unsafe temperatures, leading to spoilage and the possibility of food poisoning.

o If you see unsanitary conditions, past-due expiration dates, or other problems at your local grocery store, inform the manager. If you have done this but are still dissatisfied, report the problem to the municipal health department listed in the telephone book.

o The mold you see on cheese or lettuce is not the only problem. The poisons molds can form are found under the surface of the food, as well. You can sometimes save hard cheeses, firm fruits, and salamis by cutting the mold out, but it's necessary to remove a large area around it, too. In general, most moldy food should be discarded.

o Never use or buy a cracked egg. Even if the crack is small, the egg could have spoiled, so throw it out.

o Make sure seals have not been broken when you buy sour cream, yogurt, and the like. Bacteria can grow under an open seal, so avoid eating the product.

o Some cheeses can spoil and should be used within a few days. Check to see if there is an expiration date on the package, or ask your grocer.

o Store eggs in their original package so you'll always know the expiration date.

o If you are in doubt as to whether an egg is fresh, place it in a bowl of cold water. A fresh egg will remain on the bottom while an older egg will float slightly. Discard any egg that floats on the surface.

## Preparing Food Safely

○ According to the U.S. Food and Drug Administration, you should wash your hands thoroughly with hot soapy water before and after handling any raw food.

○ Even if you wear gloves, you should wash them. Gloves can cause contamination if not thoroughly cleaned before and while handling food.

○ Dr. Schaffner adds, "During food preparation, you should wash your hands (or gloves) after handling raw meat or poultry and before handling other foods. When you stop food preparation to do something else, be sure to wash your hands again before continuing. Also, if you have a cut or sore on your hand or arm, be sure to keep it covered by a plastic glove. (This protects you and the food.)"

○ Be sure to wash the counter, cutting board, and any knives, tongs, or other utensils that you use. An acrylic cutting board is recommended, since it is easier to clean than a wood one. A common source of food poisoning is salad chopped on a cutting board that was used for raw meat and not properly cleaned in between. One way to prevent this is to use two cutting boards. Use one for raw meat, and clean it well with hot, soapy water before and after each use. A cutting board can be sanitized by pouring a kettle of boiling water over it. Another way to sanitize is to soak it in a solution of 1/2 teaspoon bleach to 1 quart water, then rinse with clean water. The cutting board should soak for at least one minute.

○ Thaw frozen seafood, meat, and poultry in the refrigerator. Gradual defrosting overnight is best because it helps maintain quality. If you must thaw food quickly, seal it in a plastic bag and immerse it in cold water for about an hour, or microwave it on the "defrost" setting if the food is to be cooked immediately. For fish, stop the defrost cycle while the fish is still icy but pliable. If you must thaw in water, remember to cover the food completely with water and to change the water every 30 minutes.

○ Cook food immediately after thawing. Do not thaw a food and then refrigerate it to cook later!

○ Marinate food in the refrigerator, not on the counter. Discard the marinade after use because it contains raw juices, which may harbor bacteria. If you want to use the marinade as a dip or sauce, reserve a portion separately before adding raw food.

o Do not taste any meat, poultry, fish, shellfish, or egg dish while it is raw or being cooked.

o Never let raw meat or poultry juices come into contact with other foods. If you use a cloth to wipe up spills, don't use the same cloth that has wiped raw meat juices. Use another to clean the counter or wipe out a serving dish.

o According to Dr. Schaffner, "Use a meat thermometer to determine the temperature inside pieces of meat or poultry that are more than 2 inches thick. Red meat should be cooked until this internal temperature is 160 degrees F. or higher. Poultry products require an internal temperature of 180 degrees F. or higher. When you are cooking in a conventional oven, the USDA recommends that the oven be set at 325 degrees F. or higher.

o If you cook large pieces of meat in the microwave, use the temperature probe. If your microwave oven doesn't have a probe, use a regular meat thermometer, and check the temperature in at least three different spots. If the temperature is not above the recommended safe level in all the spots you check, then continue heating.

o Pieces of meat less than 2 inches thick should be cooked until their centers aren't pink and the juices are clear (and not bloody). If you stick a fork into the piece of meat (or poultry) and the juice that runs out still has some red in it, continue cooking.

o Never partly cook foods and then refrigerate or set them aside to finish cooking later. If you cook a food partly before grilling, do it immediately before putting the food on the grill. A food you don't finish cooking until later is likely to make you sick.

o Dr. Schaffner also cautions, "Beware of recipes that call for 'cooking without a heat source.' Placing raw poultry in a pan of boiling water, then turning off the heat and setting the pan aside is a good way to cause food poisoning. Also, to place a roast in an oven preheated to 500 degrees F. and then turn off the oven to allow residual heat to cook the roast is a good way to 'cook up' a case of food poisoning!"

○ Never place a cooked food back into a dish or container that held the uncooked food until that container has been thoroughly washed. Many cases of food poisoning are caused by not following this simple rule.

○ "While microwaving food, be sure to use a rotating turntable, or periodically stop the oven and rotate the food by hand. It's important to make sure the whole food reaches a safe temperature, and any cold spots remaining in a microwaved food could be the cause of a food-poisoning incident," adds Dr. Schaffner.

○ Packaging deli meats in smaller amounts in resealable packages will help avoid spoilage. Often a resealable bag is left open and air causes the meat to spoil.

○ Sliced lunch meats must be used in two to three days, or one to two months if frozen. If you are unsure, throw it out. If it smells funny, never eat it!

○ Never stuff a holiday bird ahead of time, because this can encourage bacteria to grow.

○ A cooler does not always keep things cold enough, so beware of the temperature and don't leave food sitting out or trust that the cooler is cool enough. Many coolers still need ice, so be sure to read the instructions when purchasing one.

## Serving Food Safely

○ Whether you fried the chicken or broiled the hamburgers, never ever leave meat out ahead of time until dinner. Let it cool for 10 to 15 minutes, and then refrigerate.

○ If a serving bowl or container of perishable food has been sitting out, do not refill it. Always use a clean dish with fresh food. Otherwise, the bowl could be contaminated.

○ Do not mix fresh food with cooked food that has been sitting out previously. You'll never know how long something has been there and it could spoil. Also, the food that's fresh will be a different temperature and they shouldn't be mixed.

○ When serving buffet style, keep in mind that it is unsafe to let food sit out for long periods of time. Dr. Schaffner suggests that one hour is a good rule of thumb, but if you must leave the food out for a party and require it to sit out for longer periods of time, use a cooler for cold foods or a warmer for hot foods.

○ When eating out at salad bars, make sure cold food is in containers that are really cold. Eater beware!

## Storing Food Safely at Home

○ The refrigerator is another place where food poisoning can occur. To prevent this, you must make sure there is no contact between uncooked meat or poultry and other foods. Overwrap the meat package in plastic or aluminum foil before placing it in the refrigerator. Place the overwrapped package on a dish to keep the juices from dripping onto other foods.

○ If fresh produce touches raw meat, poultry, or the juices from raw meat or poultry, do not eat it! This rule also applies to any other food that will be eaten without cooking.

○ If raw meat juices drip onto a refrigerator shelf, clean the shelf immediately. This will prevent contamination of other foods.

○ It is important to clean the inside of your refrigerator regularly to help improve food safety.

○ Always read food labels and refrigerate items marked "refrigerate after opening" or "keep refrigerated." Check every package since you'll sometimes be surprised at things you never thought should be refrigerated.

○ Never eat things that might have been in the refrigerator too long—when in doubt, throw it out!

○ "An inexpensive way to avoid food poisoning is to purchase a thermometer. The temperature inside your refrigerator should always be 40 degrees F. or colder," suggests Dr. Schaffner.

○ Place only fresh or freshly cooked items in the freezer, because freezing doesn't make an unsafe food safe again. Frozen items don't spoil as quickly as those in the refrigerator, but they will lose quality and flavor when they are stored too long. Be sure to date your frozen packages so you know how long they have been in the freezer.

○ According to the FDA, "Acid foods should not be stored in

cans after opening. This includes foods such as tomato juice, fruit juices and drinks, and other fruits. Storage in opened cans increases iron accumulation. Further, metallic off-flavors result from acid foods left in the opened cans. If you are not going to eat food left in cans immediately, empty the contents into clean, hot-water-rinsed glass or plastic containers. It is important to place the containers in the refrigerator immediately."

○ If you ever notice that a can is leaking or the ends are bulging, dispose of it properly so no one, including your pets, can get to it.

## Handling Leftovers Safely

○ Leftover foods are cooked foods that you or your family do not eat within two hours after they are cooked. Leftovers include foods that you may eat before or after they have been stored in the refrigerator or freezer. The chance of food poisoning increases the longer you store a food after it is cooked. Improper handling or storing of cooked food is one of the most common causes of food poisoning in the home.

○ Dr. Schaffner strongly advises, "All cooked foods should be reheated to 165 degrees F., refrigerated, or frozen within two hours after cooking. In hot weather, that time limit is only one hour. Remember that the safe period starts after the food is cooked. It includes the time that the food sits before being served and the time it sits on the table while the meal is being eaten. This period lasts until the food is actually in the refrigerator or freezer."

○ Wash your hands with soap and water and dry them thoroughly before handling any cooked food, especially food you store to eat later. Use clean utensils to handle the food, and store it in clean containers.

○ You should place foods to be refrigerated or frozen in small, shallow containers, three inches tall or less, and cover them completely. Don't stack these containers right next to other containers, but leave some air space around them. By using shallow containers and by leaving air space around the containers, you can promote rapid, even cooling of the food. When you refrigerate or freeze cooked food in a large, deep container, the food in the center of the container remains warm for a longer time. Dangerous bacteria may grow in this warm spot without making the food look or smell bad and if you eat this, you could get food poisoning.

o As a general rule, Dr. Schaffner recommends, "Never keep leftovers for more than four days."

o When reheating leftovers, make sure you heat them completely. Leftovers that are merely warmed and not heated throughout are much more likely to cause food poisoning. Cover any leftover sauces, soups, gravies, and other wet foods and heat them to a rolling boil before they are served. Heat all other foods to 165 degrees F. throughout. Be sure to also stir foods while you reheat them to make sure that all the food reaches the appropriate temperature.

o Be careful about bringing home doggie bags from a restaurant. After a two-hour meal and then a trip home, meat could spoil.

## Seafood Safety Tips

o According to the U.S. Food and Drug Administration, when choosing seafood, buy only from reputable sources. Be wary, for example, of vendors selling fish out of the back of their pickup trucks.

o Buy only fresh seafood that is refrigerated or properly iced.

o Don't buy cooked seafood, such as shrimp, crabs, or smoked fish, if displayed in the same case as raw fish. Cross-contamination can occur.

o Don't buy frozen seafood if the packages are open, torn, or crushed on the edges. Avoid packages that are above the frost line in the store's freezer. If the package cover is transparent, look for signs of frost or ice crystals. This could mean that the fish has either been stored for a long time or thawed and refrozen.

o Put seafood on ice, in the refrigerator or in the freezer, immediately after buying it.

o Recreational fishers who plan to eat their catch should follow state and local government advisories about fishing areas and eating fish from certain areas.

o If seafood will be used within two days after purchase, store it in the coldest part of the refrigerator, usually under the freezer compartment or in a special "meat keeper." Avoid packing it in tightly with other items; allow air to circulate freely around the package. Otherwise, wrap the food tightly in moisture-proof paper or foil to protect it from air leaks and store in the freezer.

o Discard shellfish, such as lobsters, crabs, oysters, clams, and mussels, if they die during storage or if their shells crack or break. Live shellfish close up when the shell is tapped.

o When selecting fish, look for scales that are shiny, not dull.

o When in doubt, throw it out. If your fish smells too fishy or has a strong odor, it could mean spoilage. It's better to be safe than sorry.

o Before purchasing prepared lobster, make sure you know when it was cooked to ensure freshness.

o Never buy oysters with an open shell.

o Wait until the end of your grocery shopping to purchase your seafood. You can also have it packaged on ice to ensure freshness.

o Avoid cutting cooked and uncooked seafood on the same cutting board. Cross-contamination could occur. Use separate boards, dishes, and utensils for raw and cooked seafood.

o Seafood leftovers should be immediately refrigerated.

o Never refreeze thawed fish.

o Always wash seafood in cold running water before preparing.

o Never leave seafood out to thaw. Thaw overnight in the refrigerator.

o It's always best to cook seafood. It's a must for at-risk people who have sensitive health conditions.

## Resources

o Call the U.S. Food and Drug Administration's hot line at 1-800-FDA-4010 (332-4010) or 1-202-205-4314 in the DC area. This toll-free food information line is for consumers in the United States. It is located in the Center for Food Safety and Applied Nutrition, in Washington, DC. The hot line offers information to consumers in English and Spanish, twenty-four hours a day, seven days a week. Over twenty recorded informational messages are offered, as well as almost seventy-five publications, which may be mailed or automatically faxed to callers. Information is available on safe sea-food purchasing, handling, cooking, and storage, as well as on nutrition, labeling, economic fraud, additives, pesticides, contaminants, and general food safety. Public affairs specialists are available from noon to 4 P.M. EDT, Monday through Friday, to answer your specific questions.

   o Visit http://vm.cfsan.fda.gov/list.html on the FDA's Web site.

   o Write to the FDA's Center for Food Safety and Applied Nutrition, Consumer Education Staff, HGS-555, 200 C Street SW, Washington, DC 20204.

# Garage Sales

Garage sales are a great way to get organized, clean up your home, and earn some extra money along the way. A garage sale might sound like a lot of fun, but the truth is it is also a great deal of work. While I have consulted on citywide and celebrity sales that appeared on local and national television, I always reinforce how important it is to plan ahead for every detail. Your time and effort will pay off, since you ultimately end up with some extra cash and, it is hoped, a clutter-free environment.

If you've had a garage sale before, then this chapter should help you fine-tune your technique. If you've never had one, then it'll probably save you quite a few headaches. While a garage sale sounds like a good thing to do, there are many things to consider before you have one that will help prevent your effort from turning into a disaster!

What could go wrong, you ask? What if someone enters your property and an item falls on them and they sue you? Or, what if they trip and fall over a toy left in your yard and get hurt? What if someone gives you a bad check for your most valuable items and has already left with your goods? What if you put up signs on telephone poles and later discover it's against the law? What if you sell something that doesn't work or is broken?

These problems and more have actually happened to some unassuming people who thought that having a garage sale was going to be a breeze. To hold a successful sale, you must arm yourself with important information and strategically approach the event like a business. Think of it like opening a retail store in your own backyard! The following ideas should help you plan, prepare, and prevent your garage sale from failure or potential problems.

## How to Prepare for a Successful Garage Sale

○ Don't wait until the last minute. A garage sale is more successful if you start early. The more you have to sell, the more attractive your sale looks to a buyer. Try the shopping bag trick! Months ahead of time, hang a shopping bag on the back of every door in the house and begin filling it with items you wish to sell. Before you know it, you'll have lots of garage sale goodies!

○ Keep in mind that almost everything might sell! Good-condition items go quickly, but you'll be amazed to find that everything from coat hangers to torn linens have sold at garage sales before yours. Don't assume anything won't sell; give it a chance. You just might be surprised.

○ Check every nook, cranny, and corner of your house for items to sell and group like things together, such as one bag for stuffed animals, another for socks. Check every drawer, closet, and cabinet. Get rid of everything you haven't used or no longer want. Encourage everyone in the family to do the same and don't overlook any area of your home.

○ Make sure you have a great location. If your home is not easy to find and doesn't have a great deal of traffic, consider teaming up with a friend who has a better location and do the sale together. If another location is not available, consider joining a few neighbors, or even your entire neighborhood. Strength in numbers really does work since your cooperative ad could give more details, indicate more items for sale, and illustrate that your sale is worth the trip!

○ Choose a date for your sale and think ahead. Garage sale pros suggest that having a two-day sale over the weekend works best. If you have the time and energy, try three days (Friday, Saturday, and Sunday). This way you'll have time to evaluate what's selling and what's not, and reduce the price of the items you really want to get rid of. Two days also gives you a chance to add more items you might have forgotten or decide to sell. You'll find that different people come on each day, so you also increase your number of customers and purchases.

○ Consider a rain plan. You must know what you will do with everything in case your sale will be held outdoors. I prefer a garage or enclosed space for security, but if you don't have one, team up with a friend who does. An enclosed area makes a huge difference, since you can also start preparing for your sale way ahead of time and attractively set up your belongings.

○ Get the facts. You must check out your city's requirements and tax guidelines. Can you hang signs or is it illegal? Are you allowed to hand out fliers to surrounding neighborhoods or not? Be sure you know the law and what your limitations and regulations are before you decide to have a sale. Check with your city/town hall to see if you need a permit.

○ Consider purchasing a few yard sign holders if you can't post announcements. These work well and can be placed in a variety of visible positions, including the top of your street. Be sure to get permission if you wish to place your sign on someone else's property.

○ Check your insurance and see what liability you have. This information is crucial, especially in the event that someone has an accident on your property. Know your liability and prevent safety problems beforehand.

○ Call your accountant and find out what your tax responsibilities are. What do you need to report about the income you earn at your garage sale?

○ Have a valuable or custom-made piece of furniture for sale? Don't be shy when promoting the best pieces you are selling. If it's a quality item and desirable, say so!

○ If an item you are selling is too large to bring outside or perhaps even too valuable, take pictures of the item ahead of time. Enlarge the photographs and make a special sign displaying the piece or pieces for sale. You'll be surprised how many people will be interested even with just a picture. Post the size of the piece and any details that might help sell it, including the original price, where it was from, the condition it's in. This works especially well for dining room suites and china cabinets or items that are too heavy to move.

○ In the event that you have too many valuable items, feel overwhelmed by the idea of a garage sale, or need professional assistance, consider hiring an expert to run your sale. You can expect them to take a percentage of the profits and sometimes charge an hourly fee depending on the way they work. The good news is that they will take care of everything that relates to your sale, from pricing the items to running the sale from start to finish. Find an expert by speaking with friends or calling antique dealers, or by checking the Yellow Pages under "Organizing Services" or "Estate Sales."

o If your sale is going to benefit a charity, be sure to work closely with the charitable organization to ensure that you have followed all of the necessary rules. Get all the facts ahead of time in regard to receipts, sales, donations. Don't assume anything.

o If you are organizing a sale for someone who is ill, older, or a relative who is deceased, be sure to go through every suitcase or drawer, since valuable papers, jewelry, and other sentimental items might be hidden very carefully throughout the house.

## Publicizing Your Sale

o Advertising is a must and will definitely increase your earnings by announcing your sale. Ask your local newspaper if they have any garage sale ad specials.

o Include directions to your sale or a familiar landmark in your ad. This is an absolute must for any location, especially those that are off the beaten path. Avoid listing your telephone number, since that requires too much of your time and is often not productive.

o Check if your ad can also be placed on the Internet. Many classified advertising departments offer an additional listing on their Web site for little or no extra charge.

o Check out the garage sale listings in the classified ad section, and see which ads would attract you. Model your ad similarly. Don't forget to emphasize your most attractive items. Use bold type for key words.

o If you are selling good-quality clothing, highlight the fact with a description like "designer clothing."

o When placing your ad, be specific, since you are competing with dozens of other sales. What will make yours more exciting?

o When placing your ad, you can save money with abbreviations. And don't be shy with the classified representative. Ask for their help with suggestions and ways to save money on your ad, but be sure to announce your sale in capital letters or boldface if you want it to stand out from the others. Don't compromise your ad. It's your best selling point.

○ Be specific with the time of your sale—for example, 9:00–5:00 *only!* Be prepared for early-bird shoppers, and don't negotiate at the beginning of the sale or everyone there will be countering your prices. Keep your sale prices firm on the first day and don't bargain unless you feel it's necessary or the traffic at your sale is slow.

○ If you live in a hard-to-find neighborhood that is off the beaten path or doesn't have a lot of traffic, be sure to include clear directions. Experts prefer not listing a telephone number since you'll be besieged with callers who won't come but are looking for something specific.

## How to Set Up Your Sale

○ If you are having your sale in an enclosed area like a garage or a house, begin setting up your sale a few days ahead of time. People usually underestimate the amount of time they need to set up, so get a jump start.

○ If you are having a yard sale, have everything ready to move out on the day of the sale. Make sure you have ample helpers, since it's a big job and takes time.

○ Merchandise your items. As you set up your garage sale area, create aisles and set up a shopping area just as you would if you were setting up a store. Keep the paths clear and group things together in an attractive manner. Arrange your items on tables when possible. Presentation is the key!

○ Take your possessions seriously if you wish to sell them. Keep in mind that you once bought them, too! You're bound to make more money at the sale if you display your belongings in an appealing way. Use tables, hanging racks, and anything else that will help your things be easily seen and appreciated. Take it seriously and it will sell.

○ Price items with removable self-sticking labels and use a permanent marker with a medium tip so the price is easy to read. Write prices on masking tape for larger items or objects that stickers might fall off of easily during the sale. If you decide to price each piece of clothing separately, attach a hanging price tag on a string to a button or a label.

○ Clothing sells better if displayed on a rack. There are many portable rolling racks, but be sure not to put too much on it or your shopper will have an impossible time looking through it. Call attention to your best things and create a designer rack by grouping better clothing together.

○ Keep your merchandise looking fresh and not picked over. If you leave a pile of clothes on the ground, it's not likely to sell. People want things that have been cared for, so be sure to clean up your sale as you go.

○ Move things around during the sale. Often, a vase takes shape when displayed on a piece of furniture. Clean silver and crystal so they look their best. Take pride in what you're selling.

○ Put a price on everything! If you choose to reduce it, cross out the original price and give it a significant reduction. Get a second opinion if you are in doubt, and if you have any antiques, call an appraiser. You might have something quite valuable.

○ Have an extension cord on hand that works. Keep it rolled up in a corner away from the traffic so no one trips on it, but available to test any electronic items to make sure the item is in good working condition. If you can't do this, make a sign that says *sold as is*.

○ If something is not for sale, mark it *nfs*. This will prevent your shoppers from being disappointed. Plus if it's already purchased, be sure to mark it *sold* and with the name of the buyer.

## Tips for Conducting Your Sale

○ Give your garage sale some street appeal. Many people will drive by a sale and make a one-minute decision to stop or not to stop. Give them something that might intrigue them to come in—add some curb appeal. List your best items on a sign or put a few objects out front that are really exciting or interesting.

○ Be an energetic salesperson! Greet people as they arrive and make them feel at home. They are bound to stay longer and spend more time at your sale if they feel welcome.

○ If possible, have a lot of plastic grocery bags, boxes, or shopping bags on hand in case someone needs them to pack up their purchases.

○ Wait until the last day or few hours of your sale to reduce items when possible. This takes willpower, but often pays off. You can tell customers who choose to offer you less than you want on an object to come back and take their chances. Sometimes this even encourages them to grab the item at the price you have it marked.

○ If someone tries to negotiate with you for a single item, you could give them an incentive to buy more. Offer a small reduction or a package deal if they purchase more items. If your sale isn't really busy, this can work in your favor.

○ Don't miss a sale! If someone is really interested in an item but makes you a low offer, write down their name, amount offered, and telephone number. You'll be glad you did this in the event that the object doesn't sell. This way you can call them back and tell them the item is theirs.

○ If you have the sale in your garage or outdoors, do not let people use your rest room or come into your house. Keep the house locked and make sure to stick to this rule.

○ Keep a portable telephone nearby in case you need to make a call. You won't have to go in and out of the house and leave your sale.

○ Have a few hundred dollars broken down into smaller bills for change. You'll need at least one hundred one-dollar bills, so be prepared. If your sale is really big, have additional change but keep it locked in a safe place. Make a note as to how much money you are putting in the money box each time. This way you can determine how much you earn overall.

○ Guard your money carefully. Set up a small table and put one person there as your official checkout area. Designate this person as the individual in charge of the money box. Have a lot of change for cash purchases and never leave the money unattended. Some people prefer to wear a fanny pack if they don't have extra help and must run the sale by themselves.

○ Enlist a few friends to keep an eye on items throughout the sale. Display valuable possessions in a highly visible place.

○ Accept cash only. Know where the closest banks are and hold an item until the person can bring you back cash. For more expensive items, arrange for a later pickup and request identification. If someone must write a check, get all the pertinent information and a telephone number. Check the telephone number to make sure it's correct, or wait until the bank is open to conduct your transaction. If you plan to accept only cash at your sale, be sure to mention that in your ad.

○ Be a creative salesperson! You are your own best advocate, so go to work. Create signs that give information that will make the object more desirable. Have you seen the item for a lot more money? Was it from a well-known shop? Is it an antique? Show the original price you paid for the item if you are offering it at a huge savings. Be a creative merchandiser.

○ If you have clothing, give it all one price. It makes your job and the buyer's shopping easier if everything on the rack is $5.00. You'll make a little more on one item and possibly less on another; however, it's appealing to your shoppers and a quick way to price things.

○ Shoes are often the hardest thing to sell unless you get lucky and a size 7 arrives and every pair fits. Price shoes inexpensively and make a package deal for a buyer who can take all of them.

○ Avoid pricing things under $1.00. It's better to group inexpensive items together, such as four magazines for $1.00. You can also put them in a plastic bag, but stay away from pricing things at 25 cents, and so on.

○ Involve the kids and let them help. They will enjoy being part of the sale and feel great about the money they earn from their contributions.

○ Let it go to a good cause! Arrange for a nonprofit organization to pick up whatever you don't sell. Pull the few items you still love or prefer to save and donate the rest immediately following the sale.

○ Deduct your expenses from the sale and calculate what you earned. Check with your accountant about the earnings you must list and get the facts on what is necessary to report.

○ Avoid having too many sales. Your neighbors will think

you're running a business, and garage sale junkies won't take your sales seriously.

    ○ If you are having a multiple-person sale, color code the items. Your checkout person can help tally and divide the money later. Or, let each individual person collect his or her own money at the time of the purchase.

    ○ Add a special touch and sell water, coffee, and muffins. Early birds will especially appreciate this personal touch. Or consider a good ole lemonade and cookie stand during hot weather. The kids will love running it and enjoy the rewards.

# Gardening and Lawn Care

Gardening is one of the few hobbies that can be all things to all people. But not all of us were born with a green thumb. Thank goodness for plants that are hard to kill and gardens that thrive even when we forget what to do next! Still, we all know people for whom summer wouldn't be summer without big, juicy, red tomatoes and other vegetables fresh from their garden, or people who like to spend their free time babying rosebushes, looking for that perfect bloom. And every neighborhood has at least a few carpetlike lawns.

But even if your idea of gardening is limited to a few flower pots on an apartment rooftop, you have to admit there is something very satisfying about coaxing flowers, fruit, or foliage from a plant. Gardening doesn't even have to be just a warm-weather activity. Many gardeners consider sitting by the fire with an armful of seed catalogs and a head full of plans a most enjoyable way to spend a winter evening. Of course, there are many plants that grow well indoors, giving year-round opportunities to exercise your green thumb.

Another wonderful thing about gardening is that you always learn something. Whether you've never planted a seed before or whether you've been gardening since your grandmother made you help pull weeds as a small child, there's always more for you to learn. The sources for expanding your gardening knowledge are nearly endless. Talk to the people who run a local nursery, and you'll find out about plant varieties specially developed for your neck of the woods. Visit a hardware store or home improvement center, and you may run across some new tool or gadget to help with your yard work. Reading a seed catalog can be very informative. And there are gardening classes at local colleges or adult education centers.

Your county Extension Service is another source of free help and advice on gardening and lawn care. While many rural residents are familiar with the Cooperative Extension Service, residents of more urban areas might not realize that they, too, can take advantage of the program. The Extension Service can provide you with free pamphlets and fliers on topics of interest to you, help you to identify pests that are attacking your garden and set you on a course of action to combat them, and can provide testing of your soil. The service also offers free classes on topics related to gardening. Because extension agents work in your specific county, they are experts on the gardening conditions and problems that you are most likely to run into. (These tips were provided by the Cooperative Extension Service of the University of Georgia, and county agent and horticultural expert Walter Reeves.)

## The Real Dirt

o Proper soil preparation is the key to happy, healthy plants. Work the soil well, to a depth of at least 12 inches, and add organic matter to help loosen the soil. By loosening the soil, you improve its capacity to hold moisture, and help improve drainage as well.

o A soil test will help you develop and maintain more productive soil in your garden. The results of the test will help you select the proper program for adding lime and fertilizer so you'll get the best possible growth from the lawn or garden you plan to plant.

o Soil tests are available through the Cooperative Extension Service in your county. The Extension Service phone number is listed in your phone book among the county government listings—look for a listing for "Extension Office," "Extension Service," or "Extension Agent." The county Extension Office can provide you with specific instructions on how to collect your soil sample and other information you will need to have your soil tested successfully.

o When having your soil tested, remember to test areas of your yard separately. For example, if you have different kinds of grass in the front yard and the backyard, each of those areas should be tested separately. The lawn and the vegetable garden should also each be separate samples.

o According to the Cooperative Extension Service, soils can be tested at any time of the year, but it's best to have them tested well in advance of when you want to plant. It's especially important in areas where lime may need to be added to the soil, because lime reacts fairly slowly and has to be absorbed several weeks before planting.

o Once good fertility levels have been established, the soil in lawns and areas for ornamental plants should be tested every two to three years. The soil in vegetable gardens should be tested annually.

## Flower Gardens

o Flowering plants vary considerably in their tolerance of sun or shade, and in the amount of water they need or are willing to put up with. That's why it's extremely important to do a little research before selecting the plants you will put in your garden. While the country has been divided up into a number of zones to help indicate which plants will thrive in certain regions (those are the multi-colored maps you see in seed catalogs and plant books), that's only part of the story. The conditions in your own yard can vary widely. You could easily have a sunny, dry location for a garden in the front, and a damp, shady spot where you'd like to do some planting in back—and the plants that do well in one of those locations would be unlikely to thrive in the other.

o A primary consideration in choosing plants is how much sun they will receive. Plants listed as needing full sun usually need at least six hours of sun, though many would prefer eight or more hours in the summer.

o Shade plants are those that require less than six hours of sun a day. Few plants flower in full shade, while most will bloom in dappled sun.

o Most flower gardens need about 1 inch of water per week, in the form of either rainfall or water you apply from a hose, sprinkler, or watering can.

o Before planting flowers, spread 2 inches of organic matter on the bed, then work it into the soil. During the winter, when your perennials have died back, spread compost or other organic matter on top of the bed and let the earthworms work it into the soil for you.

o Many flowering plants will rebloom if they are "deadheaded"—

that is, if you pinch the faded flower off. This trick doesn't work for all plants, but go ahead and do it; you can't do any harm to the plant by removing an old flower.

○ Mulching will help you minimize the amount of water your flower garden needs and will also help combat weeds. Organic mulches are preferred, the Cooperative Extension Service says. But don't put mulch over the crown of the plants, especially in the winter.

○ To avoid spreading disease among the plants, don't work in the garden when the foliage is wet.

## Your Own Produce Stand

○ Tomatoes need to be planted very deep. Strip the lower leaves off the seedling tomato plant so that only a tuft of leaves shows, and then plant it to that depth.

○ Tomato plants are particularly susceptible to diseases that can be spread from the soil. To keep the soil from splashing up onto the plant and possibly spreading disease, be sure to mulch your tomato plants immediately after planting, before watering. A layer of newspapers covered by a layer of more attractive mulch works well.

○ If you have very limited gardening space, you can still grow "patio tomatoes" in a planter. Be sure to get the biggest container you can for each plant. Go for a minimum of 5 gallons of soil per plant; 10 gallons would be better. Even though one tomato plant looks very lonely in a huge pot, tomatoes need a great deal of soil and water.

○ Once you plant carrot seeds, cover the row with a board to keep the ground moist until the seeds sprout. In about a week, you can remove the board and reveal the tiny plants.

○ Corn does better if it is planted in a square or block configuration rather than in a straight line. That's because the pollen will remain more concentrated in the square area, resulting in better pollination.

○ For trouble-free fruit, plant raspberries, blueberries, or blackberries. These plants will thrive in most areas of the country and they don't need to be sprayed, as fruit trees do.

○ Your apple tree will be healthier and will have larger fruit if you thin the apples when they are about the size of a walnut. There should be about 6 inches between each apple. Discard the apples you remove. Do not let them remain on the ground around the tree.

○ A strawberry plant won't bear well for more than one year, but it will send out runners that can be counted on to provide fruit the next year. Dig up and discard the "mother plant"; allow the "daughter plants" to provide your berries and to send out runners so you can repeat the process again.

## The Grass Is Greener . . .

○ Every kind of grass has a proper mowing height. Check with a local nursery or Extension agent to find out how high you should be mowing the grass in your yard. If you have different kinds of grass in the front and back yards, it's very possible they will need to be mowed at different heights, and you will have to adjust your mower when you move from one area to the other.

○ You know it's time to mow when you will have to remove about one-third of the grass blade to return your lawn to the proper height. For example, if the proper height for your grass is 2 inches, you need to cut it when it is 3 inches tall.

○ Grass should be cut when it is dry, and it's important to maintain a sharp mower blade.

○ Most lawns need about 1 inch of water a week, either from rainfall or a sprinkler. To make sure you are giving your grass enough water, set a couple of soup cans out in the lawn to catch the water, so you can see how much your sprinkler has put out. Many people simply run the sprinkler for a certain amount of time, assuming that's the right amount of water, but sprinklers vary greatly in how much water they deliver.

○ The best time to water your lawn is between midnight and 10 A.M. Doing so allows the grass to dry off in the afternoon sun. The longer your grass stays wet, the more opportunity fungus has to develop. The worst time to water is in the evening, after 5 P.M., because the grass will remain wet until sometime the next morning.

○ Let the grass clippings remain on the lawn when you mow,

rather than bagging them. It's commonly believed that grass clippings are a major part of the problem known as thatch, but research has shown that thatch buildup is caused by grass stems, shoots, and roots. Grass clippings left on the lawn rapidly decompose and release valuable nutrients into the soil.

o Not bagging those grass clippings saves you time while it nourishes your grass. According to a study of so-called grasscycling, the practice may require an extra mowing a month, but it reduces the time per mowing. Over a six-month period, homeowners who took part in the study had saved an average of seven hours of yard work.

o Mulching attachments for your mower, which chop grass clippings into smaller pieces, can improve the mower's grasscycling performance. However, any mower can be used for grasscycling without any special attachments, the Cooperative Extension Service says.

o Slow-release fertilizer is better for grass than quick-release formulations. That's because with the slow-release fertilizer, the lawn is getting a more steady diet of nutrients. With the quick-release kind, the grass is subjected to periods of feeding and starvation.

## Trees and Shrubs

o One-fourth of the foliage on a shrub can be taken off in any growing season. You can cut it back even more during the nongrowing season.

o Most shrubs should be pruned yearly to maintain their shape and size. When pruning shrubs, it's always better to prune back to an existing limb, rather than just shortening a limb. Taking a hedge trimmer and simply shearing is not the recommended way to prune a bush.

o Putting mulch under your shrubs does more good for them than fertilizing does. Mulch will help keep water in the soil, prevent heat from reaching the plants' roots, and prevent the growth of weeds.

o The most important thing you can do when planting a tree is dig a big hole, so there is plenty of room for the roots to spread out.

Research indicates that adding organic matter to the soil when you plant a single tree doesn't give any real advantage, as it does with flowers or other small plants.

## Parsley, Sage, Rosemary, and Thyme

o Herbs are good candidates for a container garden, window garden, or for the gardener with limited space. Just a few plants can result in a "crop" that is plentiful and useful.

o Herbs should be planted where they will get at least six hours of sun a day. Choose a sunny area that has good drainage.

o Many herbs originated in the Mediterranean region, so they do not like acid soil or soil with a low pH. Herbs do best when the soil they are planted in has a pH of 5.8 to 6.5. (You can have your soil tested through your county Extension office to find out the pH level.)

o If your soil has too much acid for an herb garden, you will need to add lime to the soil to reduce the acidity. Experts from the University of Georgia's Cooperative Extension Service recommend using granulated dolomite lime, because it is easier to work with than powdered or hydrated lime.

o Herb plants should not be set deeper than they were in the container they came in from the nursery. A good plan is to lift or mound the plants about 1 inch above the ground, then rake up soil or mulch to cover the root ball. That ensures good drainage at the crown and gives the plant a better chance of surviving in wet weather.

o Once they are well established, most herbs prefer the soil to be on the dry side, rather than too wet. When you first plant herbs, however, you will need to water them every few days for the first two weeks, unless Mother Nature takes care of the task with a good soaking rain.

## Houseplants

o If you are looking for a houseplant that can put up with a lot of neglect and still thrive, some good choices include philodendron, Swedish ivy, geraniums, and peace lily.

○ Many popular houseplants are poisonous if ingested, including dumbcane (dieffenbachia), philodendron, and English ivy. Dozens of common landscaping and flowering plants can also be dangerous if eaten, including azalea, caladium, daffodil, delphinium, morning glory, holly, and wisteria. If you are unsure about the poison status of a particular plant, contact your local poison control center for advice. The telephone number is included in the emergency numbers listing in your phone book.

## Resources

www.garden.org
www.gardentown.com
www.gardensolutions.com
www.vg.com
www.garden.com

# Health

Whoever said, "If you have your health, you have everything," understands the real priorities in life. However, with all the information that bombards us daily about our health risks, options, and threats, it's often difficult to sort out the details and determine what to do next.

When it comes to keeping ourselves healthy these days, we are fortunate to have an incredible amount of information available from hundreds of books and magazines, Internet sources, physician advice lines, and health-oriented television programs. But while we tackle this abundance of information, the day-to-day questions and little things can sometimes get lost in the shuffle.

While the field of health is changing every second, this chapter includes practical information from a wide variety of resources. Some of the information may be as familiar to you as Grandma's chicken soup, while others might be things you really didn't know. The advice presented, however, is in no way, shape, or form a substitute for medical advice. As quickly as I write this book, there could be new information that affects your life. Similarly, your individual situation might demand a different approach. So get the facts, stay up to date, and be a smart consumer when it comes to your health.

## Allergies/Asthma

According to Dr. Dennis L. Spangler, medical director of Atlanta Allergy and Asthma, "22 million Americans suffer from seasonal allergic rhinitis, otherwise known as hay fever. Those with hay fever experience 2 million days of restricted activity, 6 million days of bed rest, 3.5 million days of work loss, 2 million lost school days, and 8.4 million physician office visits." Dr. Spangler offers the following tips to help us through the spring and fall allergy seasons:

○ To decrease allergies, keep the windows closed in spring as bushes and trees begin to bud. These plants can trigger allergies.

○ Everyone prays for rain during pollen season. A prolonged rain will effectively wash pollen out of the air; however, a brief downpour may in fact cause particles that had settled to the ground to once again become airborne.

○ Pets can bring pollen into the home. If your pet goes in and out of the house, limit his access to the home and wash him more frequently.

○ Spring pollens may be most bothersome at midday or mid-afternoon, as the wind picks up the pollen particles and distributes them through the air.

○ Cutting grass can cause significant allergic symptoms for some. If you must cut your grass, wear a mask and take a shower, including shampooing your hair.

○ Even though fall temperatures are mild, keep windows closed and use air-conditioning to reduce allergy problems. Air-conditioning filters out pollen particles and reduces indoor mold.

○ If there is moisture, there is mold! Mold can grow on almost any surface. Keep humidity low by using a dehumidifier or your air-conditioner.

○ Mold can cause allergies, so be sure you have no breeding ground for spores. Check your basements, filters, and other areas of your home that might need help.

○ Fall is the season for "wheezing." High mold counts and viral illnesses that occur as the kids go back to school can cause increases in asthma symptoms.

○ After sunset, many of the airborne pollen particles will settle out of the air as the wind drops off. Therefore in spring, it is best to exercise in the morning.

○ Don't use your attic fan in the spring. It sucks the pollen into the house.

○ Keep the pets out of the bedroom and if you're allergic to dust mites, buy hypoallergenic pillows and bedding treated with anti-microbial agents.

○ Check your heating and air-conditioning filters and change them at least every six months.

## Bones

o Cracking your knuckles isn't harmful. The sound might drive you crazy, but this action does not lead to arthritis or enlarged joints.

o If you break a bone and it must be in a cast, be sure to check out all your options. Casts now come in a variety of colors and patterns; there are even waterproof ones that can be worn in the shower.

o Seventy-five percent of all lower-back pain problems can be prevented by building your abdominal muscles. Aim for twelve to fifteen properly done crunches a day.

o Here's a travel tip that might save you from pain! After long drives, avoid lifting heavy objects like luggage when you arrive. You have an increased chance of injuring your lower back.

## Colds

o Chicken soup really works for congestion. Studies show that hot chicken soup loosens sinus secretions, allowing them to drain more quickly. Be sure to add some garlic to the soup for added benefit.

o Colds are caused by viruses, not the weather.

o Frequent hand washing is the best defense against colds. Colds arrive in your system through your nasal passage and often get there by your hands.

## Cosmetic/Plastic Surgery

The news from the world of cosmetic surgery is "mini-procedures." These simple operations let surgeons zero in on specific problem areas. Today's mini-procedures yield better results than the traditional, more invasive operations cosmetic surgeons have traditionally used. According to Dr. Arthur Simon, board-certified plastic surgeon, "these procedures are safer, less costly, and allow faster recovery." Dr. Simon provides the following tips to help ensure the best outcome.

o A common problem, turkey neck, which is droopy skin on the neck, is now treated with microsuction of the neck. The surgeon simply sucks out excess fat from underneath the neck skin using a suction tube (cannula) inserted through pinhole incisions. Microsuction leaves more of a natural look and causes no scarring.

○ Droopy eyes can now be treated with a laser that vaporizes excess skin, and fat can be removed through an incision inside the lower eyelid. Typically, laser surgery involves less bleeding and bruising. The laser can rejuvenate the skin, while the internal incision eliminates external scars. It also prevents the "deer-in-the-headlights" look.

○ The usual approach to correcting facial wrinkles is to fill them with injections of collagen. However, some patients are allergic to collagen. And because collagen rapidly absorbs back into the skin, wrinkles usually reappear within weeks. A better way is to utilize injections of fat that has been removed from the patient's own body. With proper technique, 30 percent of this fat stays in place indefinitely.

○ In some cases, fine lines can be improved or eliminated with a nonprescription cream, lotion, or gel containing salicylic acid or alpha-hydroxy acid.

○ To treat deep wrinkles, doctors have traditionally used chemical acids that remove the damaged outer layer of skin. Deep peels can leave the skin looking mottled or permanently lighter; they're unsafe for people with dark complexions. A better way is laser resurfacing. It works against wrinkles and scars, leaves the skin looking soft and natural, and is less likely to cause color changes.

○ In picking a cosmetic surgeon, ask someone who has undergone the same procedure you're considering for a referral. Interview at least three cosmetic surgeons before picking one to do your surgery, and make sure they have the proper credentials and board certifications. Find a surgeon who has performed *many* of the procedures you are considering with satisfied patients.

## Dental

According to internationally renowned Atlanta dentist and author of the best-selling consumer book *Change Your Smile*, 3rd ed. (Quintessence Publishing Co., Inc., Carol Stream, Illinois, 1997) Dr. Ronald

Goldstein, and his partner Dr. David Garber, a world-renowned author and teacher, these are some helpful dental do's and don'ts:

o Regular dental checkups help keep your teeth healthy, but they also help discover certain other diseases. Adults with cavities and dental infections or gum disease increase their risks of having strokes, respiratory problems, underweight babies, and even heart problems.

o Sucking excessively on a bottle is the leading cause of tooth decay in children under the age of three. The milk or juice lies on the teeth for an extended period of time and initiates the decay process.

o Adults and older children should use a drinking straw whenever possible. A straw limits the amount of contact between your teeth and sugary sodas or fruit juices. Never swish drinks around your mouth.

o Chewing sugar-free gum after a meal will increase saliva in the mouth and that may help prevent decay.

o Painless dentistry is now available. Dentists can actually spray away decay with mini sand blasters almost before it starts and becomes an invasive cavity that needs to be filled. However, if further treatment is needed, there is now a painless delivery system for anesthesia. No more needles needed if you get there in time.

o Request that your dentist put your dental plan in writing. Make sure you know what you are getting and how the treatment is being done.

o Supply yourself with multiple toothbrushes. They will last longer and stay firmer. Soft, round-ended nylon is best. Natural-bristle brushes take longer to dry. If it isn't used properly, a brush can damage gum tissue because the bristles are too firm and coarse. Angled brushes may help in reaching some areas. Caution: Too-vigorous brushing can wear grooves in tooth enamel. When used correctly, a toothbrush will not abrade tissues or teeth. Hardness or bristle material is not as significant as the way the brush is used and the time spent brushing.

o Alternate your regular toothbrush with a site-specific mechanical rotary brush system with fine filaments instead of bristles that can more effectively remove the deposits just under your gum tissue.

○ Never chew ice, which can cause sudden temperature changes as well as microcracks in your teeth.

○ Protect your dental work with a night guard to be worn during sleeping hours. A high percentage of people clench or grind their teeth while they sleep. It may take only one episode of clenching or grinding to crack restorations or your own natural teeth, so protection with a bite guard can be a wise investment.

○ It is important to see your hygienist three to four times yearly to minimize the formation of bacterial plaque buildup under the gums, which can cause bone loss if it is not removed, or to evaluate any changes in your dental health. Make sure your dentist or hygienist periodically does a "periodontal probing," as well as X rays, to see if you have the beginning of any periodontal disease.

○ Daily flossing is extremely important in overall daily dental care to help prevent decay and periodontal disease. However, it is just as important to use floss properly. Improper use can cause damage to the gum tissue between the teeth and wear grooves in the teeth themselves.

○ Be proactive in your dental care! In this age of high-tech dentistry, ask your dentist for a "video" exam performed with an intraoral camera. You can discover potential filling fractures, microcracks, or hidden decay.

○ If you have a tooth knocked out, you must take immediate action. A tooth must be replaced in its oral socket within 60 minutes. If the tooth is dirty, gently rinse it with water, but do not scrub, scrape, or disinfect the tooth. Place it back in the socket and press it down or bite into a small towel and go to the dentist! If you can't put the tooth back yourself, keep it in your mouth wet with saliva and go to your dentist. For small children who may swallow the tooth, put it in a container of cool milk or water and take it with you.

○ To protect a winning smile, brushing and flossing may not be enough. New research indicates that getting plenty of calcium might also be crucial. Adults who consume too little calcium are one and a half times more likely than those who drink milk to have periodontal disease.

o For further assistance, check out www.goldsteingarber.com or call the American Dental Association at 1-800-621-8099. They can refer you to a specific state dental society. As an alternative, call the American Academy of Esthetic Dentistry at 1-312-321-5121, or the American Academy of Cosmetic Dentistry at 1-800-543-9220, for a referral in a city or state near you.

## Eyes

Dr. Peter A. Gordon, board-certified ophthalmologist, offers the following tips for eye health:

o Everyone should have a thorough eye exam before turning forty, and anyone with a family history of glaucoma should go yearly. After that, an exam every two years until age sixty-five is fine. At this age there is a big jump in the risk of contracting a disease that can lead to blindness, so it's wise to get a checkup every year.

o If your eyes itch, your problem is probably allergies. A cold washcloth held over closed eyes will shrink blood vessels and reduce redness. If your eyes burn, the problem is fatigue or dry eyes.

o With computers coming into mainstream use, a common eye problem is blurry computer vision. If the problem persists, get it checked out. The solution may be as simple as a pair of reading glasses.

o Ever wonder why the eyedrops you put in aren't very effective? Most people leave their eyes open, which can pump out much of the medication. Keep your eyes shut for 3 to 5 minutes after putting in eyedrops. It prevents your eyelids from moving.

o Glaucoma affects 2 million Americans and nearly half don't even know it. Effects from glaucoma can be prevented, reduced, or delayed with laser treatment, eyedrops, or other treatment. To minimize the risk, you should have regular medical eye examinations—generally every two to three years if you are age forty or over and annually if you are black, elderly, have a close relative with the disease, take steroids, or have had a serious eye injury in the past.

○ Several common medications can cause vision problems. While most of these problems fade when you stop taking the medication, some may cause permanent harm. Drugs or medical conditions that can affect your eyes may include some drugs given for diabetes, cardiac problems, or hypertension. Be sure to find out the side effects for any medication you are taking and be aware of any symptoms.

## Foot Fitness

Podiatrist Dr. Irving Miller, founder of Action Podiatry in Atlanta, Georgia, offers the following tips for foot fitness:

○ Your feet take thousands (9,000) of steps a day, so it's no wonder that they are worn out! Feet need care, and the experts agree that if the shoe doesn't fit, do not buy it. Shoes shouldn't be purchased if they are too tight, especially since most foot problems are caused by ill-fitting shoes that compress the bones in your feet.

○ It's best to try on shoes later in the day or after you've walked a lot. Feet swell a little and if you buy shoes that are too tight or fit perfectly now, they might tighten up later on when your foot swells.

○ Most shoe salons have carpet, which feels good on feet. The trick is to try on shoes and then walk on uncarpeted flooring. This gives you a better idea of how the shoe really feels. Since shoes typically hurt once you've gotten home, save yourself some time and effort and don't be too quick to judge.

○ Purchase shoes that have a similar shape to your foot—wide enough in the front and a snug heel fit.

○ Feet shouldn't hurt. If they do, you should consider listening to them before a potential problem gets worse. If you have corns or areas of your feet that frequently hurt, talk to a foot doctor and see what you can do about it. There are many simple solutions. They might recommend including corn pads, which ease the pain of constant pressure from your shoes.

○ If your feet are always cold, cover and layer them. Put on warm, dry socks in loose layers that insulate heat and help keep you warm.

○ To avoid blisters, apply a light coating of petroleum jelly to your heels and any other hot spots on your feet.

○ To help prevent athlete's foot, always wear flip-flops or some type of shoe in a fitness facility, and dry your toes thoroughly.

○ To ease the itch of athlete's foot, sprinkle baking soda on your feet and between your toes, or apply a paste made with 1 tablespoon of baking soda and lukewarm water. Wait 15 minutes, rinse, and dry your feet thoroughly.

○ If you have corns that repeatedly are being aggravated, try using a foot aid such as the nonmedicated Dr. Scholl's corn or callus protector without acid.

○ When purchasing shoes, remember the lower the heel the better. Statistics show that there is a 2 to 1 ratio of pressure exerted on the forefoot by a 3-inch heel compared to a 1-inch heel.

○ Men get athlete's foot more often than women because their feet are frequently enclosed in shoes for longer periods of time. You should change your shoes regularly so they have a chance to dry out from the previous day. Also, if you wear the same shoes every day it will cause corns and calluses, because your shoes will rub the same place on your foot.

○ Your feet take all the beating when you exercise, so don't forget them in the process. Feet need exercising, too. Roll the center of your foot over a can or a tennis ball for several minutes. This will help the foot stretch and relax. You can also put some uncooked large beans in your slippers and walk around for a few minutes. The rolling beans, similar to the tennis ball, create an instant massage.

○ To help prevent future foot pain, you need to exercise your feet. Place some marbles on the floor and try picking them up with your toes. This will help strengthen your feet. Don't forget to clean up the marbles when you finish!

## Digestive Check

Dr. Alan Sunshine, board-certified gastroenterologist with Atlanta Gastroenterology Associates, L.L.C., offers the following tips to help keep your digestive system in check:

### Heartburn

o Heartburn, acid indigestion, or gastroesophageal reflux can present with chest pain and be misdiagnosed as heart disease.

o Heartburn is very common, but when associated with difficulty swallowing, hoarseness, cough, asthma, loss of appetite, or weight loss, a physician should be consulted.

o After eating a spicy meal, chew a stick of sugarless gum. Chewing gum for half an hour after a meal can prevent or reduce heartburn by increasing saliva flow. Saliva is very effective in neutralizing stomach acid.

o If you are suffering from indigestion and don't have an antacid handy, mix one of the following items in a glass of water: ½ teaspoon of baking soda or 1 teaspoon of apple cider vinegar. Then take a walk or remain upright without lying down. This can help digest your food 40 to 50 percent faster.

### Peptic Ulcer Disease

o Upper abdominal burning pain that occurs between meals or at night and is relieved by eating food is characteristic of ulcer disease.

o People at increased risk for ulcers are individuals with a previous history of ulcers, who use pain relievers, or who have high tobacco and alcohol usage.

o *Helicobacter pylori* is a bacterium that lives in the stomach and is responsible for over 90 percent of all ulcers. Its detection and eradication with antibiotics can cure over 90 percent of all patients with a known history of ulcer disease.

### Gallbladder Disease

o Abdominal pain that occurs from thirty minutes to two to three hours after a meal, is sharp and cramping, and radiates to the back or right shoulder is characteristic of gallbladder disease. Signs or symptoms associated with gallbladder disease include nausea, vomiting, yellow skin or eyes (jaundice), dark urine, and fever.

o People at most risk for gallbladder disease include those over forty years of age, obese, female, fertile, with a family history of gallbladder disease, and who have experienced rapid weight loss.

o Gallbladder disease is diagnosed in approximately 500,000 cases a year in the United States and is treated by a simple surgical procedure whereby the gallbladder is removed.

### Pancreatitis

o The onset of severe abdominal pain that radiates into the back, associated with nausea, vomiting, diarrhea, and fever, is characteristic of pancreatitis.

o Pancreatitis can occur with patients with gallstones, heavy alcohol use, certain drug use, family history, and trauma to the pancreas; 10 percent of cases have an unknown cause.

### Inflammatory Bowel Disease

o There are two well-known inflammatory conditions of the intestines—Crohn's disease and ulcerative colitis. Ulcerative colitis is confined to the large intestine or colon, and Crohn's disease can involve the entire intestinal tract.

o Ulcerative colitis is characterized by the development of diarrhea, urgency, and intestinal bleeding. Crohn's disease typically presents with pain, fever, and an abdominal mass or bleeding.

o Both types of inflammatory diseases can be successfully treated with medication or surgery, and despite the severity of these conditions, those affected are able to lead normal, healthy lives.

### Diverticular Disease

o The development of lower abdominal pain, constipation, and fever are characteristic of diverticular disease. The presence of infection and swelling that occurs in these little saclike projections, which arise off the colon, lead to the above symptoms.

○ Eating a high-fiber diet, drinking four to six glasses of water per day, and doing frequent exercise can prevent diverticular disease.

### Colon Polyps and Cancer

○ Colon polyps and cancers frequently are present without symptoms. The most common finding is blood in the stool.

○ Colon cancer kills more Americans that any other malignancy except lung cancer.

○ Once colon cancer develops, surgical resection of all malignant tissue is the only reasonable curative therapy. Unfortunately, only 30 to 40 percent of tumors are cured by surgery, because the tumor has already spread beyond the wall of the colon.

○ Colon cancer screening is very important in preventing the disease. The recommendations are as follows:

Annual fecal occult blood test beginning at age fifty
Screening flexible sigmoidoscopy every five years beginning
at age fifty
Colonoscopy for individuals with a positive test
Colonoscopy for patients with a first-degree relative with a
history of colon cancer

○ Studies indicate that dairy products may reduce the risk of colon cancer. Aim for 1,000 mg of calcium per day.

## Germs

Dr. Winkler G. Weinberg, author of *No Germs Allowed!: How to Avoid Infectious Diseases at Home and on the Road* (Rutgers University Press, 1996), suggests the following tips:

○ The number of infections you get has nothing to do with being too hot or too cold. Temperature changes do not affect your resistance. Illness has to do with contacting germs.

○ Wash your hands frequently, especially after sneezing and before you touch shared items. Do other people a favor and avoid handshaking until you've recovered from a cold. Avoid coming into direct contact with anyone with a cold. People are contagious for even up to five days, so don't believe them when they say it's not a new cold. A cold is a cold.

○ Most respiratory viruses are contacted via your hands rather than through the air. You then touch your nose or eyes and make direct contact.

○ Sponges in the kitchen may be a problem, so be sure you replace yours weekly, or use paper towels instead.

○ Viruses can hang around for hours on doorknobs, toys, coffee mugs, and anything else that has come in contact with a cough or a sneeze, or has been touched by an infected person.

○ A sneeze projects germs approximately 3 feet. A single sneeze can carry up to 100,000 airborne droplets traveling with velocities of over 200 miles per hour! If you are going to sneeze, or if someone around you is going to sneeze, try to establish a "buffer zone" of safety.

○ Respiratory illnesses are commonly passed from person to person and transmitted on inanimate objects. When anyone in your family comes home and has a respiratory illness such as influenza, clean any surface he or she touches with paper towels and a disinfectant.

○ Food safety is critical for effective reduction of germ transmission. When purchasing food, check expiration dates.

○ Buy a thermometer for the refrigerator. Proper temperature should be between 38 to 40 degrees F. If the temperature remains above 40 degrees for any length of time, bacteria begin to grow.

○ Paper products are the safest way to clean off countertops and cutting boards. Achieving a dry surface is one of the most effective ways to create a sterile surface in your kitchen. Using a germicide is added protection.

○ Cleaning and disinfecting are not the same thing. Regular cleaning of surface areas will remove dirt and most germs, but disinfecting offers that extra ounce of protection. While surfaces may look clean, many infectious germs may still be lurking.

## Heart Smarts

Dr. Winston H. Gandy Jr., board-certified cardiologist with the Atlanta Cardiology Group, P.C., located in Atlanta, Georgia, offers the following tips for the heart:

○ Major causes of heart disease include family history, smoking, and high blood pressure, and minor causes include cholesterol, being overweight, and lack of exercise.

○ Quitting cigarette smoking cuts the risk of heart attack by up to 70 percent within five years. After five years ex-smokers have about the same risk as people who never smoked.

○ High blood pressure is known as the silent killer. Up to 50 million Americans have high blood pressure and many exhibit no symptoms. Almost half of the people with high blood pressure don't even know they have it.

○ Ninety percent of the time, the cause of high blood pressure is not known. Some major risk factors are family history, being African American, age, and in women, menopause. Minor risk factors include being overweight, excessive alcohol consumption, eating foods high in salt, lack of potassium, cigarette smoking, and lack of exercise.

○ Cardiovascular disease accounts for almost half of all deaths in the United States, and people who have high blood pressure have an increased risk for developing cardiovascular disease. Controlling high blood pressure (hypertension) decreases the risk 2 to 3 percent for each one-point drop in total cholesterol among people with elevated levels.

○ Decreasing one's blood cholesterol cuts the risk 2 to 3 percent for each 1 percent drop in total cholesterol among people with elevated levels.

○ Exercising even moderately can reduce the risk of heart attack by 35 to 55 percent. Minimally, this means at least once a week.

○ Eliminating obesity cuts the risk of heart attack by 35 to 55 percent. Obesity is defined as more than 20 percent above your desirable weight.

○ Your blood pressure is read as systolic (the first number) pressure and diastolic (the second number) pressure. For every point your diastolic pressure drops, your heart-attack risk falls 2 to 3 percent.

○ Before a cholesterol test, avoid eating a high-fat meal such as fried chicken with french fries, or consuming alcohol. Even if you fast for 12 hours before the test, the fat from your last meal affects the outcome.

○ To help prevent heart disease problems, you should have a ratio of total cholesterol to "good" cholesterol (HDL cholesterol) of 4.5 or less to 1.

○ Stroke, which is when a blood vessel in the brain bursts or becomes clogged, is a consequence of high blood pressure. About half a million Americans annually have a stroke, and stroke is the third leading cause of death in the United States after heart disease and cancer.

○ Warning signals of stroke include:

Sudden weakness or numbness of the face, arm, and leg on one side of the body
Loss of speech, or difficulty speaking or understanding speech
Dimness or loss of vision, particularly in only one eye
Unexplained dizziness, unsteadiness, a sudden fall

○ Many African Americans are salt-sensitive. Since cigarette smoking and being overweight also contribute to hypertension, changes in lifestyle are very important.

○ If you drink, make sure you limit your alcohol intake to no more than one or two drinks per day. Large amounts of alcohol can raise pressure in the arteries.

○ Reducing fat in the diet helps the heart. Buy foods in which fat is not a major ingredient. Don't purchase foods containing more than one type of fat. Select the appropriate serving size.

○ If you believe you are suffering a heart attack, have someone call 911 for help. While you are waiting for an ambulance, cough vigorously, as you may be able to kick an irregular heartbeat back to normal. Also, take an aspirin and chew it. The medicine will enter the bloodstream more quickly and may prevent the formation of a clot.

○ Heart attacks are the major cause of death in women in the United States. While men get heart attacks earlier in life than women, a woman's risk increases with age.

○ Many women consider hormone replacement therapy (HRT). Estrogen can be beneficial to the heart, yet there has been some controversy regarding HRT and an increased incidence of breast cancer. Keep in mind, however, that approximately 40,000 American women die of breast cancer each year while almost 500,000 women die from heart disease. Carefully weigh your options.

## Medication Time

○ Many children's medications are often prescribed up to four times daily; a serious overdose could occur if given improperly or a medication could not go to work properly. Always read the label carefully, know the medication that is being given, and know how to properly use the measuring device (infant dropper, measuring syringe, calibrated cup) when dispensing the medication. Many dosages are effective only if based on weight. Make sure you know your child's true weight.

○ A teaspoon isn't always a teaspoon. Silverware varies in size and can lead to either overdosing or underdosing your child. Use the measuring device that comes with the medication, or purchase a syringe or calibrated cup at your local pharmacy. Look for one that has both metric and conventional measurements.

○ Children's medications, including the same brands, come in different strengths. Infant drops might be concentrated and much stronger than liquid formulas, so always check and read the label and instructions carefully. Never assume anything when giving a child medication, and never rely on your memory.

○ Some pharmacists offer special services, such as adding flavors to liquid medicines. Check with your physician first and see what options and incentives you might try if your child repeatedly spits out medicine.

○ Read the list of side effects. Children's medications can have side effects just as adult medicines do. Make sure you know what to watch out for.

○ Medicines work best when they are taken as prescribed. Don't play catch-up if you miss one; always check with your physician. Dosages should not be altered in any way. Don't play doctor, and be sure to read all information you are given about the drug. If the medication says a side effect is drowsiness, then don't drive or do anything that could be harmful to you while taking it.

○ Some pills are time-released and should never be crushed and added to food or water for easier swallowing. If you have a problem swallowing a pill, talk to your doctor and pharmacist about your options. Many common medications come in a variety of forms.

○ Be sure to tell your physician if you are taking other medications, even over-the-counter antacids. Don't assume anything is safe to mix until you have gotten the facts. Drug interactions can cause serious side effects.

○ Sometimes medications are better tolerated if swallowed with a full meal, while others are better absorbed on an empty stomach and might not work at all if taken with food. Check with your physician or pharmacist before taking any medication.

○ Did you know that the bathroom can be the worst place to keep your medication? Because of the shower and moisture that builds in a bathroom, excess heat and temperature changes can occur and harm your medications, depending on your ventilation. It's best to store drugs in airtight containers or their original bottles in a cool, dry place out of the reach of young children and away from warm air that might destroy their effectiveness.

## Massage

○ According to Kimberly Segale, a certified massage therapist, "lactic acids are metabolic wastes that can accumulate in the muscle tissue on a daily basis. Many of these toxins may be released into your bloodstream as a result of having the muscle tissue massaged. It is important to increase the amount of water you drink after receiving massage to help flush your system and avoid any feeling of nausea."

○ Always tell a massage therapist about medical conditions that might preclude a massage. This is critical, because massage can briefly cause your blood pressure to rise, possibly resulting in a hazardous reaction.

○ If you don't know how to find a certified massage therapist, call the American Massage Therapy Association (1-847-864-0123), which keeps a national list of qualified therapists.

## Nail Care

○ It is recommended that both women and men take care of their fingernails and toenails with regular manicures; however, men can go longer between manicures because their nails are stronger and shorter.

○ Runners and exercisers need to keep their toenails cut short so they don't get jammed while exercising.

○ To avoid ingrown toenails, don't cut the nails too short. You should file your toenails straight across and then gently round the corners.

○ If you want to take off artificial nails to let your natural nails grow, never let the technician peel the nail tip off, because it will strip layers of your own nail with it. Soak the nail off completely.

○ The best time to clip cuticles is after you've taken a shower and rubbed your tips with a good cuticle cream. The combination of steam and lotion softens those hard-to-fix flakes.

○ Always be sure to thoroughly clean your nail tools, especially your nippers, after use with a cotton ball whisk of rubbing alcohol.

○ Safety first! You want to treat a nail salon as you would treat a restaurant. You would not want to eat in a restaurant that has dirty utensils, and you do not want to use a nail salon that uses dirty utensils, either. The instruments should be kept in a sanitizer. Clippers should not come out of a drawer. For added safety, bring your own instruments and keep them cleaned!

○ Brittle nails are usually not a sign of a vitamin deficiency. Most likely, nails are brittle because they are dried out. Certain ingredients in nail care products are rough on nails. Use the gentlest formulations—formaldehyde-free polish and acetone-free remover—and do not apply them more than once a week. Also, apply a moisturizing cream frequently and protect your hands by wearing lined rubber gloves when washing dishes and using household cleansers. In some cases, brittle nails may signal an underactive thyroid.

## Nutrition

o The American Cancer Society recommends eating five or more servings of fruits and vegetables a day. One-third of cancer deaths are caused by a variety of dietary factors. Call 1-800-ACS-2345 to talk to a representative and for more educational information. (Reprinted by the permission of the American Cancer Society, Inc.)

o Artificial sweeteners can actually make you hungrier. Be careful about consuming too many sugar-free and fat-free items.

o Eat broccoli, spinach, carrots, squash, or other fruits and vegetables that each contain powerful antioxidants. All are rich in glutathione, the body's prime antioxidant, according to Dr. Theodore Hersh of Thione International, a developer of glutathione-based antioxidant healthcare products. Antioxidants help reduce the risks of developing many types of cancer.

o To cut the risk of prostate cancer, remember the color red. Two to four servings of tomato sauce a week can cut your risk for prostate cancer by 34 percent. Incidentally, there is greater benefit from tomato sauce than from tomatoes. The heating process "energizes" the sauce for maximum benefit, containing the antioxidant lycopene.

o Spicy foods, such as Indian, Mexican, or Italian, taste great and offer some health benefits. Your metabolic rate will increase significantly, and when your face sweats, it's a sign that your body is burning more calories.

## Ouch

o The best way to take off a sticky bandage is to remove it slowly, in an advancing way. As you pull the bandage up with two of your fingers, use your other fingers to push down on the skin hairs.

## Skin

o There are hundreds of products out there right now that claim to reduce fine age wrinkles and make us look "years younger." But those products can be expensive. While not the most glamorous, petroleum-based products can do the trick just as well, says dermatologist Dr. Richard Sturm. Put the cream on immediately after a bath or shower. If your feet are dry, put cream on your feet, and put on a pair of cotton socks to hold the moisture in during the night.

o O.K., you probably know this one, but we get more sun exposure walking to and from our cars than we even realize! Make a habit of wearing a moisturizing sunscreen every time you are outside, even during the winter. Age spots and wrinkles and even skin cancer can result from a lifetime accumulation of sun damage to your skin.

o Long baths—even with water loaded with moisturizers—are potentially too drying for our skin. If you want to take a good bath, remember to moisturize your skin immediately after exiting the tub to seal in moisture.

o In sunny climates it is recommended to wear dark clothing outdoors, because the colors protect the skin better than lighter shades by absorbing more of the sun's UV rays.

o Here's a "just in case." You can soothe a sunburn by applying a compress dampened with cool water, or try soaking a cloth in cold tea or applying a mask of yogurt.

o Does chocolate really cause acne breakouts? Although there are no current data to support this belief, it's important to use common sense. If you find that you break out after eating certain foods, stop eating them and see if it makes a difference.

o Parts of our body age differently. The heart, for example, barely ages at all. On the other hand, sweat glands will stop working as we get older and eventually you won't perspire under your arms like you once did.

o According to Egleston Children's Hospital in Atlanta, Georgia, "Studies show that one in every seven children will develop skin cancer as an adult, usually as a result of too much sun—especially severe sunburn—during childhood. Just one bad sunburn can double your child's chance of getting skin cancer."

○ Use a sunblock made for children with an SPF (Sun Protection Factor) rating of at least 15; apply as directed, then reapply according to the sunblock directions. If she swims, use waterproof sunblock. Shield your child's sensitive shoulders, neck, and back with a T-shirt and have her wear a hat with a wide brim to protect and shade her face.

○ Children's sunglasses with 100 UV protection are also a good idea. Even with all of these precautions, don't let your child stay in the sun too long, especially from noon to 3 P.M. or in climates where the sun is stronger.

○ If you get sunburned, take an oatmeal bath. You can do this without a lot of mess by wrapping a handful of oatmeal in a piece of thin cloth and hanging it from the bath faucet. The water will run through the bundle of oatmeal as the tub is filling. This will soothe the sunburn pain.

○ If you get a splinter and it's wood, try to remove it immediately. If you can't get it out easily, then try soaking the area in warm water. The soaking makes the wood swell and sometimes the splinter will pop out on its own for easier removal. If you have trouble locating the splinter, press a small light to the area of entry. The light will pass through the skin, showing the angle and depth of the splinter.

○ No one likes to get up and shave first thing in the morning. Take a break! Have breakfast and move around for half an hour. Then shave. Your face won't be as puffy and you'll get a closer shave.

○ If you're out of shaving cream, don't despair. A few drops of olive oil will do the trick.

○ If you've come in contact with poison ivy, you have a few minutes to wash the area and prevent a skin reaction. Use soap and water.

○ To reduce the inflammation from an insect bite or sting, put ice on it. After the ice, rub some meat tenderizer (or aspirin if you're not allergic to it) on the bite to break down the venom. You can relieve some of the pain and itching with a paste of baking soda and water.

○ To relieve a minor burn, place the area in cool water until the pain subsides. You can also use a bag of small frozen vegetables (carrots, peas, beans that would mold around the skin) or shaving cream.

## Sleeping

○ If you can't get to sleep, the National Sleep Foundation has free brochures, such as "When You Can't Sleep," that may help you. Call 1-202-347-3471 or check them out on the Web at www.sleep-foundation.org.

○ Many people wake up with "Monday morning grogginess" after a hectic weekend. To help prevent this, avoid sleeping late on Sunday mornings. It throws off your body clock and makes it difficult to get up for work on Monday.

## Women

Dr. Michael D. Randell, board-certified OB/GYN, Atlanta, Georgia, offers the following tips for women:

○ Vaginal infections are the most common reason American women see their OB/GYNs. Vaginitis can be caused by a variety of organisms, and each must be treated differently. Avoid self-medicating, which might mask the symptoms and make the diagnosis more difficult. A healthcare professional should diagnose the cause of a vaginal infection and prescribe the proper therapy.

○ Oral contraceptives offer several noncontraceptive benefits: clearer skin, and protection against pelvic inflammatory disease (PID), cancers of the ovary and endometrium, recurrent ovarian cysts, and benign breast disease. The pill can also ease the problem of menstrual cramps and discomfort.

○ Make absolutely sure you know how to self-examine your breasts, and get regular mammograms according to your age and individual history. Request that your doctor show you how and when to do self-examinations, and that you are also checked by a health professional regularly. Don't assume you are doing it correctly; get the facts.

o Avoid sexual intercourse, tampons, and vaginal creams 24 to 48 hours before having a Pap smear. These could cause your Pap smear to be misread. Don't have a Pap smear if you have a discharge or are menstruating. Infection and blood can hide abnormal cells and make it difficult to interpret the smear.

o Know who reads your Pap smear, mammogram, or any other test. Don't assume anything. Make sure they have the correct certifications. Ask your doctor about new technologies available to enhance the overall accuracy of various medical tests.

## General Health Tips

Mitchell J. Ghen, D.O., offers the following health tips for longer living:

o Stay on the perimeter of a supermarket; you are more likely to buy the right foods to keep you healthy. This is because fresh fruits and vegetables are in this area. The white flour, sugar products, refined foods, and most unhealthy products are usually within the body of the supermarket.

o We change our skin every 91 days, our red blood cells every 120 days, our stomach lining approximately every week. Change is okay, but we must remember to provide the appropriate food and nutrients so that our new cells are healthy.

o Use your stomach to get the most out of your environment. When you take a deep breath, your abdomen should expand; when you exhale, your abdomen should contract. Watch a healthy infant breathe and imitate him. Chest breathing is shallow and unhealthy. Think about your abdomen the next time you take a deep breath.

o Just because it tastes good does not mean it is good for you. Often foods that taste good may be laden with sugar, and sugar can reduce your immune system's first line of defense for up to four to six hours. Keep sweets to a minimum.

o More is not any better. It is not necessarily true that the more you take of vitamins and minerals the healthier you will get. As a matter of fact, vitamin and mineral therapies can be toxic. Consult a healthcare practitioner to find out the optimal dosages for your individual needs.

o There is no *always* or *never* when it comes to health. What is good for one person may not necessarily be good for another person. It is unfair to think that one person's medicine or nutrient regimen would be appropriate for you. We are unique in our makeup. Make sure that your health program is unique for you.

o Water means water!!! When counting your water intake in a day, other fluids such as coffee, teas, and sodas do not count as your overall healthy water consumption amount.

o Waters are not all the same. Water can differ based upon its acid, base, mineral, and energy content. The best water still remains that which comes out of a reverse osmosis purifier. Bottled purified water is a second to a good home unit.

o Drink eight glasses of *pure* water daily. Pure water means using a high-quality filter such as for reverse osmosis. A good rule of thumb is to take your body weight in pounds and divide by two; that number in ounces is what you should drink in water.

o Laugh until it hurts. Laughing has been shown to improve the immune system for up to twelve hours, so make sure that you watch a funny movie, read an amusing book, or listen to a hilarious tape every day.

o We cannot tell the difference between reality and nonreality. If we close our eyes and concentrate or meditate on a place we love to go that is safe and relaxing to us, the body cannot tell the difference whether we are there or not. So, with such meditation, the immune system will become enhanced. Our hormones will become balanced, and in general our bodies will slow down the aging process. If you cannot physically get to a place you love every day, then 20 to 25 minutes a day of thinking about it will renew your cells and refresh your spirit.

○ Get the chlorine out. Do you remember how you used to tell your children to wash off after being in a swimming pool? Well, chlorine is a toxin and implicated in many chronic diseases. A good water filter both on your tap for drinking and in your shower will protect you.

## Web sites

www.WebMD.com
www.onhealth.com
www.rxlist.com
www.thione.com
www.netwellness.com
www.healthanswers.com
www.intelihealth.com

# Holiday Hazards

Holidays are a special time, but staggering reports show that during the holidays there are more accidents than at any other time of the year, and many of them could easily have been prevented. From Halloween pranks to Christmas tree fires, Easter egg food poisoning to July the Fourth fireworks burns, carelessness during the holidays can have terrifying results.

Most often the victims of accidents are children and pets. According to health and safety experts at Egleston Children's Health Care System, homes change during the holidays and there are new things that are of particular interest to children. You may have a tree, ornaments, candles, lights, decorations, new toys, or many other gadgets that appear for holiday enhancement. While all of these things liven up the occasion, they can also be threatening.

This chapter might not solve all the problems that pop up during the holidays, but it is hoped that you will pay careful attention to everyone's safety and well-being. The most precious part of the holiday is your family, so do everything possible to keep them safe and healthy and happy. Even though you might not have young children, if friends or family will be visiting you during the holidays and they have young children, then it's important to follow all of these rules!

## Food

○ According to Egleston Children's Health Care System, "About 2,700 children under the age of five in the United States are treated in emergency rooms every year for choking." Children can choke on small round foods like candy, peanuts, carrots, grapes, hot dogs, or popcorn. Keep them away from preschoolers.

○ Check your child's trick-or-treat bag for unwrapped or tampered-with candy, and also hard candy or candy that could cause choking. Many area hospitals also offer complimentary X-ray screening services for candy during Halloween. When in doubt, throw it out!

○ Keep alcoholic beverages, including wine, eggnog, and holiday punch, out of your child's reach. Don't leave unfinished alcoholic beverages around on tables. Clean up glasses immediately after entertaining. Alcohol poisoning is serious, and it doesn't take much alcohol to poison a child.

○ Keep coffeepots and hot drinks away from children where they might fall, spill, or tip and a child could be scalded. Remember tablecloths could be pulled down by a child, and whatever was on them could spill on and hurt a child.

○ When mixing adult's and children's festivities, consider serving foods and beverages that are safe and appropriate for *everyone*.

## Decorations

○ Avoid decorating with latex balloons for young children's parties. They are a leading cause of infant death by choking.

○ Stay away from tablecloths when decorating for young children. A child can be injured if he uses the cloth to climb up, and objects from the tabletop can topple onto him.

○ When decorating, keep small objects that a child could choke on out of reach. Also make sure that small pieces can't break off and pose a threat to your child or pet.

○ Avoid leaving burning candles unattended, even for a few minutes. This is a common cause of fires. If young children are around, avoid candles altogether.

○ Hang all ornaments high enough on your tree so that your child can't reach them. Keep small toys, toy parts, ornaments, and small round foods out of your child's reach, because if your child can reach it, then he could potentially choke on it, too.

○ Young children can choke or cut their mouths on ornaments or tinsel.

○ Older ornaments and tinsel might contain lead, which could poison a child. Avoid those nostalgic ornaments with young children around.

○ Glass ornaments should be saved until children are older.

○ A Christmas tree should be anchored so that a child cannot pull it down on himself.

○ Seasonal plants can be very dangerous to a child. For example, both holly and mistletoe are poisonous, so keep them out of a child's reach.

○ Poinsettias do not pose a life-threatening danger; however, they are still hazardous. Keep them out of a child's reach.

## Fire Hazards

○ Avoid putting too many plugs in one outlet. Repeatedly blown fuses and tripped circuit breakers are signs of an overloaded electrical system.

○ Turn off all electrical appliances when you go to bed.

○ During Hanukkah, keep a lit menorah out of the reach of children. Also, do not leave candles in a menorah unattended. They could fall or a child could knock them over.

○ Candles, lights, trees, and fires in the fireplace all increase the chances of a fire during the holidays. Make sure you have your fireplace checked if you haven't used it recently, and know what you are doing. Keep all matches and lighters out of a child's reach.

○ Keep your tree away from all heat sources, including the fireplace and heating vents.

○ Keep burning candles and space heaters away from the tree and anything flammable.

○ Before stringing lights on a Christmas tree, make sure there are no shorts, faulty bulbs, or frayed cords that could catch on fire.

○ Don't overload outlets with extension cords.

○ Water your tree regularly, since dry needles burn faster.

○ Don't try to hide electrical cords under a carpet or rug. A damaged cord can cause a fire.

## Toys

○ Choose toys that are age-appropriate. Follow the warnings on the toys and use judgment when buying them. Just because everyone has a pop gun doesn't mean they are safe. In fact, toys that shoot rubber darts can also shoot sharp pencils and other potentially dangerous items.

o Consider younger siblings when buying older ones toys. What's safe for a six-year-old could pose a dangerous threat to a two-year-old.

o Create rules. The only time she can ride her bike is when she wears a helmet. Also, make sure you read the chapter on safety and follow the directions for safe play.

o If you have questions about toy safety, for more information you can call the United States Consumer Product Safety Commission at 1-800-638-2772.

o Follow labels that give age recommendations. Look for "flame resistant" labels on fabric products and "washable/hygienic materials" labels on stuffed animals.

o Tie plastic toy packaging in a knot and dispose of it immediately so a young child does not play with it and become smothered.

o When opening a gift, be sure to immediately get rid of packing materials that a child could choke on. Be aware of everything and play it safe.

## Ten Toy Hazards to Avoid

The Toy Manufacturers of America advise the following toy safety suggestions:

1. Toys left on stairs
2. Toys with small parts for children under three
3. Toys for an older child in the hands of a younger child
4. Toys with sharp points or rough edges
5. Uninflated or broken balloons for children under eight
6. Toys with heating elements for children under eight
7. Sports equipment without protective gear
8. Broken toys
9. Toys not played with properly (hitting, throwing, etc.)
10. Any toy used without sensible supervision

For a free copy of TMA's "Toy Safety and Selection Guide," call toll-free 1-800-851-9955 or visit TMA's Web site at www.toy-tma.org.

## Pets

○ Just as with young children, there are many holiday culprits that are very dangerous for your pets. From cleaning supplies while you're getting the house ready for entertaining to festive foods left for guests, think safety when it comes to your pet, too.

○ Holiday foods like turkey and chicken or anything on a bone could cause choking. Keep these foods out of the reach of your pet, and your pet out of the reach of these foods! If your pet can't be trusted, make sure it is kept outside or in a safe place during your holiday preparing and entertaining.

○ Beware of mistletoe and holly that have berries, which can both be poisonous to pets. Almost everything that is on a Christmas tree can also be harmful if a pet swallows it, including tinsel and metal ornament hangers. Pets can easily knock things over, so make sure wires and decorations are off-limits.

○ Foods of many kinds can be dangerous to a pet, especially chocolate, alcohol, nuts, and many holiday favorites that are often left out for company during the holidays. Be sure to keep them out of the reach of your pets and clean up quickly, since most household pets are well known for grazing the floor for unwanted tidbits.

○ Streamers, decorations, and balloons can be choking hazards for pets. Be sure to keep a keen eye on these if you have pets, or avoid them entirely if possible.

○ Some flowers that are seasonal and often used during the holidays are very dangerous to pets. For example, daffodils, hyacinths, and even Easter lilies can be harmful.

○ Easter eggs that aren't found during a hunt and some eggs that have been painted with toxic paints can be harmful to your pets.

○ Small toys, candy, and other holiday favors can be choking hazards to your pet, so don't forget to keep all of these out of your pet's reach.

○ Make sure your trash cans lock, since many pets get into the overloaded trash during the holidays. Most pets will eat anything in sight, including spoiled food. Keep the trash out of the path of your pet, since pets are famous for knocking over trash cans and getting into things they shouldn't.

○ Keep pesticides and poisonous or toxic items locked up, or avoid having them at all. And keep in mind that many things can be dangerous, including lotions, beauty products, and shampoos.

## Safety

○ While safety precautions are important all year long, during the holidays there are increased reports of crimes. Take every precaution possible, from always locking your house when you leave to keeping the drapes or shutters closed so people can't look in and see what there is to steal. Also, avoid leaving your holiday presents sitting out for days. Many people put a Christmas tree at the front window as a decoration and surround it with gifts. This is an open invitation for a thief!

○ Avoid going shopping alone or late at night. While crime occurs 24 hours a day, consider every safety precaution, from locking your car doors to hiding packages in your car. Thieves are looking for cars that are filled to the brim, so don't be an invitation for a robbery or shop without a companion. Safety in numbers really does help.

○ Consider that your purse or wallet is a gold mine for a thief. Only carry with you the items you need while shopping and especially reduce them to a minimum while traveling. Be sure to keep all receipts in a safe place and be certain that each time you use your credit card or checkbook you put it back in your purse safely and securely. One wrong turn and you just might regret it!

# Home Ownership—
# Buying and Selling

Owning your own home is such a part of the fabric of America that we all can recite phrases about real estate without thinking about it—"location, location, location," for example, or "it's the biggest investment you'll ever make." But even though we're familiar with those phrases, the buying-and-selling process can be intimidating. After all, it's something most people do only a few times in their lives, so they never really feel that they master the task. They have to deal with a variety of professionals—agents, lenders, contractors, inspectors—whom they don't normally cross paths with. And for most people, it truly is the biggest-ticket item they will ever buy. Putting that much money on the line for thirty years is a frightening prospect.

Because it is such a big investment, no one should rush into buying a home. Owning real estate, whether it's a big home with lots of acreage or a tiny apartment in a city high rise, brings lots of responsibility. The joys of ownership—pride, the ability to decorate any way you want, tax breaks, price appreciation, and more—are many. But for some people, the problems of ownership—yard work, home maintenance, the knowledge that you could lose your home if your economic situation changes—outweigh the joys. Consider both pros and cons before deciding to join the ranks of owners.

If you've never owned a home before and aren't sure if you're ready for the commitment, visit Fannie Mae's HomePath page on the Internet at www.homepath.com, where you'll find information on whether home ownership might be right for you, and plenty of details on the process of buying a home and getting a loan. Even veteran home buyers might want to check out the page for a refresher course. Or check out www.realtor.com, the largest real estate site on the Internet, or the Web sites of your local board of realtors and the real estate companies that are members of the board.

Once you're in the market to buy or sell a home, you'll need professional help for most aspects of the deal. Whether you're looking for a real estate agent, lawyer, inspector, lender, or other person involved in the process, check references and find someone who is experienced and reputable. The same goes for choosing a contractor for home remodeling. All aspects of home owning come with a big price tag, especially if you don't do your homework along the way!

Find someone you feel comfortable working with and have thoroughly checked out, because buying or selling real estate, and improving it, can sometimes be a trying endeavor. You'll need someone who can guide you through any aspect of the process with home-run results!

## Buying a Home

o Remember, you aren't just buying a house, you're buying a neighborhood. Before making a decision on any home, check out the area. (This is what that famous real estate phrase "location, location, location" is all about.) See if the homes are well maintained, find out if the schools offer a quality education, make sure the area is economically sound, find out if the kinds of recreational and cultural activities you enjoy are available nearby, and make sure the roads and transportation system will meet your needs. Try the commute—drive or take the bus from the neighborhood to your office during morning rush hour, and make the reverse trip during evening rush hour.

o According to real estate agent Genie Freedman of R. S. Owen & Company Realtors, "Before starting the home search process, sit down with the other members of your family and create a 'wish list' of everything you would ideally like your new home to have. Consider hobbies, lifestyle changes, future plans, potential additions to the family—whether it be baby, in-laws, or pets—and what it is about your current home you like or dislike. Also, consider the more typical considerations like the size of the bedrooms, bathrooms, basement, and the amount of land you own. Once you have a complete list, prioritize your list and stick to it."

o Talk to a lender and your accountant to determine how much house you can really afford. This is a crucial step and you should take it seriously.

o Check with your local bank to see if it has a "newcomer kit" that outlines details about loans, and so on. Check out what other resources are offered, including schools in the area and maps.

o Talk to a professional real estate agent. Agents have most of this information and more at their fingertips, from how much you can afford to spend to demographics about the neighborhoods you are looking at; just ask and you'll receive.

o It's a truism in real estate that you are better off buying the worst house in a good neighborhood than the best house in a bad neighborhood. A good neighborhood is far more likely to appreciate in value than is one that doesn't have the qualities most buyers want. It's a fact that some "urban pioneers" can buy very cheaply in an area that eventually turns itself around and becomes desirable, and they make a lot of money in the end. Waiting for the area to make that upswing, however, can be a lonely and worrisome process.

o Unless you have lots of handyman skills or a pot of money to spend fixing up a home, your best bet is to look for a home that has been well maintained throughout its lifetime. The exterior of the home, including the landscaping and appearance of the house, is your first clue as to whether the house has been taken care of, said Kenneth Austin, chairman of HouseMaster, the largest home inspection franchise company in the United States and Canada. If people don't maintain the part of the house that the whole world can see, it's unlikely that they've done much upkeep on the interior, either.

o When you are out looking at homes, take a camera with you to photograph details and help you remember what you've seen. Those photographs will come in handy when you are comparing houses.

o As you walk through a house, look for signs of problems—

cracking plaster, sagging floors, and water stains are obvious to even the untrained eye, and they could be symptoms of something serious, Austin said. If you see lots of symptoms, it's possible the house could have some expensive problems. A professional home inspector can give you a better idea of just how extensive the problems are, once you decide you want to pursue the house further.

o When you're ready to make an offer on the house, remember— should this deal not work out, you will find another house that is just as good or better. Never fall in love with a piece of property, because you have lost all your negotiating power when you "just have to have" a particular house. On the other hand, a buyer who is willing to walk away from the deal might have the upper hand with a seller who must sell his house.

## Get It Inspected

o When you buy a house, be sure your purchase offer includes an inspection contingency clause, which gives you the right to have the home inspected by a professional inspector and allows a reasonable amount of time for the inspection to be performed. About 85 percent of buyers have the home inspected before buying, according to Diane J. Knapp, CEO of World Inspection Network International, a nationwide home inspection network.

o More than 300 items in the home, from foundation to roof, will be visually inspected by a home inspector who uses the nationally accepted home inspection standards. The inspector looks for clues that something is wrong. If he suspects a problem, he may have you call in a specialist (such as a plumber) to confirm his diagnosis and give you an estimate of what the repairs would cost, Knapp said. Once you have the information, you can go back to the seller and renegotiate the price, either asking the seller to fix the problem before closing, or cutting your offering price to account for the defect.

o The inspection will take about two hours, and experts such as Austin and Knapp urge the home buyer to accompany the inspector. For a buyer, it's a great opportunity to learn about how your new home functions and how to operate the various systems. The inspector can show you how to change the filter in the furnace, for example, or how to light the stove's pilot light. If you have any questions about the condition of the house, be sure to ask the inspector at this time.

○ A standard inspection will focus on mechanical systems, roof, foundation, condition of the exterior, and other concerns that can be visually checked. Before selecting an inspector, find out what services are offered and get it in writing. If you have special concerns about the house—such as the quality of the water or the presence of lead or radon—you can request extra tests for an additional charge. If you are new to the area and are not sure what tests might be advisable in your new location, ask your real estate agent for advice.

○ Many states have no certification process for home inspectors, so it's buyer beware. Look for an inspector who has completed formal training in the home inspection process and who participates in continuing education to keep up with changes in the industry. Look for membership in a professional organization, such as the National Institute of Building Inspectors.

○ Make sure the inspector you hire has professional liability insurance, which is similar to malpractice insurance, and workers' compensation insurance, which will cover him should he be injured while completing the inspection. Also, look for an inspector who offers a guarantee if you are not happy with the services you receive.

○ Avoid inspectors who may have a conflict of interest—including part-timers who use the trade to supplement their business as roofers, contractors, and so on. Austin also cautions against using inspectors you feel are being "pushed" by anyone involved in the sale, because someone may try to steer you to an inspector who will gloss over problems in an effort not to kill the deal.

○ The seller must ensure that the inspector has ready access to all rooms, crawl spaces, and operating systems, such as the water heating and electrical panels. Often, the seller's real estate agent will be present during the inspection to provide such access.

○ If possible, visit a home you are considering buying while it is raining to watch for leaks.

## The Finance Maze

o Even before you start house hunting, most mortgage lenders would be happy to give you an idea of what sort of loan you could qualify for, and many will do this "prequalifying" over the phone. Talk to friends and coworkers who have recently purchased a home to get recommendations for lenders. If you are working with a real estate agent, she can suggest a lender; the agent will want to know how much house you can afford, anyway, so you don't waste time looking at houses you can't buy.

o Generally, mortgage lenders estimate that your monthly housing cost—which includes the mortgage payment as well as property taxes, homeowner's insurance, and private mortgage insurance—should not be more than 28 percent of your monthly gross income.

o Other debts you have, such as a car loan, student loans, or large credit card bills, could reduce the amount of money a lender would be willing to advance. If you can pay off some of those bills before you start looking for a home, you may qualify for a larger mortgage.

o Special programs for first-time buyers and people with low down payments have proliferated in the last few years. Even people with spotty credit, which once would have kept them from buying a home, are now better able to find a lender who will give them a mortgage. Federal, state, and local agencies offer various plans to help people get into a home of their own. A good lender can suggest programs you might qualify for, so be sure to ask when you are calling around.

## Selling Your Home

o Be careful not to make the mistake of letting the price you would like your home to sell for be the determining factor in your choice of real estate agent.

o Choose a company as well as an agent based on reputation and check them out carefully. Many sales are co-ops with competing companies, so make sure your home is listed with a company that is affiliated with a multiple listing service. Also, consider a company that is a member of a relocation network, particularly if you live in an area that has a history of corporate transfers.

○ Interview at least three real estate agents before giving one the listing to your house. To get the names of agents to interview, talk to neighbors who have recently sold or purchased a home and see if they would recommend the agent with whom they have worked. Drive around your neighborhood and see which agents and real estate companies currently have listings in the area. Some agents will specialize in a specific neighborhood, which means they already know about sales trends in the area and may know of buyers who are looking for a home.

○ Each agent you interview should provide you with a list of recent sales in the area, showing what homes comparable to yours have sold for. These comparable sales will be the basis upon which you determine the asking price for your home.

○ Ask each agent for his or her marketing plan for your home. Anyone can stick up a "for sale" sign. How else will the agent make sure that potential buyers know about your property?

○ Walk though your home with an agent and view it as a prospective purchaser might. Replace anything that you have no intention of selling (i.e., a family heirloom chandelier). For security reasons, put away calendars, personal invitations, plane tickets, planners, and anything else that tells a perfect stranger too much about your personal life. Take all valuables and put them in a safety-deposit box. Anything that is irreplaceable should be put out of sight.

○ A home that is clean, tidy, and uncluttered will sell faster than one that is messy and cramped. Before putting your house on the market, wash the windows, scrub the bathrooms, and get rid of old toys, clothing, furniture, and other items that are cluttering your closets, basement, attic, and garage. Now's a great time to hold a yard sale or to donate to charity. You don't want to pay to move all that stuff to your new house, anyway. If you have lots of things you want to keep but that are causing clutter, rent a storage space and move as much as possible out of your home.

○ If you are a smoker or have a pet, it's possible that there are odors in your home that you don't even notice, but that would turn off a potential buyer. Ask your real estate agent or a friend you trust to tell you if your home has offensive odors. If it does, have the upholstery and carpeting cleaned, air the place out, run the exhaust fans, and do everything else possible to eliminate the odors. Ban smoking indoors and keep the pet outdoors, if possible, to keep your home smelling more pleasant.

o On the day of an open house, try baking something that smells delicious, like cinnamon buns or chocolate chip cookies, for a special touch.

o Open up all the shutters, draperies, and blinds and let the light in! If there is an area that is dark, leave a light on or put a lamp on a timer for the most logical hours that your home may be shown. A bright, fresh, clean overpriced home will sell more quickly than a dark, dirty well-priced home.

o If an agent brings someone to look at your property while you're home, leave! Take a walk, go visit a neighbor, or get in the car and run a few errands. Buyers feel uncomfortable about "kicking the tires" and really inspecting a place when the owner is there—they worry about invading your privacy. If you're gone, it's likely that they will spend more time visualizing it as their own home.

## The Presale Inspection

o Have your home inspected before you put it on the market. The eventual buyer is almost certainly going to have it inspected, anyway, so you might as well be aware of any problem areas. When your presale inspection is completed, it's a good idea to fix the major problems, which could become a stumbling block during sales negotiations. You can also disclose the problems to potential buyers and price your house accordingly.

o Real estate experts say that a buyer will discount the value of your home by $200 for every $100 worth of needed repairs, so you will more than recoup your investment when you fix up the home prior to putting it on the market, according to Kenneth Austin of HouseMaster.

o Be sure to let your inspector know of any recent upgrades, mechanical repairs, or service contracts in effect on any appliances or systems. It might enhance a potential buyer's view of the home when this information is included in the inspector's report, said Diane Knapp of World Inspection Network International.

## Biggest Home-Buyer Turnoffs

○ The exterior of the home and the appearance of the yard are the first things a buyer will see, and first impressions really count, said Austin. Dirty peeling paint, loose railings at the front door, a broken doorbell, and cracks in the driveway are some of the things potential buyers will notice before they even step in the house.

○ Obvious plumbing problems also scare off buyers. The original leak may have been fixed, but if there are dark brown stains on the ceiling below the bathroom, buyers are going to be very leery, Austin said.

○ Any signs of a damp basement, such as water marks on the wall, a dank, musty odor, or mildew, will scare off buyers.

○ The kitchen is one of the most important and most used rooms in the house, and any signs of neglect there will make a bad impression, Austin said. Dirty appliances, loose handles, poor flooring, and bad lighting can all turn off a buyer.

○ A house that's chilly in cold weather or too hot in the summer will make buyers feel uncomfortable and may cause them to think there is a problem with the heating or air-conditioning system, even though the seller may just have set the thermostat at a level to save on the power bill. Energy conservation is a good thing, but don't let it backfire on you while your house is on the market.

## Home Maintenance

○ Expect to spend between 1 and 3 percent of your home's value, on average, each year doing routine maintenance on the house, says HouseMaster's Kenneth Austin. The actual amount you will spend could differ, depending on factors such as age and design of the house, the geographical area you live in, and how well it was maintained by previous owners, but for the typical $100,000 house, annual maintenance costs will average between $1,000 and $3,000.

○ When it comes to maintenance, little fix-ups can save big repair bills in the end. HouseMaster suggests lots of jobs you can do around the house for $25 or less that could save you hundreds or even thousands of dollars by preventing serious damage. Spend a little time sealing the roof flashings and replacing missing roof tiles, and you can prevent roof leaks. Clean the gutters, and you stop roof drainage and basement leaks. Caulk the exterior trim, windows, and doors, and you prevent water seepage and leaks. Apply deck preservative, and you stop premature wood wear. Clean and replace the kitchen exhaust fan and clean the clothes dryer vent, and you have eliminated two possible fire hazards.

○ Visit HouseMaster's Web site at www.housemaster.com for more home maintenance information.

## The Contractor

According to the State of Georgia's Office of Consumer Affairs:

○ Ask for the complete business name, address, and telephone number of the contractor and verify them. Do not accept a post office box number without a street address.

○ Check with the Better Business Bureau (BBB) in the area where the contractor's business is located to see if any complaints have been filed against the company. Ask about any unresolved cases and how long the contracting company has been in business under its current title. Unfortunately, some of the less reputable companies may frequently change names in order to avoid being located.

○ Ask to see the contractor's business license and then check with your county or city business license department to verify that it is valid.

○ Check the records at the local magistrate's state and superior courts to see if any claims have been filed against the contractor or company.

○ Ask if the contractor is a member of a professional or trade association that has a code of ethics and a process to arbitrate disputes, such as the National Association of the Remodeling Industry.

o Compare construction costs by getting written itemized estimates or bids from several contractors. Similar building specifications, materials, and time frame for completion should be listed in each estimate.

o Verify prices for building materials quoted in the estimate by contracting building-supply companies. You may also ask the supply company about previous dealings with a prospective contractor.

o Be cautious if a contractor tries to pressure you into quickly signing a contract, and do not automatically select the lowest bid.

### What You Should Know About the Contractor

o Ask for a list of previous customers whom you can contact for references on the contractor's work. If possible, inspect some of these properties.

o Ask to see a copy of the contractor's insurance certificate or the name of the insurance carrier/agency and verify the coverage. Contractors should have personal liability, workers' compensation, and property damage insurance to protect customers from lawsuits if an accident happens on the customer's property. Do not do business with any contractor who does not have this coverage.

o Depending on where you live and whether it's possible, request that the contractor apply for a building permit under the name of the business, or his name and not yours. This will protect you from any additional expense if the work does not comply with the building codes.

o Consider asking the contractor to post a bond to assure payment to all subcontractors and suppliers for any sublet work, and require subcontractors to sign a lien waiver when payments are received. Be aware that any subcontractor or supplier who is not paid by the contractor may file a materialman's lien (a legal claim) against your home.

o At a minimum, require the contractor to provide an affidavit of completion when the work is finished.

### Tips to Consider Before Signing a Contract

o If you need to borrow money to finance the work to be done on your home, add a clause to your contract stating that it is valid only if financing is obtained.

o When writing a contract, limit your down payment to no more than 25 percent of the contract price. The remaining payments should be made depending upon the progress of the work, but you should withhold 10 percent until the work is satisfactorily completed.

o Never sign a partially blank contract. Fill in or draw a line through any blank spaces. If you have any questions about the contract or do not understand something, ask before you sign.

### What Records Should You Keep?

1. The contract and any change orders
2. Plans and specifications
3. Bills and invoices
4. Canceled checks
5. Letters, notes, and correspondence with the contractor
6. Lien releases from subcontractors and material suppliers
7. A record sheet on each subcontractor listing the work performed and the length of time on the job
8. Warranties
9. Samples, swatches, or identifying information on materials used in your project

### What Should You Do Before Making the Final Payment?

o Thoroughly inspect all work before making the final payment. Remember to specify in the contract that you will withhold 10 percent of the total price until the job has been completed, you are satisfied with the work that has been done, and you have proof that all subcontractors and employees have been paid.

o Review the entire project with the contractor. Immediately point out any defects and be sure they are corrected before making the final payment.

o Never sign a completion certificate until the city/county building inspection department has certified that all work was performed in accordance with code standards, you have proof that all subcontractors have been paid in full, and you are completely satisfied with the job.

## Resources

Two good videotapes you might want to purchase are *Pricing Your Home to Sell* and *House Hunting,* by David S. Knox, CRS. Call 1-800-533-4494.

## Web Sites

www.askbuild.com—Visit on-air radio personality Tim Carter and his Home Improvement Center Web site. His helpful site features information on home building and remodeling.

# Insurance

Insurance can be a scary subject. It brings to mind a lot of things we'd rather not think about, such as fire, tornadoes, illness, accidents, and death. Then there's the small print, the confusing language, and the cost. No wonder most of us tend to purchase the cheapest policies we can find and file them away unread.

That's not wise, say experts. You want to give insurance the critical attention it deserves, because when the small or large disasters of life hit, one of the greatest comforts can be insurance. First, find an agent who will listen to your needs and tell you the advantages and disadvantages of policy options. Your agent must know what you do, where you work, and a great deal about your life to make sure the appropriate insurance is recommended!

Second, make your insurance effective. Read the documents you sign and know your coverage. The time of a loss or illness is *not* the time you want to find out that you are not properly covered or, as most discover, underinsured. Finally, prices for the same coverage can vary by hundreds of dollars, so comparison shop.

Today, it's much easier to be a savvy shopper. Insurance companies freely make educational brochures available. Corporations have benefits managers who can explain insurance options, and most national insurance organizations have Web sites that can add considerably to your knowledge.

Insurance is an ever-changing field, so whether you're a long-standing consumer or preparing to purchase your first policy, you can benefit from these tips from the professionals.

## General Advice

o Every state has an insurance commissioner who can answer questions, provide basic information, and field complaints about providers or claim disputes.

o Purchasing your homeowner's and auto insurance from the same company can earn you a discount of 5 to 15 percent on your premiums.

o One of the best buys in insurance is an umbrella policy that gives you additional liability coverage over and above your homeowner's and auto policies. Purchase enough liability insurance to cover your assets and then some.

o Insurance deductibles (your out-of-pocket costs for any claim, or for the year in the case of health insurance) vary from $200 to $10,000. By taking the highest deductible you can afford, you can reduce the cost of an insurance policy.

o Don't ever cancel an insurance policy until you have a new one in place. Make sure it makes sense to switch before doing so, and that you are never left without proper insurance at all times during the change.

## Homeowner's Insurance

o Cost should never be the only factor when choosing a homeowner's insurance policy. The company's stability, experience, and reputation for service are equally important. You want to know that they'll be in business when you need them. Look for an A.M. Best Rating (a national rating system for insurance companies) of A or A+.

o When purchasing homeowner's insurance, be aware that all policies are not the same. Since your home is one of your greatest assets, the coverages of your homeowner's policy should be inclusive of the broadest protection. Andy Siegel, CPCU, CIC, AAI, believes that you should have your agent compare various companies' coverages along with the price to see where you can get the best value. "Besides insuring for all perils available on your dwelling and contents with replacement cost, you should be concerned about sewer backup, limits on computers, rebuilding to codes (on older homes), replacement cost on your home without regard to limit, and the full replacement cost cash option. Some policies will cover the increase in mortgage rate due to refinancing because a larger loss occurred and your mortgagee wants to eliminate your favorable rate," says Siegel.

○ Flood and earthquake insurance must be purchased separately. Be sure to discuss this with your agent and consider what additional protection you might need based on where you live.

○ A homeowner's policy doesn't just cover your home. It includes liability insurance to help protect you from financial disaster if someone files suit for accident or injury on your property or anywhere (excluding auto accidents).

○ While $100,000 worth of liability coverage is standard on most homeowner's policies, seasoned agents advise purchasing at least $300,000 worth of coverage (costs about $15) and more if you can afford it. You don't have to be a millionaire to be sued like one!

○ It is also extremely important for condo owners and renters to purchase at least $300,000 of liability insurance to cover their negligence in damage to the building they occupy.

○ Did you just get remarried or inherit valuables? One of the biggest mistakes that homeowners make is undervaluing the contents of their house and not paying attention to limitations on valuables such as jewelry, computers, silver, or hobby collections. Compare limits on your policy with an inventory of your possessions once a year. Remember to add things you have bought or inherited and drop insurance on things you no longer own.

○ When adding a personal property rider to your insurance on a high-ticket item, get an appraisal and insure the item for the "agreed value." That way you get the insured price for a $10,000 diamond ring, not what it would cost at a discount jeweler.

○ Want to save money on homeowner's insurance? Stop smoking! Smoking accounts for more than 23,000 residential fires a year, and some companies offer discounts to nonsmokers.

○ Beef up home security. Some companies also offer policy discounts for smoke alarms, dead-bolt locks, burglar alarms, and sprinkler systems.

○ Buy a brick house on the East Coast (better resistance to wind damage) or a frame house on the West Coast (better resistance to earthquake). It can save 5 to 15 percent on a policy.

○ Your cheapest homeowner's policy may be through your job, college, or business association. Groups can negotiate for cheaper rates.

o Do you travel with your laptop computer, or does your child have a computer at college? Check your policy to see about limitations on items stolen away from home. You may need a separate renter's insurance policy if your child owns a lot of electronic equipment, expensive cameras, and the like.

o Condominium owners need to know about their building's insurance coverage. "All-in" coverage is the most comprehensive. "Bare-walls" coverage means that you would be responsible for replacing the interior walls, plumbing, and light fixtures and would need additional insurance. "Original specs" coverage would pay to put the building back to its original condition, not for owner upgrades in appliances, flooring, or lighting. In any case, you will need condo owner's insurance to cover your possessions and liability.

o In many condos, commonly owned property isn't covered under the building policy. When the pool cabanas are destroyed during a windstorm, for instance, you could be assessed a fee to replace them. Adding "loss-assessment insurance" to your policy would cover that expense.

o Renters need insurance. If there is a fire, the building is covered by the owner's insurance policy, but your possessions are not. Even if you're young and just starting out, you probably couldn't afford to replace everything you own from your savings.

o Make sure that your policy covers items at their "replacement value," rather than actual cash value. Cash value pays according to the age of an item. An old TV would be worth a fraction of its cost, but "replacement value" would pay for a comparable, new TV.

o After a disaster, when insurance agents are swamped with calls, do what you need to do to stop further damage—that is, put a tarp on a damaged roof, board up broken windows, and save your receipts. Your policy should cover the costs of those materials.

o When deciding how much you would need to rebuild your home, ask a dwelling construction contractor to advise how much it would cost per square foot to build your house. You will have to know the square footage per floor—both finished and unfinished space. Multiply the cost per square foot by the size of your house and you will have the proper replacement cost. Ask your agent to check the *Boeckh Dwelling Replacement Cost Guide*, a resource used by

224 • Bet You Didn't Know

insurance agents and companies to determine the replacement cost of a home.

o Be wary of builders or contractors who go door-to-door selling their services. Investigate their record with insurance agents or claims adjusters.

o Never pay for repair work in advance or in cash. If asked for a deposit, pay no more than one-third of the total price by check or credit card, and the balance only after the work is completed to your satisfaction.

o Be skeptical of contractors who encourage you to spend a lot of money on temporary repairs. Those repairs will be part of your insurance settlement and may not leave you enough to cover a permanent solution.

o An estimated 12 million people operate a part-time or full-time business from their homes. Don't assume that your home-owner's insurance will cover business equipment, inventory, or liability if a customer or supplier gets injured on the premises. You need home-based business insurance.

o When buying business insurance, remember to cover the inability to operate the business if your home is damaged or destroyed and for the inability to collect income due to loss of records.

## Health Insurance

o Today four out of five people with employer-sponsored health insurance are enrolled in managed care plans (HMO, PPO, POS) that change frequently. To get the most from any plan, stay informed. Talk to your employer's benefits manager. Read the policy, member handbook, and newsletter.

o While most plans give basic health coverage, they differ on whether they cover prescription drugs, obstetrical care, mental health counseling, physical therapy, mammograms, and so on. Consider your health priorities, then choose the plan that offers the services that are the best match at a price you can afford.

o How can you know if you are getting quality care? Managed care providers are regulated by federal and state agencies. Indemnity plans are regulated by state insurance commissions. Look for accreditation standards. Ask how a plan reviews its own services and corrects problems. Ask about data on customer satisfaction.

o Need to choose a new doctor? Ask for recommendations from medical societies, friends, or referral services. Ask the office about the doctor's training and experience, or look him up on the AMA Physician Select service (http://www.ama-assn.org). If he is board certified in a specialty, you can call the American Board of Medical Specialties (1-800-776-2378) for more information. You can also call the state medical licensing board to make sure that no complaints have been registered or disciplinary actions taken.

o Finally, you can make a "get acquainted" appointment to interview the doctor and see how his experience matches your health conditions. Many don't charge for this service.

o Set up a health file for every member of your family. Include histories of shots, illnesses, hospital stays, copies of lab reports, a list of medicines taken, and side effects experienced.

o If you travel for work or have a child in college, know how your plan provides care for those outside the service area. Following the correct procedures for emergency care can ensure that you won't meet with unpleasant surprises when you file a claim.

o All plans have an appeals procedure if a claim is turned down. Call member services to file an appeal or grievance. When you do, keep written records of all correspondence, claim forms, invoices and phone conversations, noting person talked to, date, time, and subject of call.

o If you get no satisfaction within the system, go to your employer's benefits manager, your state insurance commissioner, the state health department, or a lawyer.

o If a claim is rejected because the procedure is "not covered," and you think it is, check to make sure that the doctor's office entered the right diagnosis or procedure code on the claim form.

o One clause that customers often overlook is "reasonable and customary charge." This means your plan will pay most of the prevailing costs of a medical service within a geographic area. If your doctor charges more, the difference comes out of your pocket.

o Experts advise consumers to look for "lifetime limits" clauses in their healthcare coverage policy. Anything less than $1 million in today's market may be inadequate in the case of a chronic or catastrophic condition.

o The Health Insurance Portability Act of July 1997 has been good news for people with coverage who have preexisting conditions. Previously, people feared changing jobs and insurance carriers because of the waiting period. Now if you have been insured for the past twelve months and join a new group plan, there is no waiting period. If you haven't been insured, the longest you'll have to wait before coverage is twelve months.

o Trouble getting insured? Check with your state insurance commissioner to see if there is a "risk pool" to cover those who can't get insurance elsewhere.

o Under some state laws, following an employee death or divorce, the family has the right to continue that health coverage up to three years, providing they pay the premiums.

o Between jobs or out of college and not yet employed? You can buy an interim or short-term policy to cover hospital and surgical care for two to six months. The policy can be renewed once.

o Generally, individuals pay higher insurance premiums, but if you're self-employed, a partner in a partnership, or a shareholder in an S corporation, you are allowed to deduct a certain percentage of what you pay for health insurance for you and your family. Under the Taxpayer Relief Act of 1997, the deduction increases each year from 1998 (45 percent) to 2007 (100 percent). It doesn't apply for any month that you are eligible to participate in a subsidized health plan maintained by your employer or your spouse's employer.

o People sixty-five or older can purchase Medicare supplementary insurance to cover the gaps, without having to worry about being rejected for previous medical problems, if they apply within six months after enrolling in Medicare. Also, people eligible for Medicare now can get private Medicare coverage through an HMO or a PPO.

o According to certified life underwriter Bruce Weinstein, who is president of Professional Planning Services, "If you have a choice of plans, either individually or through your group policy, look over the list of network physicians of each plan to see which one has the majority of doctors you use or that has the ones closest to you."

o Weinstein adds, "If you have no health insurance coverage and you have health conditions that preclude getting an individual policy, there are still a few ways of getting coverage. Many employers with group coverage of ten or more people have plans that let new people on with no medical questions. Preexisting conditions usually aren't covered for twelve months, but everything else is. In addition, if you are leaving a company, ask about COBRA, which allows you to keep the plan at your own cost. Once COBRA runs out, most carriers give you the opportunity to convert to an individual plan. While they have limited benefits, it does give you some coverage."

## Auto Insurance

o Auto insurance is a highly competitive business. When comparing sticker prices, make sure you are comparing policies that offer the same amounts of coverage. The policy can, but doesn't have to, include coverage on six distinct risks: bodily injury liability, medical or personal injury protection, property damage liability, collision, comprehensive (fire, theft, missiles, flood, etc.), and uninsured motorists coverage.

o One way to reduce your premium is to drive a "low-profile" car. Cars that are expensive to repair or favorite targets for thieves cost more to insure. To find out which cars get stolen most, write to the Insurance Institute for Highway Safety, 1005 North Gleve Road, Suite 800, Arlington, VA 22201, and ask for the Highway Loss Data Chart, or check out www.highwaysafety.org. This organization is an independent, nonprofit research and communications organization dedicated to reducing highway crash deaths, injuries, and property damage losses.

o Another way to save money is to drop the collision and/or comprehensive coverage on older cars worth less than $1,000 because any claim wouldn't substantially exceed the annual premium cost and deductible amounts.

o Ask about discounts. Some companies offer discounts for more than one car, accident-free driving, older drivers, driver training courses, antitheft devices, automatic seat belts, air bags, antilock brakes, and good grades for student drivers.

o Fight insurance fraud by reporting any instances to your company, your state insurance department, or law enforcement agencies. Did you know that auto insurance fraud adds $112 to the typical auto insurance premium?

o You can lower your auto repair costs by up to 33 percent by using certified replacement parts found to be equal in quality and warranty to the manufacturer's original parts.

o If you're planning to rent a car, check your auto insurance policy to see if you're covered and by how much. Make sure anyone driving the rental car is also listed. With the average new car costing $23,000, you can't afford to make a mistake on rental car insurance.

o You probably don't need the additional liability insurance when you rent a car (at $8–$9 a day) if you have an auto/home umbrella insurance policy. Have other questions about rental coverage? Call the National Insurance Consumer Hotline (NICH) at 1-800-942-4242.

o When you purchase an additional car and have an existing policy, you have thirty days to report it to your insurance company.

o Consider your budget, driving record, and the risk of where you drive when deciding how high to set your deductible.

## Life Insurance

o Life insurance should cover five needs: income, repayment of borrowed monies (mortgage, credit cards), major future expenses (a child's college education), emergency funds (burial, legal, and accounting expenses), and estate taxes. These needs change over time, so review your life insurance policies every two years.

o A common myth is that you don't need as much insurance when you're older. You may need more if your estate has been growing during your lifetime.

o Haven't heard from your insurance agent in a while, or looking for one in your area? Try the World Wide Web. Many insurance agents and companies are posting their own home pages to share information about agents or new insurance regulations and products.

○ One of the advantages of life insurance is that proceeds payable to a named beneficiary pass outside of probate. Instead of being subject to the lengthy and costly probate process, the beneficiary receives the money immediately.

○ Be specific in naming beneficiaries and keep them up to date. Write your spouse's name, not "wife" or "husband." An ex-spouse could end up with the proceeds if the designation isn't clear. Remember to add younger children's names to your policies as they are born.

○ Try to cover every contingency. If a child beneficiary should die before you and you want her benefits to go to her children, you need to put it in writing.

○ Think twice before dropping an in-force policy for a new one. Remember that you have already paid acquisition costs (first-year overhead, medical exam cost, agent commissions) on the existing policy and would have to pay those again. Also, if your health status has changed, you may not be insurable at standard or preferred rates. On the other hand, if the new policy offers more benefits at an economical price, it may be worth the cost of switching.

○ According to CLU Bruce Weinstein, "It is important to have an agent that will review and help you assess your insurance needs at least every year. It is to your benefit to have an agent with a Chartered Life Underwriter (CLU) degree, as he would have a more in-depth knowledge of planning and product. The most important thing is to have the proper amount of insurance for your needs and situation. The ownership and beneficiary arrangements should give you the most tax-advantaged protection and fit in with your specific situation."

○ "The basic types of life insurance available today are annual renewable term, level term, whole life, universal life, variable life, and survivorship life. Based on whether your needs are long or short term and your financial abilities, you choose what type, or combinations of each, that is best for you," states Bruce Weinstein.

○ To receive benefits you have to file a claim, but what if you can't find the policy that you know a relative held? Write to the

Missing Policy Service at the American Council of Life Insurance, 1001 Pennsylvania Avenue NW, Washington, DC 20004-2599. Include a self-addressed business-size envelope. For a nominal fee, they will forward your inquiry to nearly 100 large life insurance companies.

## Disability Income Insurance

According to CLU Bruce Weinstein:

○ The chances of a disability lasting ninety days or more before the age of sixty-five are fifteen times greater than dying before age sixty-five. Even with these statistics, less than 20 percent of today's workforce has long-term disability coverage.

○ One way of getting disability coverage is through an employer-sponsored plan. These plans usually have rigid eligibility and definition requirements, but are inexpensive and sometimes even paid for totally by the employer. Check out your options. You can also purchase an individual policy, which is more expensive but will have more liberal benefits and definitions and is more tax-advantaged.

○ It is most important to get with a company that guarantees your premiums and guarantees the policy renewability (noncancelable and guaranteed renewable).

○ Some policies are occupation specific and some just protect your income. What you choose should be based on your occupation and its specific job requirements, your income, and how many other assets you have.

## Long-Term Care Insurance

According to Bruce Weinstein:

○ Long-term care insurance is one of the most important coverages a person can get as he or she gets older. It protects finances, assets, and estates from being drained to meet the huge costs associated with illnesses that require personal care or supervision due to cognitive impairment. Keep in mind, the earlier you purchase it (in your early forties verses your fifties), the lower the premiums. The later you wait, the more expensive this insurance becomes. Plan ahead.

o A good policy covers nursing homes, assisted-care facilities, community care, hospice care, and home care, along with all the services (nurses, therapists, etc.) that are required. Why long-term care insurance? Nursing home costs today are between $40,000 and $50,000 annually. The average stay is between three and five years. Home care is less expensive but can last longer. These are costs that have very limited benefits through individual health insurance and Medicare. With people living longer, these costs are predicted to skyrocket. Many individuals and their immediate families have lost all their assets to pay for these costs, yet a good long-term care policy eliminates this kind of risk or exposure.

o There are various plans, with different elimination periods (0, 50, or 100 days) and different benefit periods (three years to lifetime). The area you live in and other assets you have can help determine what's best for your individual situation.

## Insurance Resources

Here are some Web sites to explore that might help you in the process:

> Insurance Information Institute—http://www.iii.org
> Health Insurance Association of America—
>     http://www.hiaa.org
> American Insurance Association—http://www.aiadc.org

# Kitchen Improvement

Our concept of the ideal kitchen, or even an acceptable one, has changed a lot over the years. Think back to your grandmother's cozy room filled with the homey scent of fresh-baked bread but only the most basic of appliances. Then flip through a recent issue of a glossy design magazine and marvel at the huge, stainless steel–equipped room with a flotilla of convenience gadgets that the publication is featuring as "the kitchen you just have to have."

Maybe neither fits your definition of the perfect kitchen, and that's as it should be. Kitchens are as individual as the people who work in them, yet yours is almost certainly the heart of your home. The kitchen is where all the guests end up when you have a party, the place where you have your first cup of coffee in the morning, and where you help your kids struggle with math homework in the evening. You want your kitchen to be special.

It's no wonder that a new or improved kitchen is a major part of so many home renovation projects. You'll enjoy a better kitchen as long as you live in the home, and you'll probably reap a reward, too, when it comes time to sell, because a kitchen renovation is one improvement that nearly pays for itself. In fact, it's estimated that when you sell, you'll recoup about 90 percent of the money you put into a kitchen improvement.

Redoing your kitchen is not a cheap proposition, however, and the cost can quickly mount up into the five digits. You are the best judge of what you can afford, but before making any final decisions, make sure the new kitchen will function the way you want it to. It's not just a matter of picking out some elegant cabinets or durable flooring. A lot of careful thought, planning, and measuring goes into designing a kitchen that works to the optimum, easing the cook's job by allowing plenty of room to work, and locating controls and storage space within easy reach. In fact, the National Kitchen and Bath Association (NKBA) has forty specific guidelines for planning a kitchen so that it is functional and accessible. Failure to follow these guidelines can result in a kitchen that doesn't work as well as it should, is uncomfortable, or has safety hazards.

If you're getting ready to upgrade your kitchen, start by studying these tips from the experts at the NKBA, whose members include companies that offer kitchen and bath design and installation services and specialists in design. Knowing what goes into a good kitchen design will be helpful, whether you're planning a minor redo by yourself or hiring a professional to rebuild your kitchen from the ground up.

## Working with a Professional

○ The National Kitchen & Bath Association certifies kitchen designers who have met minimum competency requirements. To find a certified kitchen designer in your area, you can visit the association's Web page at http://www.nkba.org and go to the Find a Design Professional area.

○ You can hire a kitchen professional to handle as much of the project as you'd like. He can be limited to designing your new kitchen, can act as a consultant for the project, or can be project manager, hiring the subcontractors, scheduling the work, and supervising the installation.

○ Before any work is started, make sure to get detailed, written estimates of the costs involved, project specifications, and signed contracts from the professionals you hire. Make sure everyone who will be working in your home is bonded and insured, and check references carefully.

○ Your designer should prepare project drawings, including floor plans and renderings that clearly represent your project. If anything changes after the project is under way, you should be asked to sign a change order.

○ You will probably be required to pay 50 percent of the total cost of the project up front when you sign the contract. You'll make another payment of about 40 percent when the cabinets are delivered or installation begins, and the balance when the job is complete. You may also be required to pay a design retainer at the start of the job.

## Know What You Want

o Before embarking on your redesign, spend lots of time looking at magazine articles on kitchens and tear out pictures of kitchens that particularly appeal to you. Whether you work with a designer or make all the decisions yourself, these pictures will help you visualize what you want.

o Cabinets account for about half the cost of a new kitchen, according to the NKBA. Cabinets come in different price ranges, depending on the quality of workmanship, the type of material they are made of, and whether they are "stock" or custom cabinets. Stock cabinets are those that are ready made and available in specific sizes, but these days they come in such a variety of materials, styles, and options that the price can be staggering. Stock definitely does not mean cheap or inferior. Custom cabinets are produced specifically for your kitchen and can be made in whatever sizes are needed, and with whatever finishing details you desire, such as glass-front doors, special crown moldings, and other unique elements.

o Other surfaces in your kitchen, including countertops, back-splashes, and floors, can be covered in a variety of products that come in a wide range of prices, from simple vinyl to synthetic solid surface materials to real marble or granite. Those items will also have a large impact on your budget, and you should investigate different surfaces to see which have the longest life, require the least care, or would otherwise provide the kinds of benefits you are looking for. Special-interest publications available at magazine stands often have good articles comparing the various products available, and reading those articles can help you narrow your choice or decide to investigate an option you hadn't previously considered. A design professional can be a resource to help you find those coverings that best meet your needs and stay within your budget.

o Even if you are hiring a professional to handle your kitchen project, there is still some work that homeowners can perform themselves to keep the costs down. Tearing out old cabinets (taking care not to damage walls and beams), removing old flooring, and handling trash removal yourself can save you some money. Doing the painting and wallpapering yourself are other options for saving money if you are on a limited budget. It pays to hire professionals for skilled jobs, however, including the plumbing and electrical work and hooking up the appliances. If you try those tasks on your own, you could end up violating local building codes or invalidating the warranties on your new appliances, the NKBA instructs.

## Design Tricks from the Pros

o By varying the counter heights, you create work spaces for different tasks and accommodate cooks of varying statures, including those who are seated. Placing counters at different heights also adds an interesting design element. The NKBA recommends that each kitchen have at least two counter heights, one between 28 and 36 inches, the other between 36 and 45 inches.

o Raising the dishwasher 9 to 12 inches above the floor makes it more accessible and easier to load and unload, because you don't have to bend over to reach the bottom rack. And raising the dishwasher is one way to add a second height to your countertops.

o Lowering some wall cabinets can result in more storage space within a comfortable reach range. For a standing person who is between 5 foot 3 and 5 foot 7 inches tall, the most accessible cabinet space is located between 15 and 69 inches above the floor.

o Drawers and roll-out shelves help maximize storage space. In base cabinets, roll-outs improve accessibility by bringing pots and other items out to you, instead of your having to reach into the cabinet to retrieve them. Drawers of various sizes also add design interest to your kitchen space.

## The Work Triangle

o The work triangle is the kitchen area from the refrigerator to the main cooking area to the main sink. If you drew an imaginary line connecting all three of those areas to one another, it would form a triangle (unless your kitchen is limited to one wall). The work triangle is perhaps the most important ingredient in your kitchen because all the key kitchen activities, such as food preparation, cooking, and cleanup, take place at or adjacent to the triangle's points. In a well-planned kitchen, the work triangle helps to ensure that your kitchen will be functional.

○ According to NKBA guidelines, the work triangle (measured from the center front of each appliance) should total 26 feet or less, based on the shortest walking distance between each point. No single leg of the triangle should be shorter than 4 feet or longer than 9 feet. The work triangle should not intersect an island or peninsula by more than 12 inches.

○ If two or more people normally work in the kitchen at the same time, a work triangle should be created for each cook. The two triangles may share one leg, but the two triangles should not cross each other.

○ No major traffic patterns should come through the work triangle, as this would be disruptive to the cook and could be dangerous if she's taking something hot out of the oven just as someone walks in her path.

○ To ensure adequate working space, the food preparation center should contain at least 3 feet of continuous countertop that is at least 16 inches deep. It should be near a water source, usually the primary sink in the kitchen.

○ If two people work in the kitchen at the same time, each needs his or her own food prep center that measures at least 3 feet long and 16 inches deep. If the people work side by side, that means the food prep area must be at least 6 feet wide and 16 inches deep.

## Landing Spaces

○ A countertop "landing space" that is at least 15 inches wide and 16 inches deep is needed for hot dishes, pots, and baking trays. It should be located either next to, above, or directly across from both the microwave and oven.

○ There should be a minimum landing space of 15 inches by 16 inches to one side of the cooktop. If the cooktop is at the end of a countertop that meets a wall, there should be at least 3 inches of counter clearance space between the cooktop and the wall, and the wall should be protected by a flame-retardant surface.

○ By the primary sink, there should be at least 24 inches of countertop frontage on one side and 18 inches on the other, providing a landing area for food being prepared or dishes to be cleaned.

○ The secondary sink needs at least 18 inches of countertop on one side, and at least 3 inches on the other to provide adequate landing space.

○ The dishwasher should be installed no more than 3 feet from the sink, with the dishwasher also placed so that there is at least 21 inches of standing room between it and other appliances and cabinets. You need at least that much space to be able to load and unload dishes.

○ By the refrigerator, the landing area should include a counter space that is at least 15 inches wide. The landing space for items coming out of or going into the refrigerator should be located on the same side as the opening in the refrigerator door, or located on a counter across an aisle from the refrigerator, such as on an island, but no more than 4 feet from the appliance door.

## Other Space Needs

○ There should be at least 12 to 19 inches of leg room beneath eating areas designed into counters, peninsulas, islands, and bar areas.

○ To ensure that aisles are wide enough for two people to pass each other, they should be 4 feet wide in the food preparation areas and at least 3 feet wide between facing cabinets.

○ In any area where people will be seated, such as a breakfast bar, allow at least 3 feet of clearance, measuring from the edge of the counter or table to any wall or obstruction, if no traffic will pass behind the seated diner. If people normally will walk behind the seating area, allow at least 65 inches of clearance, including the walkway, between the seating area and any wall or obstruction. Those measurements should give a diner enough room to comfortably move the chair away from the table without hitting the wall or bumping into someone walking behind him.

o At least five storage or organizing items should be included in the kitchen to improve functionality and accessibility. All should be located between 15 and 48 inches above the floor. Examples of storage/organizing items you might want to consider in your kitchen are appliance garages, bins/racks, swing-out pantries, interior vertical dividers, and specialized drawers and shelves. Lowered wall cabinets, raised base cabinets, and tall cabinets can also be included among items that help make your kitchen more functional and improve your access to items stored in the cabinetry.

## Think Safety

o A cooking surface should not be placed below an operable window unless the window is at least 3 inches behind the appliance and more than 2 feet above it.

o No windows located near a cooking surface should have a flammable window treatment.

o All major appliances used for surface cooking (such as a range or a cooktop) should have a ventilation system with a fan rated at least 150 cubic feet per minute (CFM).

o All electrical receptacles in the kitchen should have ground fault circuit interrupters (GFCI). GFCI monitors the balance of electrical current moving through the circuit. If an imbalance occurs, GFCI cuts off the electricity. The purpose is to prevent fatal electrical shocks. All switches, sockets, breakers, and circuits for the kitchen, as well as all the bathrooms in your home, should be GFCI protected.

o Every kitchen should be equipped with a fire extinguisher. The extinguisher should be kept in a location where it can be easily seen, yet where it is away from the cooking equipment. It should be hung at a height of between 15 to 48 inches above the floor, which is the easiest zone for people to reach. Smoke alarms should also be installed near the kitchen.

o The control knobs for the cooking surface should be located on the front or side of the appliance, and not on the area behind and/or above the cooking surface, where you would have to reach over the hot cooking area to turn the knobs. If you have to reach over the cooking surface, you risk burning yourself or having a loose sleeve catch on fire.

   ○ To eliminate sharp edges on your countertop, edges and corners should be rounded, curved, or clipped.

   ○ Controls, handles, and pulls for drawers and doors should be operable with one hand, require only a minimal amount of strength for operation, and not require tight grasping, pinching, or twisting of the wrist.

   ○ Wall-mounted controls, such as wall receptacles, switches, thermostats, telephones, and intercoms, should be located 15 to 48 inches above the floor.

# Legal

To those of us who do not speak it, the law can be an incomprehensible language. And, since some of us only get involved with the law and lawyers in times of trouble, we may tend to be uncomfortable from the start.

A lawyer is a necessary guide in most situations involving legal issues. Trying to go it alone can be costly, frustrating, and futile. Sometimes do-it-yourself legal software or forms can be dangerous. But how do you choose a lawyer and accomplish your goal while still managing the rising legal costs? How do you choose a lawyer and deal with the unknown fears while protecting your legal rights and dealing with those legal fees? Legal conflicts and disputes are one of the most stressful situations anyone can go through. In fact, even in *Life's Little Instruction Book* (Volume 1, Rutledge Hill Press, 1991) by H. Jackson Brown Jr., he advises, "Avoid legal disputes like the plague."

Individuals who have survived legal problems find the cost and time spent to be financially draining and emotionally wrenching. However, there is much you can do to put yourself in the best possible position when certain unavoidable situations do occur. And knowing what steps to take and what moves to make to protect yourself can make all the difference.

Being armed with information is often the most helpful advice. Knowing what to do first, second, and third is crucial. Understanding that you have options when dealing with an attorney is also important. Here you'll find simple tips from legal professionals on a variety of situations that may help you more than you'll ever know.

## Legal Help

The following sources of legal information and assistance are helpful, according to the United States Office of Consumer Affairs:

o Small-claims courts were established to resolve disputes involving claims for minor debts and accounts. While the maximum amounts that can be claimed or awarded differ from state to state, court procedures generally are simple, inexpensive, quick, and informal. Court fees are minimal, and you often get your filing fee back if you win your case. Generally, you will not need a lawyer. In fact, in some states, lawyers are not permitted. If you live in a state that allows lawyers and the party you are suing brings one, do not be intimidated. The court is informal, and most judges make allowances for consumers who appear without lawyers. Check your local telephone book under the municipal, county, or state government headings for small-claims court offices. Check to see if there are any free materials. To better understand the process, sit in on a small-claims court session before taking your case to court.

o If you cannot afford the cost of legal assistance, check with the legal aid offices that help individuals who cannot afford to hire private lawyers. All offer free legal services to those who qualify. There are more than 1,000 of these offices around the country staffed by lawyers, paralegals, and law students who offer legal assistance with such problems as landlord-tenant relations, credit, utilities, family issues (e.g., divorce and adoption), foreclosure and home equity fraud, Social Security, welfare, unemployment, and workers' compensation. Check the telephone directory to find the address and telephone number of the legal aid office near you. For a directory of legal aid offices around the country, contact the National Legal Aid and Defender Association, 1625 K Street NW, 8th Floor, Washington, DC 20006, 1-202-452-0620.

o The Legal Services Corporation (LSC) was created by Congress in 1974 to provide financial support for legal assistance in noncriminal proceedings to persons financially unable to afford legal service. They offer free information; to find the LSC office nearest you, check the telephone directory, call the Federal Information Center (FIC) toll free at 1-800-688-9889, or call the LSC Public Affairs Office at 1-202-336-8800.

o If you need help finding a lawyer, check with the lawyer referral service for your state, city, or county bar association, listed in local telephone directories.

## Hiring an Attorney

o Don't jump at using the first attorney you think of just because he or she is an attorney of a relative or friend. Choose an attorney who specializes in the type of problem that you are dealing with, and interview more than one. Check to see that this lawyer has the expertise you need, just as you would when choosing a medical specialist. Find out what he or she does most of the time, and make sure it is a good match with what you need. If you meet a lawyer who practices in the wrong field, ask him or her who they'd use for your case.

o Determine if you want to use a big firm, a smaller one, or even a solo attorney. Each of these differs in what he or she offers and one might suit you best depending on the resources you require and the style with which you would feel most comfortable.

o Get recommendations from everyone you know and also call your local bar association for referrals. You may also want to check with your minister, rabbi, mediator, or family counselor.

o After you have determined a list of possibilities, call each one. Have a list of questions ready, including costs, retainers, qualifications, experience, and availability. Ask to talk to the attorney. This will give you an idea how available he or she will be to you later.

o As you narrow down your list, make appointments with the attorneys you feel you could work with, and don't choose the first one you interview. If an attorney is repeatedly unavailable for an interview, you may want to scratch him or her off the list. If the attorney's availability is difficult now, it might only get worse later.

o Check your local bar association to see if there are any complaints against the remaining lawyers, and make sure they are in good standing and licensed by the state.

o Interview the remaining attorneys and choose the one who best fits your needs. Go over the facts of your case. Also discuss what your legal options are, including fees, charges, costs, and how the fee arrangement is handled. For example, every time you call, what happens? Does the clock start ticking? Find out, too, if the attorney you hire will be the exact one who works on your case and meet the others if they will be involved in your matter. Different attorneys, even in the same firm, have different billing rates.

○ If your case involves litigation in different states, be sure that your attorney has contacts and a firm knowledge of the law in these states. Laws vary from state to state, and generally lawyers cannot practice in other states, so those contacts will be important.

○ Attorneys have different ways of handling fees. Many will require a retainer fee up front. Before you pay the retainer, ask about the total charges and what will be expected of you. Is the retainer refundable if it is not used up?

○ Ask if a retainer is required and ask for an estimate of what services will cost. How will you be billed? Types of billing include hourly rates, set fees, or a contingency fee. If you are worried about the bottom line, inquire if you can contract a price with a ceiling attached, which means that for the life of the case, you won't be billed more than a specific amount.

○ If the attorney takes your case on a contingency basis, that means if he wins the case, he receives a percentage of the recovery amount, plus expenses. If he loses, typically you will be responsible only for fees and expenses incurred.

○ Different methods are used to determine the percentage—you should discuss this at your first meeting and have a written agreement with fees stated.

## Auto Accidents

○ It's pretty safe to say that, at some time in our lives, most of us will encounter a fender bender in one way or another as a driver, passenger, or pedestrian. Bruce H. Morris, a lawyer with Morris & Finestone in Atlanta, Georgia, offers the following advice: "The first thing you must do is call the police, which is 911 in most areas. Make certain that the police are notified and come to the scene of the accident."

○ There are many things you can do to protect yourself after an auto accident if you are physically able. If the other person says it was his fault, ask him to sign a statement declaring that, or ask them to admit it to the police.

○ If it is a minor accident—in Georgia, for example—the law requires that the cars be moved to the side of the road. Know the law in your state, since this could differ. Get the name, address, and telephone numbers of any witness(es), if available. Prepare a written statement for the at-fault party, which in fact states that the at-fault party admits fault. Have him or her sign it. Too many people admit they are at fault, then when the cars are moved and the police come, their story conveniently changes and they claim to be unsure who was at fault.

○ If you think the other person is under the influence of drugs or alcohol, absolutely insist he be given a breath test.

○ If you feel even the slightest bit different after the accident, tell the police officer that you don't feel right. Make sure he writes it on the report. In the next few days, if you are well, you certainly don't have to do anything. However, it is a favorite ploy of some insurance companies to portray the injured party as a greedy person. They might point to the original report that states you didn't complain of an injury.

○ If you are hurt, go to the emergency room at a hospital or to your doctor. Don't play it down; report every little feeling of pain that is different from the way you normally feel.

○ When obtaining information about the at-fault driver, ask for: full name of the driver—better yet, copy it from the driver's license; address—check by asking if the address on the license is still the same; home and work telephone numbers; insurance information—copy the name of the company, policy number, and named insured. Make sure that the car involved in the accident is the one described on the insurance card; get the license tag number and sticker number.

○ If you have a camera in your car, take pictures of the at-fault driver; any passengers in the at-fault driver's car; the at-fault driver's vehicle with the tag showing; the at-fault driver's car damage; your car damage; and the witnesses.

○ If you are visibly injured, get good pictures taken of your bruises or contusions. Pictures of injuries are worth a thousand words describing pain. Regardless of the sensitive nature of where bruises might be or even lacerations, get it on film.

○ Keep a diary of how the injuries, your treatment, and every pain (big or little) that the accident caused have inconvenienced your life. These records will assist you, since it's hard to recall all the details over time.

○ It doesn't matter whether you are at fault or not at fault in an automobile accident; you must deal with an insurance company. They will treat every aspect of every claim with a business attitude. That may be hard for you to do because you are at a loss and emotionally distraught. Be patient and keep notes, including the time, date, and phone numbers of people to whom you have spoken and the topics discussed.

○ Report the accident to your own insurance company immediately. Follow up with a letter by certified mail, stating the same facts as you have verbally told them. Be sure to call your own insurance company and report the accident even when the other party is at fault. By doing so, you are protecting your rights. They must take the report, and they must provide you with an attorney if you are the party at fault.

○ If you are at fault, instruct your insurance company by certified mail to settle the claims of the injured party(ies), if given the opportunity for a sum within the policy limits you have purchased.

○ If you are at fault in an auto accident, your insurance policy requires that you cooperate with the insurance company. If you do not cooperate, your insurance company may refuse to cover you for that accident. There must be truthful cooperation with your own company.

○ Do not allow anyone to influence what you say. You remember the truth. It's your job to tell it.

○ The only way you should ever agree to give a recorded telephone statement is if an adjuster agrees to provide you with a duplicate of the tape. The truth is your complete defense. A good attorney will always require this as well when allowing his or her client to be taped.

○ If you have paid for certain coverage and the insurance

company is slow in acting, call your state's insurance commissioner's office.

o Do not ever worry about your insurance being canceled. There are a bunch of insurance companies who will appreciate your business. That means they want your premiums, nothing else.

o In auto accidents, generally you can find an attorney who will take your case on a contingency basis. That is, if the attorney with your expressed authority settles your case, that attorney will charge you a percentage (i.e. 30%, 40%) of the gross proceeds. If the attorney does not obtain a settlement for you, then you owe the attorney no more than his third-party costs and expenses, which are usually minimal, unless your contract obligates you for more. Be sure to read your contract thoroughly and understand it. Don't be afraid to question an attorney about the contract he asks you to sign, and take your time reading it. After you sign, be sure to get a copy.

o Another reason to hire an attorney is that the insurance company hires attorneys for the at-fault party. You should be represented equally as well.

## What If You Are Sued

This is certainly not a situation anybody wants to face. But if it happens, Michael Weinstock, an Atlanta attorney, gives some tips on maintaining your cool.

o Consult a lawyer. This is not the time for do-it-yourself tactics. Have the lawyer describe his or her analysis of the nature of the case and plans for developing it in the future. Know how much the services will cost, and most of all, remember the attorney is representing you.

o If the action appears to be from a lack of understanding, try to promptly establish mediation. Mediation is an alternative dispute resolution method where both sides (with their lawyers) present their cases before a trained mediator. The mediator is not a judge, but a facilitator who will express opinions to bridge the monetary differences between the parties. The process is confidential and not admissible, should the case go to court. The idea is to try for a compromise and avoid the costs of developing the case and ultimately a trial.

○ "Mediation cuts through the nonsense," Weinstock said. "Once you're involved in litigation, fees go skyward. The next thing you know, you've got $75,000 in legal fees before the case goes to trial. On the other hand, if the differences are real, then hire an experienced trial attorney with a reputation for success."

○ "Anyone can be sued," Weinstock says, "but communication is the best way to avoid a suit. Know who you're dealing with. Be honest and get it all out on the table."

○ In business dealings, Weinstock suggests you have "as much in writing as needed, depending on the nature of the business. It all gets down to communication.

"When you're going into a business transaction such as a real estate deal, it's cheaper to plan. Invest the money and get it done right by consulting a lawyer," he said. "People want to avoid having to spend the money, then they get into problems and it winds up costing them more."

## Starting a Business

According to Steven M. Winter, an attorney specializing in contract law:

○ Many points must be considered in setting up the legal aspects of your business. The first is the most visible—the name. It seems pretty simple, but many business names or trademarks are registered. You can be sued if you use another company's name.

○ Before using a product name and trademark, before you put together a Web page or E-mail address under that name, do an Internet search to see if the name is already registered or in use.

○ Two entities can have substantially the same names if they sell different products, unless the name or logo of the first one is considered a household name or is confusingly similar.

○ After you register the mark, incorporate under that name. Depending on whether you'll operate locally or nationally, you should also register the name at the appropriate government agency.

○ Avoiding personal legal risk in a business situation is another point to consider when starting a business. Some ways of doing business are better for this purpose than others. For example, in partnerships or sole proprietorships, owners can be sued personally and as a business. Deciding what format your business should take (corporation, limited liability corporation, etc.) is a complicated issue. Consult an attorney and get the best advice possible. In some respects, the individual is always involved and may be personally liable. You basically need three players—your lawyer, accountant, and insurance agent.

## Estate Planning

○ "Who needs a will?" asks George Fox, of the Fox Law Firm, P.C. "If you have no kids, no debt, and no property, maybe you don't need one. But most people have at least one of those three." Moreover, anyone who owns or controls assets (including investments, real estate, and even most life insurance) worth more than a "credit sheltered amount" set by the IRS really needs a will or estate plan, since that's where federal estate taxes kick in. That IRS amount equals $625,000 in 1998 and rises to $1 million in 2006.

○ "Most experts advise against do-it-yourself forms for wills. An airtight will requires an attorney's expertise," Fox says, "because every asset has particular twists and turns; why else would an IRS estate tax return have forty-four pages of questions?"

○ A will should be in writing and signed and witnessed according to your home state's law; the requirements vary from state to state. The process is to show you are mentally competent to make a will, and you must be of legal age for your state.

○ A current will can take advantage of federal and state estate tax deductions and exclusions. An old will can cost you taxes, if made under "old" law. For example, you're stuck with the "marital deduction"—which limits what you can pass to a spouse tax-free—if your will was signed before 1981; the new unlimited marital deduction won't apply.

○ Also, devices come and go. Certain clauses under the Internal Revenue Code don't automatically adjust upward. "For those with considerable funds, estate planning may include other tools in addition to a will," Fox said. "These may be irrevocable insurance trusts and revocable (sometimes called living) trusts, designed to help people avoid confusion and paying unnecessary taxes on their estates. With the right planning, they can cover you during disability, too."

○ Be aware that insurance policies do count in many circumstances as part of the taxable estate. Insurance policy proceeds can be tax-free, but only with careful planning.

○ "Beware of 'snake oil salesman seminars' on financial planning," Fox says. Be sure to check out someone's credentials and expertise; know who you are dealing with. "There is no generic, all-purpose will or revocable trust. Lots of real estate people, stockbrokers, and product sellers use the title 'financial planner.' But the tax code and probate laws are incredibly complex, and no single person who's really trying to sell a product knows it all. The good financial planner will bring in professionals to help justify the product, not exclude those other voices."

○ A living trust is like a will in that it sets what you want to happen to your assets when you die. But it also deals with your assets if you are incapacitated and avoids court involvement.

○ A Living Will is different, and even better is a durable power of attorney for health care—both are tools that give a person you trust the power to make particular medical decisions for you if you are incapacitated and unable to make a decision about your medical treatment. Some points to consider are:

> Talk the idea over with your doctor and ask for any information he or she can supply.
> Be aware that the document must be drawn up properly. If it isn't, medical personnel and providers may ignore it.
> Relate to your doctor and family your feelings on life-support systems. Fill out a donor card if you wish to be an organ donor.
> List the name and number of your doctor, medications you take, allergies, chronic conditions.
> List and discuss your feelings and requests on end-of-life

issues for your family. For example, if you have terminal cancer, would you prefer to be in a hospital where everything can be done by a medical staff, or at home? When you're healthy is the time to discuss issues like this.

○ The durable power of attorney for financial matters is a different document with a totally separate purpose. It enables someone to access your accounts, investments, real estate, and so on for your benefit if you are incapacitated. It saves having to go to court for permission, and thus saves time and fees.

○ The two durable powers are very different documents, so you might name a different person under each; the person who should handle your financial matters may not be the person you want consulting with your doctor.

## Divorce

The legal system views divorce as a cut-and-dried dissolution of joint property, assets, and household, with some support issues to be dealt with, too. Of course, there's much more to it than that. Looking out for your own interests is of utmost importance. The more you can remain clearheaded and treat the divorce as a business matter, the more solid your decisions will be. Attorney Michael Weinstock says the following tips on financial matters can be helpful:

○ Collect and copy all the records you can find.

○ If credit cards are in joint names, have the company issue one in your name only. Take your name off joint accounts.

○ Either take the money out of savings and checking accounts if your name is on the account, or notify the bank that nothing can be withdrawn without both signatures.

○ Open a separate bank account in your own name at a different institution.

○ Seek an attorney's advice. This can be done without retaining the attorney, and will give you information about your immediate rights.

o Stay in your home if possible. Courts are more likely to award the home to the person living there.

o Keep a diary of important occurrences and financial and business dealings. Keeping yourself and your children on an even keel during this stressful time is a task in itself.

o Try to make college costs part of the settlement.

o Each divorce situation is different. Talk to individuals who have gone through a divorce and ask them what they wish they had only known that might help you. You are bound to get an earful!

## Web Sites

www.nolo.com—Check out nolo.com, a self-help law center filled with resources and information on an extensive variety of legal topics.

# Money Management

Many people hear the word *budget* and they react the same way as they do when they hear the word *diet*. They think it means they will have to cut out something they enjoy, do without luxuries, live on the financial equivalent of celery sticks. That's one way of looking at it, but it's not the best way.

Budgeting is actually about being in control of your money, knowing where it goes, and making sure you have enough saved up so that you can buy the things you really want, or so that you will have money when you really need it. *Money management* is a much more accurate term for the concept, because it says that this is a life-long process in which you make decisions daily about how to spend your money.

The first step is to determine where your money is going. Your checkbook and a calculator will help you figure that out. The next step is to decide where you really want your money to go, and how you can achieve those goals. If you don't want all your money to go to the credit card company, for example, you need to figure out how to pay off your debts, then learn to control your spending so you can afford the things you really want.

While for some people it seems simple, for others it's one financial mess after another. According to accountant Adrian Grant, of Aarons, Grant & Habif, P.C., "Most people really don't think about managing their money or give it their total attention, because they are so caught up in their day-to-day life that they don't have time to focus on their financial and tax planning. Everyone should consider using a professional advisor who will help direct them to do proper planning. The real problem is that by not taking action, just sitting on money and not making proper investments, you're losing money, and without proper guidance you also might be making poor investments. Most people wait until they are married and their children are teenagers and college is around the corner. My best advice? Start early! By the time you get out of college, your planning, saving, and investment strategies should begin!"

Once you take control of your money, you won't feel deprived, you'll feel liberated. Find ways to cut your expenses, knowing the reward is money you can save toward something you really want or need—a new car, a vacation, a college fund for your children. Get the whole family involved, and make sure everyone understands that paying off debts and saving for the future are for the benefit of all involved.

As your first savings goal, most financial counselors suggest that you start an emergency fund, and deposit money regularly in it until you have saved up at least enough money to cover three months' worth of living expenses. This is your financial cushion. It is hoped you will not lose your job or suffer an injury or illness that prevents you from working, but if you do, you'll have something to fall back on. Adrian Grant also believes in playing out the what-ifs and adds, "Most people aren't fully aware of how many of their financial decisions are interrelated. For example, having an excess liability umbrella clause in your insurance policy is critical, since, if you were ever in a severe accident, rising medical costs from the other party could wipe you out." In other words, make sure you have total knowledge of all aspects of your finances.

Knowing you have money in the bank if you need it is a wonderful feeling, and you don't have to be rich to experience it. You merely need to spend less than you earn and be sensible about how you invest what's left. Financial experts agree that with a little restraint, a lot of diligence, and some common sense, anyone can become a wise manager of money.

## Where the Money Goes

○ A small notebook carried in your wallet can be your best tool to stop your money's "disappearing act," financial planners say. Many people have a good handle on what their big expenses are, but they don't know where the cash in their pocket goes—they just know it's gone at the end of the day. If that's your problem, start recording all the cash purchases you make. Every time you buy a newspaper, get a soft drink, visit the dry cleaners, pay for parking, or spend as much as a dime on anything, write it down. After a week or two of this exercise, you'll know where the cash is going. (The very act of writing down all your expenses can also cause you to spend less, because you are so much more aware that you are spending money every time you turn around. For that reason, you may choose to continue keeping a cash log.)

o The next important step is to figure out your after-tax income. This means what you actually have earned after taxes are paid. This amount is what you have to work with when it comes to managing your money and knowing where your money goes and how much you have to work with.

o You should not be spending more than 35 percent of your after-tax income for housing, including mortgage or rent, utilities, maintenance, property taxes, homeowner's insurance, and association fees. If you are spending more than 35 percent on those items, you're likely headed for financial trouble. Find a way to cut costs by taking in a roommate, for example, or moving to a cheaper apartment. Adrian Grant advises, "You can reduce your monthly house costs by taking a thirty-year mortgage at the lowest interest rate available. This gives you the most flexibility, and you can always increase your monthly principal payment later on when you can afford to pay off the house in fewer years."

o Transportation costs—including auto loan payments or lease payments, gas, tolls, insurance, maintenance, and registration fees—shouldn't take more than 10 to 15 percent of your after-tax income. If they do, you are driving beyond your means and need to find a cheaper car.

o Food (including groceries, dining out, and lunches purchased at work or school) should not come to more than 15 percent of after-tax income.

o Insurance (health, life, disability, and long-term care) should not be more than 5 percent of your after-tax income; clothing, 5 percent; entertainment/recreation/gifts, 5 percent; medical and dental bills, 5 percent; child care, 5 to 10 percent. If you're overspending in one area, you need to cut your expenses there or in another category so you have enough money to pay for all the necessities.

○ Your goal should be to save 10 percent of your after-tax income for all your future financial needs, which would include retirement and children's college fund, as well as more near-term goals such as having enough money to make a down payment on a house or to take the family on a trip to the beach.

## Healthy Financial Habits

Certified public accountant Robert B. Wilensky, of Wilensky & Co., P.C., suggests some basic advice for managing your financial records:

○ The most basic way to begin organizing paying your bills is to file your bills in a folder that has a separate space for each month. Then on the fifth or twenty-fifth of the month, or every two weeks, pay the bills that are due.

○ The biggest factor in poor money management is not understanding your own financial strengths and weaknesses. Are you someone who hates to pay bills? Are you someone who is completely financially disorganized? Do you enjoy planning for your financial future? Are you someone who doesn't reconcile her checkbook? Are you someone who lives to follow the prices of stocks? Do you trust others to help invest your money or do you want total control? You must understand and compensate for your strengths and weaknesses to successfully manage your finances.

○ Be aware of your spending habits, then set out to correct them. Once you see how you are managing your money, work with a financial advisor who can assist you with your goals. Professional advice from a CPA or other qualified financial advisor can help tremendously.

○ Keep your financial records a minimum of five years after the date you file your individual tax return or April 15, whichever is later. This includes bank/brokerage statements and canceled checks, supporting invoices, and legal papers for purchase of any item you can deduct on your tax return.

○ For major purchases such as a house or other capital assets, keep your records for five years after you sell those assets. If you've owned the house for twenty years, keep the original purchase papers, proof of improvements, and so on for twenty-five years.

o Consider utilizing a computer program to help maintain your checkbook, record your expenses into categories, balance your checkbook, and prepare a budget. Take your personal financial planning seriously. A computer program can help you understand without much effort how you spend your money. Choose a program that is recommended by your accountant, such as Quicken or Money.

o Limit your credit card applications to two major cards that are widely accepted. This allows you to easily determine your overall credit card monthly spending, know the balance owed, and set a credit limit that matches your income level.

o If you don't record checks when written, use checks that have a stub attached or a check with a carbon copy. You can then record the checks at a later time.

o Most individuals do not understand many aspects of financial planning. You'll wind up much more financially secure if you take charge, consult with a financial expert, and develop a plan.

**Top Financial Questions You Should Ask:**
1. Can you save on a monthly basis?
2. Do you diversify your investments?
3. Do you understand the investments you already own?
4. Are you realistic with your investment growth expectations?
5. Do you minimize investment losses by selling timely?
6. Do you have a retirement strategy/plan and understand how much you need to invest monthly in order to reach your goal?

## Credit Cards

o Paying the minimum amount on your credit card balances every month is the biggest mistake people in debt make, credit counselors say. The less you pay each month, the longer you will be paying off a debt that's costing you up to 24 percent annually in interest. It's best not to carry a balance at all, but if you can't pay the entire balance at once, begin a concerted effort to bring that balance down. Start by sending as much extra money as you can each month to the credit card that charges the highest interest rate. Once you have paid off that card, start sending all the extra money you can each month to the card with the next highest interest rate, and continue the process until you have paid off all your bills.

o While paying off the credit card with the highest interest rate first is the smartest way to go, you may be so overwhelmed by the sheer number of debts you're paying off that you need another tactic to help you feel better. Instead you can send all the extra money you can each month to the smallest bill you have to pay off. That bill should be paid off quickly, giving you a psychological lift as you see you are making progress. Once it's paid off, start sending the extra money to the next smallest bill you have. As you wipe out those debts one by one, you'll feel you're getting control of your credit situation. If that feeling of confidence helps keep you on track to pay down your debts, it's worth the extra interest you might be paying by not concentrating on the highest interest rate first. Ultimately, picking a course of action and sticking to it is the most important element in paying off your debts.

o If your credit card company charges an annual fee, you might be able to get it waived. The credit card business is very competitive, and many companies offer cards that charge an annual fee. If you've been with a card for a while that charges an annual fee, call the company's toll-free customer service number and tell them you'd like to stay with them, but you won't if they continue to charge that fee. Some will waive the fee if asked to by a good customer. If they won't drop the fee, find a no-annual-fee card that offers an equivalent or lower interest rate than your current card.

o Those low introductory credit card rates advertised through the mail last only for a few months. Before signing up and charging a bundle that you can't pay off before the interest rate goes up, read the fine print carefully. Find out how long the interest rate will be low, and how high it will go when it is increased.

o There's a way to use those short-term low-interest-rate offers to pay off a high-interest credit card: if you have a balance on a card with a relatively high interest rate, transfer that balance to a new card that's offering a low introductory rate. Then, pay off the bill while the low rates are still in effect. Once you've paid off your balance, charge only as much as you can pay off at the end of the month, so you don't build up a balance and find yourself in the same situation you just worked out of.

o A credit card that offers a rebate (such as 1 percent of the amount charged), frequent flier points, or other bonuses can be a good deal, as long as you pay your balance off each month. But if you carry a balance on these cards, the bonus is quickly eaten up by interest charges. After all, what good is it to get back 1 percent of what you've purchased if you're paying 18 percent interest on those purchases?

o Check out using a low-interest home equity loan to consolidate charge cards and make the interest deductible.

## Saving and Investing

o Saving is a habit, and like any habit you want to acquire, you can train yourself to save. At first, concentrate on putting aside a few dollars every week. As your nest egg grows, you're likely to find that you feel good about saving, and you'll try harder to save more.

o For most workers, the 401(k) retirement savings plan offered by their employers is the best savings and investment deal around. With a 401(k) plan, you are allowed to invest a certain percentage of your income for retirement. Many companies will match the amount you save, up to a certain point. Say your company has a 50 percent match for the first 5 percent of your salary you put into the 401(k). That means for every $10 you invest, the company puts $5 into your account. That's a 50 percent return on your investment in the first year. You can't beat that anywhere. Plus, the money you put into the 401(k) earns a tax break.

o If your children are of working age and have part-time jobs, Adrian Grant advises encouraging them to set up a Roth IRA, which will build up appreciated income over a long period of time that will never be taxed. Keep in mind that the Roth IRA is not tax deductible.

o The power of compound interest, sometimes referred to as "the magic of compounding," is the *best tool available to the average person for helping your savings grow.* What's compound interest? It means that when you earn interest on money and leave the interest as well as the principal in the account, you'll earn interest on that interest. Each year the amount you are earning interest on will grow, so the amount of interest you receive will be bigger each time. As you continue to add money to the account, the power of compounding just gets stronger.

○ If you take $125 a month and invest it at a 10 percent return (which is a reasonable, long-term average to expect from the stock market), your $125 a month would grow to $25,759 in ten years. In twenty years, it'd be $95,214. And if you invest $125 a month for thirty years, you'd have $282,487—more than a quarter of a million dollars! That's the magic of compound interest and a steady savings habit.

○ Money market accounts, offered by mutual fund and other financial companies, pay much higher interest than a passbook savings account at a bank. The accounts also have check-writing privileges, so you have ready access to your money, something you don't get when you put your savings in a certificate of deposit (CD), which pays comparable interest. The drawback to the accounts is that they require a minimum deposit, often several hundred dollars, and there may be a minimum amount on checks, so you won't be able to write lots of small checks on the account. Money market accounts are a good place to park money you expect to use in the next few months or years, but not money you need to cover daily living expenses. Grant adds, "These accounts are a good place to keep emergency funds, which are usually smaller amounts. However, some money market accounts may not be insured, so you must be aware that there could be a risk. Get the facts."

○ The National Association of Investors Corp. is a nonprofit group dedicated to helping individuals learn about investing in the stock market, mainly through investment clubs. Visit the organization's Web page at www.better-investing.org for information about investing, forming an investment club, or details about chapter activities in your region. Adrian Grant suggests, "You may want to consider a 'DRIP,' which is a dividend reinvestment plan, as a vehicle to purchase stocks directly from a publicly held company without having to pay a commission, instead of having to buy a stock from a stockbroker."

○ Mutual funds have provided a popular opportunity for many investors today. A mutual fund is run by an investment company that takes money from lots of people and uses it to buy stocks or bonds. Each investor is a part owner of all the fund's assets. With a mutual fund, a small investor has the advantages of professional management, which he couldn't afford on his own, and diversification— owning stock in lots of different companies.

○ If you invest in mutual funds, be sure you understand the tax consequences. Some funds have an active turnover ratio that can cause huge capital gains. Be sure to get the facts.

○ Diversification is a strategy to help you weather the ups and downs that all investments experience. You probably know the adage "don't put all your eggs in one basket." When you diversify your investments, you spread your savings over a number of different kinds of "baskets." If one kind of basket (investment) drops in value, it's likely another one will rise in value.

○ Adrian Grant advises, "Make sure you sit down midyear and try to plan for your taxes. Part of financial planning is knowing your projected tax levels at the end of the year and preparing for them."

## Your Credit History/Report

○ Many lenders and employers will look at your credit history before giving you a loan or hiring you. Your credit report, which is compiled by large information services companies that make money by selling the data to creditors, is a history of accounts in your name and how you have paid them off.

○ Because the information contained in your credit report can have a major effect on your financial life, experts recommend you check the data in your report at least once a year. It's especially important to check your report before you apply for a mortgage or other major loan.

○ Credit report companies are listed in the Yellow Pages under "Credit Reporting Agencies." The major companies that compile consumer credit reports are Equifax, Experian, and Trans Union. They maintain toll-free numbers consumers can call to order a copy of their credit report, and you will find these numbers in the phone book.

o In some states, the law allows you to request one free copy of your credit report annually. In other states, the credit reporting agencies are allowed to charge a fee, usually less than $10, for a copy of your report.

o If you have been denied credit or other benefits within the last sixty days because of information contained on your credit file, you are entitled to a free copy of the report.

o Information on the credit report comes mainly from companies that have granted you credit, such as credit card companies, department stores, and other lenders, as well as from courthouse notes. Your credit file can contain information on missed payments and most public record items for seven years. Information about bankruptcies will remain on the report for ten years.

o You have the right to ask the company to investigate information on the report that you believe is incorrect. When you receive a copy of your credit report, you will also receive a form to fill out requesting that the reporting company check out any information that you dispute. Supply as much information as possible to help the agency investigate the situation. If the negative information is found to be accurate, it will remain on your file.

o You may request that the agency send the results of the reinvestigation to organizations that reviewed your credit report in the last six months, or employers who reviewed the report in the last two years.

## Ages and Stages

According to certified financial planner and investment advisor Kay Shirley, in her book *Live Long & Profit* (Dearborn Financial Publishing, 1997), you should pay close attention to each stage of your life and do "decade-by-decade" planning to build financial independence. Here are some important strategies to consider:

o In your twenties: Tone down on the credit cards and invest at least 4 percent of your gross income.

o In your thirties: Maximize your contribution to a tax-deferred savings vehicle; make your car last at least seven years; and don't allocate more than 5 percent of your total invested assets to your company's stock.

o In your forties: You should already have a financial plan, IRA, or retirement plan, and invest at least 12 percent of your gross income for retirement to earn at least 10 percent per year.

o In your fifties: Now is the time to aggressively invest toward retirement. Fifteen percent of your gross income should go to this category, and you should attempt to earn at least 10 percent interest per year.

o In your sixties: Plan on how to stay healthy and live wisely, as well as make plans for a surviving spouse and establish a trust for children. Be sure your credit card balances are zero.

## Web Sites

www.financenter.com
www.smartmoney.com

# Moving to a New Home

It's no secret that we have a very mobile society, but you might be surprised at just how mobile American families really are. According to Census Bureau figures, more than 42 million people moved in just one twelve-month period, from early 1996 to early 1997. That's more than 18 million households. Of those moves, 11.9 million families moved within the same county, 3.4 million moved to another county within the same state, and 2.8 million households moved to another state, according to the American Moving and Storage Association. AMSA represents more than 3,500 member companies in all facets of the moving industry.

While there are many decisions you must make in regard to moving, no matter how you prepare it is still an emotional and stressful situation. The best way to handle a move is to prepare thoroughly, do as much as possible in advance, and choose reputable professionals to help you. Even if you aren't normally a person who relies on lists, you are likely to find that there are so many details involved in a move that making lists is the only way to keep track of everything. Take my mother and father, for example. Months after the move from their home of thirty-five years to a condo, they are still looking for things they aren't sure where they put!

Everything about moving can be disconcerting to the younger members of your family, who may wonder if they will find a new best friend, worry about fitting in at a new school, or fear their favorite pet won't be able to make the move with them. Don't get so caught up in the adult details that you ignore these anxieties. Spend lots of time talking to your kids, calming their fears and encouraging their excitement about the move. If they are old enough, let them help any way they can—packing up some of their belongings, helping to pick out the color of their new room, or perhaps looking at a map with you and determining the best route to take as you drive the family to your new home.

The following tips will help make your move as smooth as possible. It takes a tremendous amount of preparation, but with an organized effort you'll be better prepared for your new home, and months from now you'll be glad you took the time and made the effort.

## Preparing for a Move

o One of the most important ways to plan for your move is to decide what isn't moving with you. The cost of the move will be directly related to how much stuff you actually move, so it's best to pare down your belongings. As soon as you know you will be moving, start going through your family's belongings and weeding out those items that you no longer need or want. Sort through everything you own and decide whether each item should be thrown out, given to charity, sold, or kept. If you have a big "throwaway" pile, call your trash hauler or local sanitation office to arrange a special pickup. Call your favorite charity to see if it can send a truck to pick up your donations. And start planning a garage sale. (Refer to the chapter on garage sales.)

o Videotape or photograph all your belongings that you plan to move. This will serve as an excellent record for you, the movers, and the insurance company, should something be damaged or lost during the move. Put the videotape in a place such as a vault or safe, since it could easily be packed and misplaced.

o Immediately begin a file for all papers and receipts related to the move. Keep it handy and file new documents as soon as you receive them. If it's a corporate transfer, your employer will require these documents to reimburse your expenses. If you are moving for a job, some expenses might be tax deductible. For details, consult your accountant or tax preparer, or read IRS Publication 521, "Moving Expenses." The publication is available on the Internet at www.irs.ustreas.gov, or can be requested free from the IRS forms distribution center, at 1-800-829-3676. For specific tax questions, you can call the IRS's toll-free line at 1-800-829-1040.

o Create a checklist of everything that has to do with your move and keep it on a pad on a clipboard. With all the excitement of a move, you're bound to forget something if you don't write it down.

○ About two months before the move, get estimates from several movers and select the company you want to use. (For tips on selecting a mover, see separate section below.) It's especially important to do this well in advance if you plan to move during June, July, or August, which are by far the busiest months for the moving industry, according to AMSA. In fact, Memorial Day weekend usually has the most moves, the organization said.

○ If at all possible, avoid moving at the beginning or the end of the month, or on a weekend, when moving companies are most often busy. If you can move in the middle of the month and the middle of the week, moving companies have more equipment and manpower available, and they can provide a more definite schedule for picking up household goods, AMSA noted.

○ About six weeks before you move, begin notifying everyone who needs to know of your new address. Banks, insurance companies, and others you do personal business with will need your new address, as will all your friends and relatives. You'll also have to provide a new address to any magazines you subscribe to. You'll find change-of-address forms included in items such as credit card bills, so you can send in a new address along with your monthly payment. Use the toll-free customer service numbers offered by mutual funds and other organizations to notify them. And order some preprinted return address stickers with your new address—these will save you time because you can stick them on change-of-address forms rather than writing out the information each time.

○ You'll also need to notify the Postal Service of your new address at least thirty days in advance. Pick up the necessary forms at any local post office. Check out the agency's Web site at www.usps.gov/moversnet for more details about the process. You can even file a change-of-address form over the Internet.

○ Arrange for your children's school records to be transferred, and start looking for healthcare professionals in your new location about six weeks before you move. That way, you'll be prepared in case an emergency comes up shortly after you move.

○ If you plan to rent a truck and move yourself, call at least a month in advance to reserve. Do your homework. Check out the truck rental company, necessary insurance, and so on. Not all trucks are created equal!

○ If you will be moving long distance, finalize any necessary travel arrangements by making reservations for hotels, airlines, or other services well in advance of your move date.

○ Start using up food you've stocked in your pantry and freezer at least a month before the move. Canned food is heavy, and therefore expensive to move. It's not advisable to move perishable items unless you are going just a short distance and can carry them in a cooler and get them in the freezer of your new home quickly.

○ Three weeks before the move, arrange to have the utilities disconnected in your old home and connected in your new home. Have a cellular phone at the old location just in case you need to be reached. You'll also need to contact the individual companies that provide gas, electric, phone, cable, water, and trash pickup services for your old and new neighborhoods. If you start this process early enough, you can comparison shop and get the best rates. You'll also have to select a long-distance carrier for your new home. If you're not moving far, you might want to have the power remain on in your old house for an additional day or two, so you can return for final cleaning.

○ If you'll be driving a long distance during the move, take your car into the shop and have it serviced a few weeks before the move. You wouldn't want the car to break down in the middle of your big move.

○ A week before your move, transfer all your bank accounts to your new location, and clean out your safety-deposit box. If your mover requires payment in cash or a cashier's check, take care of arrangements while you're at the bank.

○ Two days before you move, empty the freezer and refrigerator, defrost them (if necessary), and dry them out.

## Hiring a Moving Company

○ Get estimates from several companies before choosing a mover. You might ask friends for recommendations, and check with the Better Business Bureau about each company's record. The local

BBB will be listed in your phone book. The American Moving and Storage Association suggests you even visit the movers' place of business before deciding which company to hire.

○ Companies that are licensed interstate household goods carriers and members of the American Moving and Storage Association have agreed to abide by the terms of the organization's published tariffs and to participate in an arbitration program to settle disputes over lost or damaged goods. For a list of members in your area, call AMSA at 1-703-683-7410.

○ If you are moving across state lines, moving companies that give you an estimate are required to give you a consumer booklet, "Your Rights and Responsibilities When You Move," and information about the mover's participation in a dispute settlement program, according to the American Moving and Storage Association.

○ In local moves, movers usually charge by the hour. In interstate moves, the cost of the move is usually based on the weight of your belongings and the distance they are moved. The amount of packing and other services you require will affect the cost of either kind of move. That's why it is important that the estimator see everything you plan to move, including items stashed away in the basement and attic. Be sure to provide additional details they might need to know (such as if your new apartment is on the third floor of a building with no elevator or the new home is on a narrow street) to give you an accurate estimate.

○ There are two kinds of estimates: binding and nonbinding. A binding estimate is a written agreement that guarantees the cost of the move, based on the items to be moved and other services listed on the estimate. Make sure the estimate sheet includes all your property and all services you want the mover to provide—anything added later will result in increased charges and may delay the move, AMSA warns. A nonbinding estimate is an approximate cost, based on a survey of the items to be moved. The final cost will be determined after the shipment is weighed.

○ Ask about arrangements for payment when you get an estimate. Most movers require cash, certified check, or money order. Some will accept credit cards, but it's unlikely that they will accept a personal check. In an interstate move, it's a federal law that you pay the movers before they unload the truck, AMSA notes, so you want to be sure to have the proper form of payment ready.

○ Get the facts ahead of time for whom you would call if the unforeseen happens. What if the truck breaks down? What if a box is damaged? What if your piano is unloaded and they scratch your hardwood floors? What if they damage something? Be prepared and get the facts in writing. Carry the mover's designated contact number with you during your entire move!

○ Be sure to ask your movers what they will and won't do when it comes to reconnecting appliances and electronics. Inquire if there is an additional charge for those services. An electrical plan that has been checked out is a smart move when it comes to plugging things back in. Electrical outlets can be overlooked and overloaded, so be sure to take this into consideration when plugging things into your new home. Don't assume your loaded stereo equipment will be a perfect match for that unassuming outlet in your new living room.

## Packing Tips

○ If the mover is providing packing services, arrange for the packers to come two days before the move.

○ If you are doing the packing yourself, make sure you know how this affects your mover's insurance guarantees. (Don't assume anything and understand your risks.)

○ If packing yourself, start about a month before the move, so you can pack a little when you have time each day. Have plenty of boxes, packing paper, bubble wrap, and other cushioning devices on hand before you start packing. Don't forget you'll need lots of heavy-duty tape and a couple of permanent markers so you can label each box as you pack it.

○ Number each box. Keep a list of how many you have and what's in each one. This will help you when you arrive at the new house to unpack, and will also be a record to help you keep track of everything that moves and to make a claim if anything is lost.

○ In addition to a number, each box should be marked with a destination room, so the movers can put the box where you want it in your new home. Write "Kitchen" or "Master BR" as appropriate, or come up with a simple code (D for dining room, J for Justin's room) and have someone stand by the door as the movers bring the boxes in and direct them to the right location.

○ Be sure to put cushioning material around breakable items. In addition to packing paper, "peanuts," and bubble wrap, consider using towels, linens, and other soft items you have to pack anyway.

○ Remember, if the consumer packs a carton, the moving company is not responsible for damage to the contents unless there is external damage to the carton itself that causes damage to the contents, according to the American Moving and Storage Association. (However, once the company takes possession of any carton, no matter who packed it, it is responsible for loss.)

○ Don't overstuff boxes. A mover has the right to refuse to load a box packed by a customer if he believes it was improperly packed or if he thinks it is overpacked and weighs too much for the carton and to be transported safely, AMSA said.

○ Limit the contents of any box you pack to one room. That way, when you unpack, you won't be running from room to room putting things where they belong.

○ Have rugs and draperies cleaned before the move, and leave them wrapped when they return from the cleaners. The rolled rugs will be easier to handle, and the paper covering will help keep them clean.

○ Don't try to pack and move flammables, such as fireworks, cleaning fluids, acids, chemistry sets, aerosol cans, nonrefillable propane tanks, and ammunition, AMSA said. Safely discard such items, and buy new ones when you're in your new location. Refillable propane gas tanks can be moved, but they must be purged and sealed by a local propane gas dealer.

○ Drain fuel from lawn mowers and other machinery, and discard partly used cans of oil, paint, thinner, and other substances that might leak; don't try to move them. Check with your local sanitation office for rules on how to dispose of such items safely.

○ Don't wax or oil wooden antiques or fine furniture before the move. Some products may soften the wood, making it vulnerable to imprinting from furniture pads, AMSA said.

○ Some appliances may need to be serviced or professionally

prepared before you move. The motor in your clothes dryer may need to be checked and secured, for example, and your clothes washer may also need to have the tumbler protected and fastened in place. AMSA advises consumers to contact an appliance dealer or authorized service provider with questions about preparing appliances for a move.

○ Freezers and refrigerators must be completely defrosted and dried before the move. Leave the doors open for several hours after defrosting to air the appliance out and avoid musty odors. All pans, trays, shelves, and other removable parts should be taken out and packed separately. The motor on these appliances may need to be bolted, too, according to AMSA. Contact your dealer or service provider for details.

○ Wrap lamp shades separately in clean packing paper, and pack a few of them in a large box so they won't get crushed.

○ Ask your mover if you can leave clothing in the dresser drawers. This will save you time packing and unpacking. You'll probably have to take the drawers out of the casework, carry each to the truck separately, then put the drawers back in.

○ Invest in some wardrobe boxes—the tall ones with the rod for hanging clothes. This way, you can transport your clothing directly from the closet to the box, without removing hangers and folding individual pieces of clothing. They'll arrive with fewer wrinkles, too.

○ If you are worried about legs of chairs getting scratched during the move, put an old sock on each leg to cover and protect it.

## Loss and Damage Protection

○ All moving companies are required to assume liability for the value of the goods they transport, the American Moving and Storage Association says. However, there are several different levels of protection the consumer can choose, all coming with different price tags.

○ The most basic protection, released value, comes at no cost to you. Under this option, the mover assumes liability of no more than 60 cents per pound for each article. That means if something is damaged or lost, the settlement is based on the weight of the article multiplied by 60 cents. If a ten-pound stereo component that cost you $1,000 was lost, the mover would be liable for no more than $6. To accept this very minimal protection, you must sign a specific statement on the bill of lading agreeing to it, AMSA says.

○ The next level of protection is declared value. Under the option, the entire value of your shipment is determined by the total weight multiplied by $1.25 a pound. A 4,000-pound shipment would have a maximum liability value of $5,000. Any claim under this option is based on the depreciated value of the lost or damaged goods, up to the maximum amount based on the weight of the shipment. So if a $1,000 TV was lost, the mover would be liable for up to $1,000, based on the depreciated value. The mover can charge you $7 for each $1,000 of liability for shipments transported with this option. For $5,000 of protection, the mover could charge $35.

○ Under lump sum value protection, you can obtain additional liability protection by declaring a specific dollar value for your shipment. The value must exceed $1.25 a pound times the weight of the shipment, and the mover can charge you $7 for each $1,000 of coverage.

○ Many movers offer "full value replacement" coverage. Under this option, articles that are lost, damaged, or destroyed are repaired or replaced, or you will receive a cash settlement, based on the current replacement value of the items, regardless of the age of the original item. The cost for this protection varies, and may be subject to deductibles, similar to an insurance policy. Ask your movers for details about the plan they offer.

○ If you ship an article of extraordinary value—any item whose value exceeds $100 per pound—you must specifically list it on the shipping documents. AMSA suggests asking your mover for a complete explanation of this rule before moving day, because movers can limit their liability for such items if they are not properly declared.

○ AMSA has a dispute settlement program that provides neutral arbitration when a shipper and a customer cannot work out a claim regarding lost or damaged property that was in an interstate move. For more information about this program, you can consult

AMSA's page on the Internet at www.amconf.org or write to American Moving and Storage Association, 1611 Duke Street, Alexandria, VA 22314, and request details.

## The Night Before

o Create a schedule that outlines your "to do" list for the day of the move. Consider everything from where you will eat breakfast and lunch to who is in charge of each aspect of the move. Make yourself a list of all the things you must do to get the day off to a great start, including everyone's responsibilities.

o Keep all important papers, moving contracts, and phone numbers on a clipboard for easy access. Tie a pen to the clipboard and keep it with you at all times during the move.

o Select and set aside the clothing you'll wear the next day for a quick getaway. Also make up a "to go" bag filled with your toothbrush and any important daily medications.

o Have a cooler with ice packs ready to move those last-minute refrigerated items. Add some bottled water and snacks, especially if the ride is long.

o For last-minute cleaning, keep a broom, clean rags, and a few cleaning supplies in a bucket in case of an emergency. You'll especially appreciate this when you move into your new home and need a quick cleanup before putting a heavy piece of furniture in its permanent place.

## The Big Day

o Pack towels, sheets, and other items you will need as soon as you get to your new home in an "open me first" box. Or consider using an empty clothes hamper, which might be visually easier to locate among your belongings than an individual box would be.

o Assign at least one adult to be in the home to answer questions and give directions to the movers.

o If possible, take younger children and pets to a friend's or neighbor's home while the truck is loaded. They'll have a better time, and you won't have to worry about their wandering away through an open door or getting in the movers' way.

o If you are transporting any of your belongings yourself, place them in your car before the movers arrive, if possible, or put them out of the way so the mover won't accidentally load the goods on the van.

o Read all documents carefully before you sign them, and keep the bill of lading and inventory with you until your possessions are delivered, the charges are paid, and any claims are settled.

o Before the van leaves, take a final look throughout the house to make sure nothing has been left behind.

o If it's a long-distance move, make sure the driver and van line know how to reach you during the move.

o Be on hand at the new home to supervise unloading and unpacking of your goods. Check the number of each box against your inventory list as it is brought into the house.

o As the boxes are unloaded, check carefully for any that appear to be damaged, and check the contents of those cartons. If anything is lost or damaged, report the facts promptly and in detail on the van driver's copy of the inventory before you sign it.

o If you notice damage after unpacking, a claim must be filed within nine months, but it's smart to do it as soon as possible. The mover must acknowledge receipt of your claim within thirty days and must deny or make an offer within 120 days of receiving your claim, AMSA says.

o To save both time and money, it sometimes pays to have an interior designer or a friend (with excellent taste) on hand to give you advice or a second opinion when placing very heavy, hard-to-move furniture. A few hours of their advice on moving day will pay off later, when you don't have to move these pieces again and again. You could also have a scaled placement drawing done ahead of time to make sure all your furniture will fit properly.

o Pay very close attention to papers you sign and things you do on moving day. Read between the lines before you sign any documents that state your belongings have arrived in good condition. Fully understand all policies and procedures, since you often don't know what's in good condition until you unpack it.

o Point out any problems that you noticed occurred during the move and make a written record of these. Make sure you note any and all problems or damaged goods or boxes when taking an inventory of your list. Based on the moving company's claims procedure, be sure to make a detailed report immediately about anything missing or damaged. Submit your claim based on the mover's guidelines for a timely resolution.

## Web Sites

www.RelocationCentral.com—check out this online guide for anyone who is moving. Helpful tips and relocation advice are organized by city and categories of interest, from apartments to zoos.

# New Moms

Congratulations! If you're about to become a new mother or father, you're in for the most exciting time of your life. To paraphrase the Marines' slogan, "It's the toughest job you'll ever love." And while love, patience, and lots of hugs are the backbone of motherhood, as with any other job a little ingenuity, organization, and planning are always wise.

We all know parents who say, "I never have a moment to myself," or "I haven't been able to get a thing done ever since the baby was born." Yet, while young children do require a lot of hours of the day (what an understatement!), clever mothers and fathers have been juggling motherhood and fatherhood, hobbies, work—or just keeping up with current events—for years. One way is to make the most of nursings or nap time. Another is to get baby involved in what you're doing, so that he plays with pots and pans on the floor while you do the dishes, or he sits on a blanket in the shade while you pull weeds in the garden. Like everything else in life, it's all a balance and knowing what works in your particular situation.

More than any other time in your life, you'll want to become as efficient as possible, so you have plenty of time to play with your baby—or, once he's asleep, catch up on what used to make you happy. Most important, though, it's a time to lower your standards; meals can be less than gourmet—or even takeout—for instance, and laundry often piles up. Don't be hard on yourself. Your most important job right now is being Mom or Dad!

While this chapter was written with a slew of tips for moms, you'll also find a section of great tips for dads included.

## Before Baby Arrives

○ Pick out birth announcements now. Some stationery stores let you order the announcement in advance, so you can determine wording for all but the baby's name, date, and time of birth. You can simply call in or fax the remaining information after baby has arrived. One call—that's all! If you really enjoy doing things ahead of time, you can preaddress the envelopes as well.

○ While at the store, it's a good idea to order personalized or monogrammed stationery for thank-you notes. Most likely you'll have a lot of them to write, so pick up plenty of stamps, too.

○ Interview baby nurses, often called "doulas," if you need help after the baby comes. To find prospective candidates, look in the Yellow Pages or check out free local parenting publications for ads. Also, gather names of maid services, diaper services, and any other helpful folks you might need. Get up-to-date references and make sure you check their past history very carefully.

○ Choose a pediatrician. Like other professionals, the best ones often come by word-of-mouth. It's still a good idea to interview a prospective physician face-to-face. Some questions to ask: How many medical staffers are in your practice? Who covers for you on weekends? What are your credentials, and are you board certified? How do you handle emergencies? Who will I see if you're busy? If I am experiencing a problem or have a concern with the office, who do I call? It's always a good idea to discuss your philosophies on bottle- vs. breast-feeding, vaccinations, circumcision, and other topics to make sure you're compatible.

○ Be on the lookout for free baby samples and parenting publications at your obstetrician's office. Investigate reading material that will help raise your confidence level.

○ Yard sales are a great place to pick up inexpensive baby items; however, you must be very careful, since many products used over time could be hazardous, and some are even recalled due to safety problems. (Also beware when buying used safety-oriented items, such as car seats that may turn out to be damaged or outdated.)

○ Do cook casseroles or anything else that freezes well in advance. You'll be awfully glad one day at 6 P.M. when you're too busy with baby to cook dinner. Similarly, gather menus of take-out restaurants and delivery services to have on hand. Some women who are having their second (or later) child ask friends to give freezable meals as gifts instead of baby "staples."

○ Be photo-savvy. Have plenty of film ready for baby's first hours and days. Choose a film that does well in low light (such as ASA 400) to compensate for hospitals' lighting. Also, don't forget to take a picture of the nursery now (before toys get thrown about!) and of you, in all your pregnant glory.

○ Read as much as you can on childbirth. If you haven't already taken a course, look into that; many courses these days are for couples, and also accommodate working parents' schedules.

○ Practice the drive to the hospital. Investigate different routes in case you face rush-hour traffic. Many hospitals offer tours of the obstetrics department, a good way to get the ins and outs of a better stay.

○ Don't forget your pets. Before baby arrives, take any pets to the veterinarian for updated shots and a checkup. Consider obedience training for any puppies that have had no such education. Some people have had luck introducing doll babies to pets as a way to get them used to the idea. And by all means, have the new father bring home a blanket or burp cloth the baby has been next to so that the house dog can get used to the smell.

○ Determine if you'll breast- or bottle-feed in advance so you can dictate your wishes immediately after delivery. Pediatricians almost unanimously recommend breast-feeding as best for baby—and Mom. Check out books from your local library or pick up one at your bookstore so that you'll be informed and ready when the time comes. If you plan to breast-feed, you might want to buy nursing bras and nursing tops in advance.

○ Pick a name for baby! As obvious as it seems, many, many couples don't give this much thought until after baby is born. And while that works for some people (and others like to see what baby looks like to help choose a name), it's always a good idea to have a few choices picked out ahead of time. Don't forget a middle name.

○ Pamper yourself now. Have your pregnancy books suggested you sleep all you can now, in a "just you wait . . ." tone? Well, it's certainly a good idea to be as well rested as possible for those first few weeks. In fact, now's the time to do things you may not have time to later: get your hair cut, stock up on staples for the house, read a novel, and just watch a few movies. A few fitting choices to rent: *Baby Boom, Nine Months, She's Having a Baby, Three Men and a Baby*, and *Parenthood*.

○ Make your telephone list to take to the hospital. After birth (or even the hectic time surrounding adoption), you'll be glad you have a list of people to call. Rank them in order of importance so that calls can be done a few at a time in the proper order.

○ Pack a bag for the hospital. Some items to include: a robe (you probably will want to use the hospital's gown), slippers, an extra pillow, makeup, skin moisturizers, socks (it can be cold there), shampoo, other toiletries, baby books, a cassette or CD player with music, and a quasi-maternity outfit for going home. (You won't be ready for your old jeans yet, but most "tent" clothes will seem ridiculous.)

○ Buy a baby car seat. You can't take a baby home from the hospital without a rear-facing infant car seat. You'll also need a blanket or two and an outfit for the baby. Choose something with "legs," since the car seat's seat belt straddles the legs.

## When Baby Comes Home

○ Don't expect to be Supermom! Line up people to help you the first few days, and don't feel bad if you're blue, cranky, or weepy. Hormones do amazing things to new mothers, but most likely you'll feel better soon.

○ Keep a diary of your early days with baby, something you'll cherish for years.

○ Don't weigh yourself for a month or so. It took months for you to get the size you were, so it will take time to get back in shape, also. Consider investing in a few "transition" outfits, loose-fitting clothes for the first few months.

○ Take lots of pictures. As quickly as babies grow, you'll want to photograph him at least once a week for the first few months. A fun way to chronicle his growth is to photograph him next to a large stuffed animal or some other oversized toy every few months. You'll be amazed at how quickly baby changes. (So make sure you date the backs of all pictures.)

○ Join a support group of other new mothers or parents. You'll appreciate the exchange of ideas and empathy for frustrations. Similarly, investigate exercise classes that let you bring baby to class.

○ Relax your standards. If you're used to making a "to do" list every day, change the frequency to once a week. Send photo postcards of baby instead of long letters (ask at your photo developing store about postcard stick-ons that adhere to photos).

○ Make the most of nighttime feedings. Tape favorite TV shows that come on while you're busy bathing baby to watch later. It's also a good time to play old records you enjoyed in college or to find a new radio channel to listen to.

○ Keep a diaper bag packed at all times so that you and baby can be spontaneous. Include diapers, wipes, a changing pad, a plastic bag for dirty diapers, a change of clothes for baby, toys, and feeding supplies. If you're nursing, don't forget snacks or bottled water for you, too.

○ Experiment with ways to reduce the crying. Any time baby is crying, you first must examine if his needs are being met. Is he hungry? Have a dirty diaper? Is he too cold? Once you've determined that he's okay, try these time-tested soothers: rock him in a rocker or side to side, swaddle him in a blanket, go for a walk with a baby carrier or stroller, try him in a baby swing, burp him to relieve gas, play music, or go for a ride in the car (car seat buckled up, of course!).

○ Always put baby to sleep on his back or side, according to the American Academy of Pediatrics. According to studies, this helps reduce the risk of SIDS (sudden infant death syndrome).

○ Start the baby-proofing process. Even when your infant is very young, it's a good idea to read up on childproofing—cover all electrical outlets with plastic inserts, install childproof cabinet locks on doors with toxic or breakable items inside, and remove dangerous cords.

○ The best advice? Supervise baby at all times. Even an intercom will do the trick if baby's sleeping and you must be in the next room or kitchen.

○ Give in to some of baby's inquisitiveness. Since little ones will inevitably want to explore, dedicate areas of the house as baby's own safe places. This could be one kitchen drawer (a bottom one?) that holds plastic containers, wooden spoons, and other unbreakable items. Once he has the urge to climb, you can help make a "mountain" of pillows for him to play on, rather than the sofa next to the coffee table that could be dangerous.

## Time to Play—Fun with Baby

○ Surround baby with what he can best see now. Young babies respond best to black and white and red, so make your own flash cards by cutting out pictures from magazines in these colors (or draw your own with magic markers) and hang them around the crib or in front of his car seat. Babies love faces, also—especially other babies'.

○ Let a mirror be "baby television." Attach an unbreakable mirror in baby's crib. You can also prop him in front of a mirror in his infant seat or bouncy seat so that he gets to know himself. You'll soon find that many of babies' favorite forms of entertainment don't cost much.

○ Exercise with your baby. Lie on your back and lift him up and down gently from your chest to strengthen upper arms (you'll need it!). You can also set baby against your legs while you do sit-ups. Make sure baby does his exercises, too. You help his legs "ride bicycle" while on his back or carefully stretch his arms over his head during the "so big" game.

○ Stimulate baby in small ways. Just simply moving him to different parts of the house makes life more interesting for him. Tell him what you're doing throughout the day, also. Studies now confirm that lots of talking, singing, and, of course, hugs and kisses considerably help child development in the first three years of life.

○ Music can soothe the savage beast (or baby). Expose your child to different types of music. Dance with him, which is fun for him and exercise for you.

○ Look for "toys" around your house. As your baby gets older, you can fashion amusements from mundane items. All sorts of boxes and other containers can keep baby busy opening and closing. Clean socks can be rolled up into balls.

○ It's never too early to expose baby to museums. Put him in a baby carrier or stroller and roam the halls of your favorite educational place. (Most museums have one afternoon a week that is free; check your local newspaper.)

○ Start the baby-sitter search soon and get to know the baby-sitter even before the baby arrives! Every parent is nervous the first time away from baby. It can also be nerve-racking finding the right sitter. Since people are sometimes hesitant to give away names of their good sitters, investigate opportunities at your local college. Some sororities run baby-sitting services; nursing programs may even have bulletin boards dedicated to baby-sitting notices.

○ Start a baby-sitting co-op. To cut down on the cost of sitters, consider swapping out baby-sitting services with another couple. They get a night out while you watch their child, then you get your turn next week.

## Getting the Right Start: Recommendations from the American Academy of Pediatrics

○ The backseat is the safest place for children to ride in the car. The American Academy of Pediatrics (AAP) urges that all infants under 20 pounds and one year of age should ride in rear-facing car seats; children over 20 pounds and one year of age or older can ride in forward-facing car seats.

○ The AAP strongly encourages breast-feeding for virtually all infants as the exclusive feeding for six months, continuing with complementary foods for at least the first year of life.

○ Infants weaned before twelve months of age should not receive cow's milk but should receive iron-fortified infant formula.

○ Healthy infants should be put down to sleep on their backs, based on an evaluation of current SIDS (sudden infant death syndrome) data. Despite common belief, there is no evidence that choking is more frequent among infants lying on their backs when compared to other positions.

○ Because the sun's rays are strongest between midmorning and midafternoon (approximately 10 A.M.–4 P.M.), it is best to keep children out of the sun during this time period. Since this is not always possible, always use a sunscreen formulated specifically for babies (with a sun protection factor—SPF—of at least 15) to block damaging ultraviolet rays. Apply the protection a half hour before going outside, and reapply every few hours or as directed.

o The AAP strongly urges parents who smoke to quit. Children of parents who smoke have more respiratory infections, bronchitis, pneumonia, and reduced pulmonary function than children of nonsmokers.

o The AAP feels there is little justification for infant swimming programs, and, in fact, parents may develop a false sense of security if they think their infant can "swim" a few strokes. Parents should never—even for a moment—leave children alone near open water in homes (bathtubs, toilets, or buckets), as well as pools or lakes.

o Parents should learn CPR and keep emergency equipment and a telephone close at hand.

## Resources

o The American Academy of Pediatrics will send free brochures on a variety of subjects, such as nutrition, child care, and first aid. For a complete list of brochures or to receive one, send a self-addressed, business-size stamped envelope to:

American Academy of Pediatrics
Dept. C
141 Northwest Point Blvd.
P.O. Box 927
Elk Grove Village, IL 60009-0927

La Leche League (a support group for nursing mothers)
P.O. Box 4079
Schaumburg, IL 60168
1-800-LALECHE

o A number of Web sites offer help to parents, from picking a name to buying a baby swing to solving behavioral problems. Some to check out include:

www.iVillage.com
www.babycenter.com
www.parentsoup.com
www.thebabynet.com
www.childbirth.org
www.parentsplace.com
www.storksite.com
www.family.com

## Books

○ *What to Expect When You're Expecting,* revised ed., Arlene Eisenberg, Heidi E. Murkoff, Sandee E. Hathaway (New York: Workman Publishing, 1994).

○ *Good Behavior: Over 1,200 Sensible Solutions to Your Child's Problems from Birth through Age Twelve.* Stephen W. Garber, Ph.D., Marianne Garber, Ph.D., and Robyn Freedman Spizman (New York: St. Martin's Press, 1987).

# Organizing

We all know there are fabulous benefits to getting organized, but few of us really take the time to stay organized on a daily basis. For every file we have, there's a pile of something standing by needing our attention. What you might not fully realize about getting organized is that it's definitely a skill that can greatly contribute to the well-being and effectiveness of your life. Chronically disorganized people have more stress, lose more time, and often even have more negativity in their life. So what are you waiting for?

Betsy Wilkowsky, a member of the National Association of Professional Organizers (NAPO), an organization dedicated to all phases of organizing, advises, "Clutter is just delayed decision making. The reason people have clutter is that they choose, for whatever reason, conscious or unconscious, not to put something away. Things pile on top of things and on top of things. Before you know it, the pile is a foot high and you can't remember what's in it. Many people don't put things away because they don't have a system."

## Controlling Paper

○ There are different types of paper that must be read, filed, paid, saved, or discarded. It's critical to understand these types of paper to help get organized.

○ You will do a better job of handling paper and getting organized if you designate a work space for handling paper with all of your tools nearby, including scissors, tape, stapler, highlighter, paper clips, and files.

○ A filing system is the key to gaining control of paper. Name files by the theme and subject, such as bank account, credit cards, computer. Always choose a noun or proper noun when naming the file, and use the last name or name of a company for proper nouns.

○ Filing systems must be alphabetized to really work. If you can't quickly find a file, it will no longer be an organizational tool. Take the time to file something correctly the first time.

○ Have a file for each family member, and keep important records (for example, birth certificates, passports, marriage licenses) in a safe or metal box for safe storage. Store a set of backup copies in another place that's safe and sound.

○ Keep a few of your most frequently utilized files in a vertical sorter on your desk, in a basket, or at the front of your filing system.

○ Use a special color ink for the file header or a visual or sticker next to a file name to locate it quickly.

○ Eighty percent of the paper put in file cabinets is never looked at again. Be selective about what you file. Ask yourself, "What's the worst thing that could happen if I throw this away?" If you can live with the consequences, then toss it.

○ Add an expiration date to the papers you file so that you know when to get rid of them.

○ An index helps you keep up with files. As you add a file, put the file's name on a master list and keep it at the front of your file cabinet.

○ Warranties are usually very bulky and have accompanying booklets. Store them in a separate place that's easy to locate. Prior to filing them, put the date you purchased the item and the room it's in. You'll be surprised how many out-of-date warranty booklets you end up with over time if you don't update this file regularly as appliances and electrical items change.

○ Consider color coding files. Divide your papers into major categories and assign a color to each category. Use a maximum of six colors. This helps with easy identification.

○ Keep a master calendar for your family and save important invitations in a specific place that go with the dates recorded.

○ Handle your mail only once. Open the daily mail over the wastebasket. Either organize it or discard it—nothing in between!

Have a place for each type of paper and immediately put it where it belongs:

1. Bills or checks. An accordion file might be ideal for you, while a more elaborate system might also work.
2. Invitations. Write the event on your master calendar and then put the invitation in a clear plastic envelope in your address drawer to be saved for future reference. If there is a reply card, respond immediately.
3. Junk mail. Either discard it or put it in the "read later" file.

o Discard any paper you really don't need. Take a look at the paper you save. Sweepstakes entries? Junk mail? Coupons? If you don't have an organized place to put it, throw it out! You can cut down on junk mail by requesting the removal of your name from junk mail lists. Write a letter requesting this to the Direct Marketing Association. Include a self-addressed, stamped envelope and request the appropriate form. Its address is:

Mail Preference Service
Direct Marketing Association
P.O. Box 9008
Farmingdale, NY 11735-9008

o Consider keeping a tickler file for papers with dates and deadlines that you deal with later. A traditional tickler file consists of files labeled 1 through 31 for each day of the current month and files labeled January through December. Ask yourself, "when am I going to deal with this?" File papers based on the day you plan to do the action. You must check it every day. If you cannot complete a task on the assigned day, move it to the next available day you have time to work on it.

o Cluster like actions together to get you organized. For example, file things that need to be paid together, filed together, and read together.

## Reducing Clutter

○ Clutter can be reduced only if you agree to bring in less than you take out. The most successful thing you can do is take out something old when you bring in something new. Purchase a new book? Donate a few old ones to a good cause.

○ You should have an annual purge day to toss, recycle, donate.

○ Get rid of things that don't work. If you have a pen that doesn't write, throw it away. Have a stapler that always jams? Get rid of it!

○ Keep one master calendar for all activities for both business and personal. Write everything in pencil because you'll save time and white-out!

○ When scheduling an appointment, write in the person's telephone number and you won't spend time hunting for the number if the appointment needs to be changed.


## Reducing Your Reading File

○ It's not a surprise that we are in information overload. Be more selective about what you read. Make a decision to choose things that you are really interested in, and focus.

○ When you get a magazine, scan the table of contents. Clip the articles of interest. If you don't have time to read them, put them in a tray or file labeled "To Read" or "Read Later." If there are pages of rooms or interiors you particularly enjoy looking at, clip the pages and file them in a picture file for future decorating tips and ideas.

○ Stop the subscriptions on magazines and newspapers that are not being read. If you cancel them, you should get a prorated refund.

○ Bring reading material along with you when you'll have spare time to read it. Keep reading material in your briefcase if you carry one. Avoid office lobby materials. Use waiting time to catch up on your reading.

○ Read or listen to books on tape in the car, train, or airplane.

## Drawers

○ Drawers are important space, so don't misuse them. Not only do they keep things out of sight, but they also keep them out of mind. Name each drawer and know what you plan to put in it. Don't overload them with junk; rather, use them for a purpose.

○ Use drawer dividers. You must divide and conquer to conquer anything at all.

○ Everyone needs a junk drawer for odds and ends, but limit what you put in it. Dump it out on a towel to sort items and get your act cleaned up quickly. If you shove things around, you'll never get organized. Only by reducing what's there and keeping like things together will you be able to see what's even in the drawer.

○ Clean out your junk drawer while you're on the telephone to save time.

## Closets

○ You must try on everything in your closet at least once! That's what the experts say. If you want to have an organized closet, pull everything out and try it on; this usually works whether you keep it or not. You then have three choices: donate it, update it, or wear it within six months or start all over. If you haven't worn something in a year's time but are still convinced you'll wear it again or it's timeless, keep it for one year and try this closet rule again. After that, odds are it's history.

○ Hang a shopping bag on the back of the door in your clothing closet. If you don't have time to clean out your closet all at once, each and every time you try on something that doesn't fit or flatter you, put it in the bag to give away or sell at a consignment store. Before you know it, you will have cleaned out your closet. (Once you have enough items, consider having a garage sale; see "Garage Sales.")

○ Keep matching hangers hung in all the same directions. This gives you more space, since clothing will fit closer together and matching hangers even help your closet look more attractive.

o Dust your closet on a regular basis. If dust builds up on your clothing, it can ruin it. Move things around regularly.

o Arrange your shoes with the right toe facing in and then the left toe facing out. This little trick will save you more room!

o Add shelving to your closet wherever you can, such as an upper shelf above your hangers for purses and small things you wish to store, or consider other space-saving gadgets for walls, including a row of hooks for belts and accessories.

o Don't forget the back of the door. There are many gadgets that hang over the door or attach to it that can offer new organizing options. Hangers that attach by placing them right over the top of the door can hold your clothes that you select to wear for the next day, dry cleaning items, or other clothes. From cap racks to laundry bags, there is a super selection of space savers for every closet door. Check them out!

## Kitchen

o Space makers and organizational gadgets can transform a kitchen. Visit your local hardware store and check out the options, and bring along your measurements. Ask for a salesperson and get his help in planning a more organized cabinet.

o Clear off the counters for a clutter-free appearance. You'll have more preparation space and your kitchen will have fewer objects that collect dust, so you'll save time cleaning.

o Get rid of things you don't use. Most people have kitchen gadgets, containers, and objects they've never used and still are saving for a rainy day. By now most of these items are outdated and some might not even work. Consider how much organizational space you'll gain if you clean out your kitchen.

o Choose smaller versions of your electrical kitchen appliances. Instead of an electric can opener, you can have a manual can opener. Or instead of a large twelve-cup coffeemaker, purchase an eight-cup one.

o Keep all like things together. This rule works everywhere in the kitchen and will help you get and stay organized! From organizing pots and pans to grouping like foods together even in the refrigerator, keep this one thought in mind. Place all your salad dressings on the door of the refrigerator and all your fruit in the fruit drawer. Plastic bowls and containers can be grouped together, as well as aluminum foil and plastic wraps.

o Place the food with the nearest expiration date in the front of the refrigerator or cabinets. Organizing expiration dates will help you avoid wasting food and make sure you use what's good before it spoils.

## Desk

o When it comes to files, don't pile files—go vertical. Put an incline sorter on your desk so you can see everything. Remember, if you pile things, you can't see them.

o Have a space and place for everything, and be religious about putting things back in place. If the scissors go in the top drawer, then stick to the plan.

o Use clear file folders and envelopes to hold address books, coupons, or any items you refer to regularly, like schedules, warranties, and invitations. I organize all of my directories and loose papers that I need to save in see-through containers. They are my best weapons against clutter and disorganization.

o At the end of each day, spend five to ten minutes clearing your desk and preparing yourself for the next day. This is how the really organized succeed!

## Resources

If you can't get yourself organized, there are professionals who can help you. NAPO stands for National Association of Professional Organizers and their address is:

1033 La Posada Drive
Suite 220
Austin, TX 78752
1-512-206-0151
E-mail: napo@assnmgmt.com
Web site: www.napo.net

# Painting

Hiring a painter sounds like an easy task. You ask a neighbor who painted his house recently, or you see a sign on a friend's front lawn and inquire about the work. Claims like *dependable painting for over 20 years* sound good, but if it were only that easy! While there are many reliable and dependable painters available, finding one with an outstanding track record should be your goal. By doing your homework you can avoid costly errors, even a real nightmare.

The first mistake most people make when hiring a painter is that they trust the person they meet. Take it from me, trust has nothing to do with it. Getting smart and staying smart is key to being an educated consumer. Recently a friend of mine trusted the painters who painted her next-door neighbor's house. She gave them the keys to the house so they could come and go while she worked, and advanced them the money to buy all the paint for the entire job. They took everything down off the walls, moved all the furniture to the middle of each room, covered it with layers of plastic, and next thing she knew, the painters were history and never called or came back.

Sounds like a horror story, but it's true. The owners had a contract, but they hadn't done their homework. These painters weren't bonded or insured, and while they did a terrific job for one family in another neighborhood, they actually had a track record of previous problems. The purpose of this story is not to scare you, but rather to illustrate that trusting someone to do what he says he is going to do is not good enough. You must take the proper precautions and measures to protect your home, family, and finances.

## Hiring a Painter

o Never hire a painter without getting all the particulars. Test every telephone number given you and check all references. Don't just accept the fact that he did a good job. Inquire if the painter was on time, reliable, and finished in a timely manner. You'll be surprised what you learn when you read between the lines.

○ Make sure the painters you retain are bonded and insured. If they get hurt on your job, you could be liable and responsible for their medical bills and subject yourself to a huge problem. Check out your insurance and theirs, too!

○ Ask the painter for a paint store reference where he or she purchases the paint. This is a good idea since the paint store would know if that painter hasn't paid his bills or if there has been a history of problems.

○ Inquire exactly who will be working on your job. Some painters contract jobs to other painters or have a stable of workers that they use and you might not get the person you actually met with. Find out the names and get the facts on who will be doing your work. Meet your employees face-to-face.

○ Make sure you know the point person on your job. Who is responsible for the crew, your house, and the paint purchases? In the event of a problem, who do you call?

○ Discuss with your painter lunch breaks and other important details, like what happens if he has to leave your house and you are not there. Who locks it up at the end of the day? Get a schedule of what you can expect and what the painter's expectations of you are, as well.

○ When you interview a painter, ask him how he would handle a few problem areas. Sometimes old caulking needs to be removed and redone before new paint is applied. Learn how he would prevent future problems. A job well done is a job done well!

○ Choose a painter who is working on only one job at a time so he can give you his full, undivided attention, while also finishing as soon as possible. Get the exact hours he will be at your location and an expected completion date.

○ In the event your painter is working on more than one job, be sure to find out where else he will be working, just in case you need him!

○ Make sure you spell out your likes and dislikes when it comes to your home. If you have allergies or have a rule against smoking, then make sure your painters know this. It's also important to tell them where they can eat when they take a break. One painter left soda bottles and candy bar wrappers in our friend's basement, which attracted bugs for weeks. Not a pretty picture!

## Choosing the Paint

o Find out the exact type of paint your painter is using and do some homework. Go to the paint store where it is sold and inquire how well it cleans up if the wall gets dirty. If in doubt, purchase a small can and try your own smudge test. If you have kids or pets, choose a paint that will rise to the occasion.

o Try it out! Paint has a personality and doesn't always look the same once it's applied. For example, the higher the gloss or sheen, the more wall imperfections will show up. Some colors take on a new hue once they are used in certain light. Get the scoop on the paint you choose and try a sample before making a final decision. That shade of blue just might not be what you're looking for!

## Contracting the Job

o Everything you and your painter agree on should be in writing. From floor cloths to the type of paint and number of coats he will do, don't take anything for granted.

o Put into writing a payment schedule that directly relates to the success of the job. It's best to make a small down payment and then pay the rest of the money upon complete satisfaction and a walk-through of your job.

o Some painters don't cover carpet, marble, or wood floors while painting, and paint can do a lot of damage. Include in your contract that all flooring will be covered properly. I suggest all flooring be completely covered with heavy brown paper and taped around the edges to avoid any problems.

o Painter's ladders and metal buckets can scratch the floor, even through paper coverings. Be sure your painters will use cloths as extra protection under all potentially harmful objects, including ladders, paint cans, and tools. Have a stack of old towels handy just in case.

○ Some painters use old, dirty paint cloths to cover your beautiful furniture. Request clean, unused plastic and get the facts on how they will protect your belongings while painting.

○ When hiring a painter or any contractor, never pay them in full ahead of time—*never, ever, ever.* Pay along the way based on performance, and consider withholding a specific amount until the job is satisfactorily completed.

○ Not every painter includes moving your furniture or re-hanging your art. Check out exactly what services your painter will provide when working at your house.

○ Painters will move your furniture, and unless you take photographs of the exact placement or place tape where things go, you'll be totally lost when putting things back. If you have a lot of artwork, let the painter paint over the hook and not remove it. Trying to get art back in the exact same place can be hazardous to the walls and a time-consuming headache!

○ Find out exactly how many coats of paint your contractor is going to apply. Sometimes a wall needs more than two coats of paint because you are covering a darker color. Be sure you will not be charged extra if a color doesn't cover the wall. Paint adds up.

○ If bookshelves or other furniture are not attached to the wall and need to be painted, inquire if there's any additional charge. Sometimes a painter will add a fee if an item needs to be taken out to be painted and then reinstalled. Make sure you know what is being painted and what is included.

## Things You Should Know about Painting

○ Every time a painter changes rooms where another color will be used, make sure you are present to approve the exact paint. You can save everyone valuable time and expensive paint if you check to see that the right color is going in the right place.

○ Remove all of your toiletries, valuables, and other items you care about and place them away from the path of paint. Paint can often splatter and painters are there to do a job. Anything that gets in their way might not be handled as you'd want it to be.

○ Even if you buy all the paint from the same company and it's mixed at the same time, the color could still differ from can to can. Make sure your painter mixes all the paint for one room in a separate container.

○ Matching colors later on can be difficult. Purchase an extra can of paint for every color used in your home, and mark every paint with the formula and the room it was used in.

○ Keep a master list of the formulas and rooms in which each paint was used for future reference. Save the exact number and paint chip to remind you of each color.

○ When matching colors even with the same formula, sample a small area before applying it everywhere. Approve the match and then give the painter the go-ahead. This way, if for some reason the paint doesn't match, the painter will not have gone too far and you can make the necessary changes.

○ If there is any woodwork to be stained on your job, find out what happens if the stain gets on the paint.

○ There is an enormous amount of dust from the sanding that painters do. Discuss with your painter how he will clean up along the way or at the end of each day; otherwise you'll end up with a huge mess.

○ In case you must be away from home while the painters work and you need to call them, have a signal. For instance, let your telephone ring twice, hang up, and immediately call right back. Also consider having a neighbor serve as a point person just in case of an emergency. Make sure the painters know who it is.

○ Painters often unplug and disconnect appliances, including dishwashers, washing machines, and dryers. Make sure they reconnect each item. Test it before they finish and leave your job.

# Pets

Over the years, some of my best friends have been pets. There were Pokey, Queenie, Smokey, and Dice. From a magnificent mutt to purebred Dalmatians, these beloved dogs were considered part of our family. And I guess I'm pretty typical, because it's estimated that six out of ten American households keep at least one animal as a pet, and a good share of those families own multiple pets. Most people keep pets for the companionship, affection, and fun they provide. Other people would add practical reasons, such as the sense of security a pet dog can provide, but mostly, we keep pets because we love them.

As in all matters of love, there are some down-to-earth factors you should consider before adopting your first pet or adding another pet to your family. You must learn about and meet the animal's special needs—which could include plenty of exercise for a big dog, daily grooming for a long-haired cat, or lots of time and patience to train a bird to talk. Ask yourself if you're willing to put the necessary time and effort into the relationship before you decide on a pet.

Other issues, such as how much room you have available for a pet, how much time you can spend with the animal, and even whether you or anyone in your family has certain allergies, all need to be addressed. Research different pet options before making up your mind. There are plenty of books available at the bookstore and library on the topic. Additionally, your friends would be delighted to tell you some of the good and bad points of different pets they've owned, and your local veterinarian can give you advice, too.

The Internet is another source of information. The American Veterinary Medical Association, whose experts provided much of the information in this chapter, maintains a Care for Pets home page (go to http://www.avma.org and then click on "care for pets") with pointers on selecting a pet and providing proper healthcare for your companion. The American Society for the Prevention of Cruelty to Animals also offers information on caring for cats, dogs, gerbils, guinea pigs, and other small animals at its Web site (go to http://www.aspca.org).

When you're ready to pick out a pet, give serious thought to visiting your local animal shelter. There are many wonderful animals there just waiting for a home, and unfortunately, it's estimated that fewer than 20 percent of them will be adopted each year. But first and foremost, consider your home, your lifestyle, and your other responsibilities and make sure you are ready and well educated about taking on another precious life—that of a pet.

## Choosing a Pet

o Get the facts! There are 124 recognized breeds of dogs, grouped into seven categories: hound, working, terrier, toy, sporting, nonsporting, and herding. And, of course, there are mixed-breed dogs. While every dog has its own unique personality, some breeds have specific traits, and some of the traits, such as being very excitable, may not fit your lifestyle. Dogs originally bred for a specific purpose tend to retain those characteristics, and they may require additional training or patience. Veterinarians, books about specific canine breeds (which you can find in the public library, at pet shops, or in bookstores), and dog clubs are all good sources of information about individual breeds.

o Selecting a specific breed does not guarantee a particular behavior, but choosing offspring from animals with desirable temperaments does increase one's chances of getting the best pet, according to experts in animal behavior. When selecting a puppy or dog, ask to see the dog's parents or talk to people who own other dogs that are related to the one you are considering to make sure they are good-natured animals.

o If you decide to adopt a puppy, select one that is active, friendly, and inquisitive. Avoid a dog that appears to be afraid of everything or snarls at people. Fearful dogs sometimes become aggressive and bite—which can become a long-term problem.

o Frequent contact with people early in a puppy's life enhances its adjustment to the human family, so look for a puppy that has been raised around humans.

○ Experts believe that a puppy should become acquainted with its new home, and removed from its mother, at about six to ten weeks of age.

○ While there are far fewer breeds of cats than dogs, some felines do have specific needs you should be aware of. As with dogs, you can find many books on cats at the library or bookstore. Consider visiting a cat show, where you can see many breeds at once.

○ Use basically the same criteria in selecting a kitten as you would in choosing a puppy. Remember, a healthy kitten will actively seek affection from humans.

## How About a Feathered Friend?

○ Birds can form strong attachments to people and can make excellent companions. They are a good option for people who have only a small living space to share with a pet, or for people who have allergies that prevent them from living with a dog or cat.

○ Having a bird as a pet is not a worry-free proposition, however. Birds are sensitive to sudden temperature changes and many household fumes. They can develop life-threatening diseases, and need a balanced diet, water, light, suitable caging, and proper sanitation. A bird won't sing or talk if it is lonely, malnourished, stressed, or confined to too small an area.

○ Depending on the kind of bird, its life span can range from a few years to several decades. Costs also vary widely, depending on the rarity of the species. If you have never owned a bird before, you might want to start with one of the less expensive types, such as a finch or parakeet, before making a large investment.

○ Members of the parrot family are highly social and trainable. The drawbacks to having one as a pet are that they can bite and they can be expensive, with a large bird such as a macaw costing several thousand dollars.

○ Large parrots may live for more than thirty years.

## Keeping Your Pet Healthy

 o If your dog or cat is in ill health, you are likely to notice at least one, and probably several, warning signs. Consult your veterinarian if your pet exhibits any sort of abnormal behavior, sudden viciousness, or lethargy. An abnormal discharge coming from the nose, eyes, or other body openings is another warning sign, as are any lumps, limping, or difficulty getting up or down. Changes in eating habits—including loss of appetite, unusual gain or loss of weight, or excessive water consumption—and difficult, abnormal, or uncontrolled waste elimination are other possible signs an animal will exhibit if he is not feeling well. Pet owners should also contact the vet if the animal exhibits excessive head shaking, scratching, or licking, or biting any part of the body. Dandruff, loss of hair, open sores, and a ragged or dull coat can also signal a possible illness. Foul breath or excessive tartar deposits on the pet's teeth are likewise signs of disease.

 o Several infectious diseases can be deadly to dogs and cats. Vaccinations are available for some of these, and your vet is the best source of information on what kinds of shots your pet needs. The AVMA's Care for Pets home page on the Internet (go to http://www.avma.org and click on "care for pets") includes extensive articles on many diseases that owners of cats and dogs should be aware of, including warning signs to look for and information about the availability of vaccinations and other preventive measures.

 o Obesity can cause health problems in cats and dogs just as it does in humans. That means you need to watch your pet's diet to make sure it is balanced and not providing too many calories, which will result in unwanted extra pounds. Make sure that your animals get enough exercise—regular, moderate exercise is what you should aim for, rather than infrequent, hard workouts. (These recommendations should be easy to remember, since they are basically the same as your doctor tells you about your health.)

## Dental Care Is Important, Too

o By the time they are three years old, 80 percent of dogs and 70 percent of cats show some sign of gum disease. Bad breath can be an early warning sign of the dangerous gum disease gingivitis. Other warning signs include a yellow-brown crust of tartar around the gum line and pain or bleeding when the pet eats or when you touch its gums.

o Small dog breeds, such as Pekinese and Shih Tzu, are particularly prone to dental problems. Experts say these breeds are more likely to develop tooth problems because their teeth are crowded into small mouths, which can create a haven for plaque buildup.

o For domestic cats, cervical line lesions are the most common dental disease, with more than one-fourth of all cats examined by vets suffering from the problem. Because the lesions often begin below the gum line, pet owners are usually not aware that there is a problem until the tooth is seriously damaged.

o Prevention is the key to helping your pets maintain good oral health. It starts with a visit to your vet, who will examine your pet's teeth as part of a physical. At home, you should establish a routine of removing plaque from your pet's teeth. Your vet can give you pointers on how to do it and tips on dietary options. Dogs, for example, can be fed specially formulated foods that help reduce the accumulation of plaque and tartar on teeth.

## Common Problems

o If your pet is a nervous wreck every time you go to see the vet, there are several things you can do to calm him down, according to Dr. Nell Dopson Tillis. Bring your cat to the clinic in a carrier—the enclosed area makes the cat feel safer and protects you from a freaked-out kitty crawling around the car. Keep your dog on a leash so you can control him. Ask the veterinarian's assistants to get the animal to the examination room as quickly as possible, so the pet won't spend time around other animals that could increase his anxiety, and schedule appointments at times when the clinic is least likely to be busy—avoid weekend visits. If these tips don't work, ask your vet whether a tranquilizer would be a good option for the pet.

○ If you're having trouble housebreaking your dog, stay consistent and use positive reinforcement, Dr. Tillis said. Lead the animal to the same spot each time you take him out to eliminate, and get him outside often, especially shortly after meals and naps. If you catch the dog "in the act" inside the house, tell him no immediately and take him outside—but if you find a wet spot after the dog has walked away, it's too late. Be sure to praise the puppy and give him a treat when he goes where he's supposed to.

○ If your pet is nervous during a storm, the best thing to do is gradually desensitize the animal to the sound of thunder. Dr. Tillis suggests buying a tape that includes storm noises and playing it at a very low volume while the animal does something pleasant, such as eating. Over time, you can increase the noise level as the animal gets used to the sounds. For immediate relief, when a storm comes up, get the animal to an interior room where he won't see the flashes of lightning and the sound of thunder will be minimized.

○ If your young puppy or kitten bites, you need to redirect the play mechanism. Stress what you want the animal to chew by giving him a play toy to chew on instead of your fingers when he starts nipping. If your mature dog suddenly starts to bite, consult your vet. Biting could be a sign of a more serious problem.

## Neutering

○ Surgical neutering is recommended as the permanent solution to problems resulting from a dog's or cat's natural reproductive processes and mating instincts. And neutering guarantees that the animal's human family won't find itself with a litter of kittens or puppies to find a home for.

○ In a female animal, the vet will remove the pet's ovaries, fallopian tubes, and uterus. The technical name for this operation is ovariohysterectomy, although most people refer to it as spaying. In a male animal, the testicles are removed. The technical term for this is orchiectomy, commonly called castration or neutering.

○ Surgical neutering eliminates the possibility that a female dog or cat will develop uterine infections. It also reduces the possibility that the dog or cat might develop mammary cancer. Neutered males usually become less aggressive and spend more time at home, decreasing their chances of being injured in fights or auto accidents, the AVMA notes.

o The operation tends to make the pet more gentle and affectionate. It becomes less interested in other animals and spends more time with its human family.

o Contrary to what many people believe, neutering your pet has no effect on its intelligence.

o Removing the ovaries or testicles does affect the animal's metabolism, which can allow the neutered pet to gain weight more easily, if it is permitted to overeat. It's especially important that a neutered animal's diet be closely regulated to prevent excess weight gain.

o The AVMA recommends that the owner consult with a veterinarian to determine the ideal time to neuter the pet.

## Pets on the Go

o When traveling, a pet should wear a collar with a license tag and complete identification, so you can be contacted if your pet disappears and is found.

o Never leave a pet in a car alone. Not only can you not control the temperature, but you also expose your pet to strangers.

o When your animal is riding in your car, do not allow it to ride with its head outside the window. Letting the animal's head hang out the window exposes your pet to a variety of potential dangers, including the possibility that particles of dirt will enter the eyes, ears, or nose, causing injury or infection. Excessive amounts of cold air taken into the lungs can also cause illness in animals.

o Carry a rabies vaccination certificate with you when you travel across state lines or in another country with your pet. If you are traveling to Canada or Mexico with your animal, you may be asked to present a health certificate, so be sure to get one from your vet before you leave home.

o A dog or cat must be at least eight weeks old and weaned at least five days before flying, according to airline regulations. Airlines will want to see the animal's current health and rabies vaccination certificates before allowing your pet onto the plane, so have them with you just in case. A good idea is to also take your pet to the vet a few weeks before flying to make sure he is in good health. Depending on the size of your animal, you can also check with the airlines to see if your pet can ride in a waterproof cage under your seat in the cabin. There is usually an additional charge for pets regardless of where they fly. Get the facts!

o If your pet is flying, it's best to book a nonstop flight or one with a minimum of stops. During the summer, choose early morning or late evening flights to reduce the risk that your pet will become overheated while on the plane.

o The cage your animal flies in should be large enough so that the pet can stand, turn, and lie down. The cage should have ventilation on opposite sides and a leakproof bottom covered with absorbent material. (If you don't have a cage that meets those criteria, look for one at a pet shop, or call the airline in advance to see what they have available for you to use.) You should label the cage with the words "live animal" and draw arrows indicating the upright position of the carrier. Put your name, address, and phone number in a visible spot on the cage, too.

## Some Pets Are Too Exotic

o The AVMA is opposed to people keeping exotic animals and wildlife as pets. Such animals can be dangerous, and in many states it is illegal to buy or keep such animals. Mature wild animals can become aggressive or difficult to keep.

o The AVMA has called for the prohibition of all commercial traffic involving wild carnivore species, reptiles, and amphibians that are considered inherently dangerous to humans.

o In areas where ferret ownership is legal, the AVMA recommends that people who keep ferrets learn about the proper care, nutrition, housing, and habits of the species.

o A ferret should never be left unattended with anyone who is not capable of removing himself from the ferret.

o Canine hybrids (wild canines crossbred with domestic animals) can exhibit unpredictable behavior and pose a significant threat of severe attacks on humans, according to evidence from experts in the fields of animal behavior, animal control, and public health.

o No rabies vaccine has been licensed for canine hybrids, and if such an animal bites a human or is exposed to a rabid animal, public health officials in some states may require the animal to be euthanized, regardless of its rabies vaccination status.

o Legitimate zoos frequently will not accept wild animals that have been kept as pets, a fact many owners confront when they have to give up the animal. It's also more than likely that the animal is "too domesticated" to be returned to the wild and survive. Many owners of wild animals find that euthanasia is the only alternative when they can no longer keep their exotic pet.

# Saving Money

I don't know anyone who can afford to waste money these days. That's why I've compiled these super saving ideas for the smart consumer. From your medicine cabinet to your home to your clothing, there are hundreds of opportunities to save money . . . you just have to know where to look! I believe that saving money does not always have to mean a major lifestyle change.

The following tips are some of the best around and don't require you to be "cheap" or go without things you like. They are simply creative ideas on saving money compiled using a little common "cents." As you will see, there has been a lot written about saving money; from books to newsletters to Web sites, there is an abundance of help out there; you just need to start somewhere. Pretty soon, you'll see the savings start to add up as you begin to think like a smart shopper and come up with your own ideas for saving money. So, get ready to save! I'll bet you didn't know it was so easy.

## Automatic Savings

o Avoid buying a new car off the lot and you will save thousands. If you must buy a new car, try to purchase it near the end of the model year. This will enable you to take advantage of "model closeout sales" from the dealers who are trying to unload their old stock to make room for newer cars.

o Another option is to buy a demo car—one that is used for test-drives at the dealership. If the car has less than 5,000 miles on it, the savings can be amazing! And since the car has been under the care of the dealership, there is usually hardly any wear or tear on it. In addition, typically the same warranties will apply to the demo car as apply to new cars, but make sure you know what applies and what doesn't.

o Check out the difference between ordering a car and buying it straight off the lot. Find out if there is a savings—you just might be surprised that there is.

o Keep your car serviced on a regular basis. Your warranty may require some routine maintenance to be made or your coverage could lapse. Be sure to check out all of your warranty info and have it explained to you before leaving the dealership.

o Use a gas rebate card. Some major gas companies offer a 1 to 3 percent discount if you use their credit card. Just ask!

o Check tire pressure once a month. Correct pressure saves gas and could save you a percentage on the cost of tires as well.

o Driving 55 MPH will save 10 to 15 percent in gas versus driving 65 MPH.

o Your trunk should be kept empty as often as possible. You'll get more miles to the gallon if you reduce the weight you are carrying around.

## Credit Card Savings

o Credit cards can save you a great deal of money and even aggravation. If you have a major credit card, get the facts. Check out if usage of your card has any of the following benefits. Note that this is only a partial list and that your credit card company may offer different programs.

1. When you travel: You may be able to take advantage of free traveler's checks, discount travel clubs (save on hotels, car rentals, airfare), travel insurance, long-distance calling card service, or roadside assistance programs offered by your credit card company.
2. When you make a purchase: Some credit cards offer purchase insurance, which saves you money if your purchase is lost, stolen, or broken.
3. When you get sick: Some credit card companies are getting savvy with regard to medical bills. Some offer healthcare payment options that allow you to pay off your healthcare bills on an installment plan with lower interest rates.

4. If you lose your job (if you quit, get fired, or get injured): Most credit cards offer a program whereby you pay a monthly insurance premium based on your balance so that if you lose your job, your credit card insurance plan will provide a grace period during which interest on your balance does not accrue.

5. When you shop online: Credit card companies are beginning to offer programs such as security for online shopping, which saves you money by protecting you against fraud when you make purchases over the Internet. Note that some cards will send you discounts and coupons to local and national retail stores with your monthly statement as well.

6. When you send a package: To help you keep track of your mail, some credit card companies will offer package tracking services for major private carriers. Check it out!

Note: Beware of disappearing benefits! These programs all sound great, but be careful. Some credit card companies will entice you to sign up by offering extra benefits, but may cut back on these extras without the fanfare that launched them. Be sure to read annual disclosure of changes, and switch cards if need be.

○ Last but not least, don't be afraid to negotiate with your credit card company for a lower interest rate and search for the best deal. Check out credit unions as well, since they might offer lower fixed rates.

## Dry Cleaning/Laundry for Less

○ Dry cleaning—for reasons that are not clear—is not an equal opportunity provider! Some dry cleaners traditionally charge almost double for ladies' blouses compared to men's dress shirts. One solution may be to put your ladies' blouses in with your men's dress shirts to try to take advantage of the lower cost, or choose a cleaner that doesn't do this.

o Most dry cleaners or Laundromats will mend garments for you at an extra charge. If you have a button replaced at a dry cleaner, bring in your own to save money!

## Make More "Cents" of Your Clothes

o Buy separates that are neutral—black, brown, tan, navy, cream. They will all go together and can be mixed and matched for many outfits. Or, do what the pros do: Build your wardrobe around one color—basic black.

o Organize your closet by color, formality, outfits, garment. You will see many more outfit options and save on impulse buys.

o Just like with smart grocery shopping, you should make lists of specific articles of clothing you need before you go shopping, including color and fabric type. Be systematic about what you buy.

o Take out clothes that need repair—buttons, hems, shoes, etc.—and have the repairs made. This will cost less than replacing the items, and will make the garment feel like new.

o Resole or reheel shoes. Don't just throw out your favorite shoes because they are too worn! Men's shoes will sparkle like new with a polish, resole, and new laces. Women's shoes (even fabric ones) can be cleaned or polished and resoled as well.

o When purchasing ladies' pumps or heels, be wary of shoes that have leather-wrapped heels. The heel is an easy target for bumps, scratches, and rips (especially caused by driving!) and will make the shoe look old long before its time. Leather heels cannot be replaced or repaired easily to look like new. Buy shoes that have stacked or wooden heels instead. They will last longer and save you money in the long run.

o Before you ever wear a pair of pantyhose, wet them thoroughly and then gently wring them out. Place them in a plastic bag and put them in the freezer overnight or until they are actually frozen. Hang them in the shower to thaw out and then dry. This process will make them last longer and run less often.

o Consider spraying your pantyhose with starch, which will stiffen up the fabric some, and let dry. This will help prevent runs.

## Managing the Cost of Medicine

○ Most of us already know that generic prescription drugs can save you money, but few of us are as familiar with the savings that can be accrued by purchasing generic or store-brand over-the-counter medications as well. For instance, generic cold medicine, cough medicine, pain relievers, and nasal sprays might have the same active ingredients and work just as effectively as the more costly national brands. Check the ingredients and consult with your doctor and pharmacist for advice on generic buying.

○ Make sure you understand your health insurance plan. Make sure your pharmacy participates in the plan.

○ Check with your doctor and insurance plan to see if you can get your regular prescriptions filled in larger quantities. Compare the savings before doing so.

○ Comparison shop over the phone and then choose the pharmacy that has the best buy on your medicine. You'll be surprised how much you can save.

○ Ask your pharmacy if they offer discounts for seniors or for parents of young children.

○ Ask your doctor for free samples. Pharmaceutical companies give physicians thousands of dollars' worth a year, and besides saving you money, you can also test a drug before buying a prescription.

○ Important tip: In the event you are on different medications and you purchase them from different places, be sure all medications are properly coordinated and managed carefully!

## Get More at the Grocery Store (While Spending Less!)

○ Ever wonder why you have to weave through the aisles of the drugstore to get to the pharmacist or why you have to pass the aromatic bakery section and beautiful desserts in the grocery store to get to simple items like bread or milk? According to "$avvy Discount$" newsletter, it's because stores know that for every minute they can delay you, you will spend money on things you hadn't planned to buy. Some stores estimate that impulse buying goes as high as 50 percent, even in grocery and hardware stores!

○ Beware of the impulse items displayed by the cash registers. These include chocolate and other candy, sodas, magazines, and toys. If you buy an item on impulse, chances are you didn't really need it (or it would have been on your list) and you paid too much.

○ You can often save money at the grocery if you buy unsweetened food products and sweeten them yourself. Compare the price of presweetened items such as instant tea and packaged lemonades. With the sugar often comes a higher price.

○ Notice that food stores are starting to accept charge cards. Why? According to "$avvy Discount$" newsletter, studies have shown that people spend approximately 20 percent more with charge cards than with a check or cash. This is perhaps the worst way to use a charge card, since you are charging a short-term purchase and paying it off long term. In 1999 you could be paying for a meal you ate in 1995.

○ When shopping at a grocery store, keep this rule in mind—look high and low for savings! You see, most of the expensive brands or products will be at eye level on the shelves as you walk down the aisles.

○ According to Hinshaw Enterprises, a recent study reported that 80 percent of all U.S. households collect and use some coupons. Over $400 billion worth of coupons were distributed last year by manufacturers in the United States. However, only 6.25 billion dollars' worth were redeemed, which is a little under 2 percent. The main reason so few coupons are redeemed is that people do not receive the coupons for the products they want; they receive coupons for the products the manufacturers want them to buy.

○ Aside from grocery store circulars, coupons in automatic dispensing machines in the actual grocery aisles, and coupons advertised in newspapers and magazines, there are other ways to get coupons. One is to call the manufacturer's 1-800 phone number directly and request coupons. A 1-800 number for customer service can usually be found on the product's packaging.

○ After shopping, when storing items in your pantry or cupboards, make sure to group like items together so you will be able to easily see what you have and don't have when making out your next grocery list. How many of us have six cans of tomato soup or green beans in our pantry because we didn't see the cans we had hiding in the back?

○ Shop near closing time, since many stores discount items at the deli counter and bakery.

○ Get to know your store manager and ask if there are any specials. Sometimes when a store buys too much of an item, it's discounted.

## Beauty Savings

○ If you are hooked on a name-brand, salon-quality shampoo, conditioner, hair spray, or mousse, you may be able to purchase the generic brand of that item at a beauty supply store for much less money.

○ Many companies hire volunteers to test their products. This is an excellent way to get your favorite brands for free and actually have some input as to the design, packaging, or product. To find out if a manufacturer needs volunteers to sample products, simply call their customer service 1-800 number.

## Clean for Less

○ Little known fact: Ammonia can be used to clean virtually everything in your house and it's much less expensive than buying several different name-brand products! Just use about 1½ cups to a gallon of water.

○ Do-it-yourselfers beware: *Never* mix bleach with anything other than water . . . toxic fumes may result!

○ For wall and floors, use 1½ cups ammonia and 1 cup liquid detergent mixed in a gallon of water.

○ Don't waste your money on expensive window cleaners! For windows, use 1½ cups ammonia and a little vinegar and baking soda mixed in a gallon of water.

○ For sparkling clean bathroom sinks and tiles, use 1½ cups ammonia and a little baking soda mixed in a gallon of water.

○ An inexpensive way to freshen up the kitchen is to pour ½ cup baking soda and ½ cup vinegar down your drain. Wait 5 minutes and then rinse with warm water.

○ I've tried many expensive stain-removing products over the years, but I've found these household products to work better. To remove stains on upholstery, try shaving cream; to remove ink stains, try hair spray; to remove crayon stains, try toothpaste. Be sure to test a small area before going for it, since these ideas are definitely an untraditional approach to cleaning.

## Dining Out

○ Many restaurants these days are serving double the normal size portions at pretty high prices . . . not too healthy for your body or your pocketbook. To help save money when eating out, if you know the restaurant will serve large portions, you can ask your server to have the item (salad, entree, or dessert) split back in the kitchen before it is brought out. This way two can eat for the price of one. I *don't* recommend you do this with all three items during one meal—it may upset the kitchen—but you should feel comfortable doing so. If a restaurant has a problem with this, it's usually indicated on the menu. (Splitting desserts is always a romantic idea anyway!)

○ Read over your bill! There are a zillion different opportunities for your bill to contain an error. Everyone from your server to the computer could potentially make a mistake, so you should always serve as a "second set of eyes" to help keep costly errors from occurring.

○ If you order bottled water when eating out, specify the size, such as small or large, since most restaurants will bring a large bottle, which will go to waste if the entire table isn't drinking it. Some restaurants will also continue opening new bottles and refilling your glass if you don't give clear instructions.

○ If your meal isn't up to par, ask to see the manager. Most restaurants care greatly about a customer's satisfaction, so be assertive if something isn't right—send it back!

○ If eating out is your downfall and you need to spend less, set a designated amount for eating out and only take cash when you go. This also works for shopping, especially if you are famous for buying things you don't need.

## Gift Giving

○ Check out my book *The Perfect Present: The Ultimate Gift Guide for Every Occasion* (Crown Publishers, 1998). I spent sixteen years researching the best gifts across America and have identified a fabulous array of presents in all budgets for every occasion. You'll also discover free and fabulous catalogs and their 1-800 numbers. This is a terrific way to shop from home and save time, money, and energy. Consider ordering a selection of catalogs that are complimentary and give them with a gift certificate or check. Tie them up in brightly colored ribbons, put them in a flower pot or basket, and add your greetings. Talk about a shopping lover's dream gift! You did all the work and even threw in some spending money! You can also visit my Web site at www.robynspizman.com for more information.

○ Save newspapers from special dates to give later as gifts. From the day a baby is born to someone's fiftieth birthday, this is a great way to preserve time and give an inexpensive gift that will be appreciated later on!

○ Videotape someone's life story for a truly perfect present!

○ Fill creative and useful objects with jelly beans or chocolate kisses. From baby bottles to pretty canning or decorative jars, this makes a great gift with a big savings.

○ Save money and create your own edible gifts. Fill a glass jar with the ingredients from your favorite muffin, brownie, or cookie recipe. Layer the dry ingredients and include the recipe, notating the additional items that must be added later (i.e., combine these ingredients and add two eggs, a cup of milk, and mix with TLC!). You can also layer an assortment of trail mix ingredients like pretzels, M&Ms, peanuts, miniature marshmallows, and so on for a fun instant snack that's really colorful.

○ While at the beach, create your own souvenir by filling a jar with sand and shells and tying it with a pretty bow. You'll be surprised how easy it is to make and how much fun this activity becomes while searching for those take-home treasures!

○ Looking for an inexpensive alternative to traditional wrapping paper? Try using the comic portion of the Sunday paper or a child's artwork for wrapping children's gifts. Use the newspaper's want ads for wrapping college graduation gifts, or the bride and groom's wedding announcement for wrapping their wedding gift. If the newsprint easily comes off on your hands, put the gift in a clear plastic bag and tie it with a great big ribbon and bow. You can also use clean empty food containers for a clever presentation. Empty cookie bags with their resealable opening make a quick gift wrap. Or, try fast-food containers for a quick wrap. Avoid plastic bags, however, when wrapping gifts intended for young children.

○ Have a gift too big to wrap? Purchase a paper picnic tablecloth and you'll be surprised how far it'll go. Or, use an extra large trash bag for an easy wrap. Just a bow and you're ready to go.

○ Plan ahead for birthdays, anniversaries, and holidays by taking advantage of after-holiday sales throughout the year. You will save money by being able to take advantage of sales all year long and will spread out your holiday spending over twelve months instead of cramming it into two weeks. This system will be easier on your wallet and credit cards!

○ Make a list on January 1 of everybody and every occasion for which you'll need a gift throughout the year. Make a miniature copy of the list and keep it in your wallet or pocketbook all year long so that when you decide to spontaneously visit a Labor Day sale, you will have your holiday gift list with you!

○ Yard sales and garage sales are two good places to find unique gifts (especially antiques and collectibles) for a fraction of the price you'd pay at a department or specialty store. If you are savvy enough, you'll develop an eye for the good deals and truly valuable objects. For example, furniture, decorative accessories, and books can be excellent deals at these sales. Porcelain keepsakes, knickknacks, and pottery can make beautiful gifts for friends and family, especially if there is a special story linked to an object.

## Home (Run) Savings

○ Always fill out and redeem the manufacturer's warranties in a timely manner for all appliances or major electronic items you purchase (including computers, dishwashers, microwaves, cordless phones). This will save you money down the road should something happen to your items.

○ Purchasing big-ticket items on a credit card that provides buyer's insurance can give you some added protection. Check with your credit card company to see if you can take advantage of this program.

○ One of your best allies in the fight to save money is right inside your house and chances are you see it every day. Your refrigerator is good for much more than just keeping food from spoiling! It can also keep nail polish from thickening, perfume from getting stale and changing its smell, and unexposed film from deteriorating.

○ Before purchasing an expensive item like an appliance or a television set, ask the salesperson if this is their very best price. Inquire if there is any upcoming sale or special on this item and find out if they can do any better on the price. It doesn't cost you anything to just ask and you just might save a bundle.

## Powerful Savings!

Here are some "powerful" tips for saving money on your electric bill from Georgia Power, a southern company and provider of electricity in the state of Georgia:

### Saving during the Spring and Summer Months

○ Peak demand for electricity occurs when air conditioners, automated factories, and household appliances run at full speed. Peak demand usually occurs in the later hours of hot summer afternoons during the workweek, when businesses are still operating. Use major appliances during off-peak hours, when demand may be lower.

○ Check your home for adequate insulation, the most important factor in controlling the amount of energy required to maintain comfortable temperatures. Insulation is measured in R-value, which is a measure of resistance to heat flow. So, the higher the R-value, the better the insulation value. Experts recommend you use an R-value of R-30 in ceiling areas.

○ Set your air-conditioner thermostat to 78 degrees F. or higher in the summer. For every degree you set your thermostat below 78 degrees, you use from 3 to 5 percent more electricity. However, if you are going to be away from your home for a long time, you should set it above 80 degrees.

○ During the heat of the day, close your draperies, shades, or blinds to reduce the extra heat caused by direct sunlight.

○ Use fans whenever possible and install ceiling fans in the rooms you use the most. Note that fans should turn clockwise in the summer to draw the warm air up toward the ceiling.

○ Set your water heater thermostat to a lower setting—about 120 degrees F.

○ Purchase a higher SEER rated unit when replacing cooling equipment or a heat pump. The higher the SEER (seasonal energy efficiency rating), the more efficient the unit. Experts recommend a 12 SEER.

### Saving During the Fall and Winter Months

○ Keep the thermostat on your heating system at the lowest comfortable setting. You add 5 percent to the operating time of your heating system for every degree above 68 degrees F.

○ If you are going away for several days, lower the thermostat to 60 degrees but not to Off. By setting the thermostat at 60, there will be less strain on your heating system to reheat the house, and having some heat in the house will prevent damage from outside freezing temperatures, such as frozen or burst water pipes.

○ On sunny days, open the drapes or blinds to allow natural solar heat to warm the house. Keep drapes and blinds closed on cloudy days and at night. Use insulated or heavy curtains on windows facing the north side of the house.

○ Cover bare floors. Carpeting adds to comfort and heat retention, especially if there is little or no floor insulation.

○ Use a humidifier to keep your home more comfortable. It allows you to reduce the thermostat setting without feeling chilled.

○ Reverse the direction of your ceiling fans so that the blades push the warm air down into the room. Fans should turn counterclockwise in the winter.

○ Insulate your water heater with at least R-6 insulation. You can save enough money on energy bills to cover the cost of the materials in just a few months, and then just keep on saving.

○ The next tip may not save you money, but it will help ease the strain of unexpectedly high power bills. Some power companies will allow customers to take the surprise out of their electric bill by averaging their monthly power bills over twelve payments. You would pay the same amount each month. While your electric use might actually be more one month and less the next, since you are paying a steady amount it usually ends up balancing out. To find out whether your power company offers this billing system, call the customer service number on your bill.

○ Dimmers use less wattage, which can mean savings on your electricity bill. Replace standard light switches and you'll be enlightened by the savings!

○ Save on your water bill, too, by turning off the water when you are brushing your teeth.

## Saving on Telephone Expenses

○ The best tip I can pass along to you about saving money on your phone bill is to question everything! Don't hesitate to call your phone company and speak to a customer service representative firsthand. Explain to that person exactly how you use the phone and see if there are any special programs you can belong to that would save you money.

○ Read your phone bill all the way through! They often communicate new savings programs and most people don't even bother to read the enclosures. You'll be surprised how much you can learn and save. Make sure you aren't being charged for long-distance calls you didn't make. This is especially important when using a cellular phone.

○ Update your telephone service program every six months and make sure you are getting the best fee structure available. Recently,

I actually saved close to one hundred dollars a month on long-distance service when I questioned my telephone service provider and switched to a different plan. On one line alone, we were being billed at the highest rate, and recently it had dropped to ten cents a minute. I took advantage of the new plan and saved a whopping amount of money!

○ Use 1-800 numbers to your advantage. Call 1-800-555-1212 and check to see if a company has a toll-free number. Also keep in mind that catalog shopping can be a great way to save time and money, and most are available through 1-800 numbers.

## Don't Go Broke Saving Money!

○ Beware of discount super clubs that sell items in bulk. Unless the items are nonperishable (i.e., toilet paper, paper towels, shampoo, lightbulbs, socks), you may not save money buying them. For instance, if you are a single person or even a family of four, you may not need a 10-pound bag of cereal that will go bad before it's ever finished. The cost per ounce may be lower than that of your grocery store, but you will waste money on all those ounces you never get to eat!

○ Beware of long-distance telephone companies that solicit your business over the phone. If a competing company calls up to offer you a deal that's too good to be true, chances are it is! Be very wary of these calls; ask for everything to be sent to you in writing and compare the rates for the times you use the phone the most. For example, if a competing company offers you 5 cents per minute on "off-peak hours" but defines their off-peak hours as 12 midnight to 6 A.M., chances are you won't be seeing a lot of savings!

○ Just in case: If you find yourself unable to save money, consider talking to your bank about an automatic withdrawal. Budget the amount in and deduct it from your checkbook monthly.

○ Sales are not always the best time to buy an item. Some sales that occur yearly are not really sales—rather just advertised specials. Shop a store and get to know a particular salesperson who can alert you to real savings. "Buy the best for the least" is always a good motto when shopping for quality and things that will last. Watch for holiday sales and after-holiday sales, but don't purchase things you don't really need.

   o Beware of magazine subscriptions being sold door-to-door. They are not always a savings or even legitimate, so check them out thoroughly before spending.

## Travel

   o Consider working with a travel agent; they can often find the best deals.

   o Book air travel way ahead of time or travel standby; these are typically ways to get the best deals.

   o Use reference materials from the library, bookstores, the Internet, and friends to investigate hotels, restaurants, entertainment, and transportation within your budget. There are several guides out there that will give you excellent advice about price ranges for these different aspects of your trip.

   o Budget! Experts say that if it takes more than three months to pay off your vacation, chances are you spent too much.

   o The quickest and often cheapest way to book a hotel or motel reservation and save money is to talk with the local desk instead of the central reservation office of a hotel chain. Call the 1-800 number and get the local telephone number of that hotel. Then, call them directly and make sure you speak to someone who has the authority to negotiate, such as the manager.

   o Request the lowest, rock-bottom rate when booking a hotel room. Check also to see if the hotel has a club, since that might help you get a better rate if you're a member. Ask about any special rates and keep asking for a better deal! Some chains offer special deals to different organizations, and if you can't get a better rate, then ask if they will include breakfast.

   o Before you book and arrive at a hotel, make sure you know what the rate includes. There are many miscellaneous charges, from telephone to parking, so get the facts. Some deals aren't so great after you add up all the incidentals.

   o When you arrive at a hotel, ask again for the best possible room rate. If the hotel isn't completely booked, you might even be able to get an upgrade for no extra charge.

○ Before traveling, request any special offers for tourists that the local visitors' bureau might have. They often have coupons and special deals in booklets and magazines looking for your business.

○ When traveling, you can save money if you purchase refillable bottles for your favorite cosmetics and products and make your own travel-sized portions. The only product that you may not be able to refill is shaving cream.

## Resources for More Money-Saving Tips and Ideas

### Newsletter

"$avvy Discount$" newsletter is an extremely helpful tool when trying to save money. It gives tip after tip and anecdotal stories about lessons learned and how to save smartly in a spend-happy world. The newsletter costs $9.95 per year and is published quarterly (16 pages/issue) with a full money-back guarantee. To subscribe with a Visa or MasterCard, call 1-800-308-1901. For a special eight-page free sample issue of "$avvy Discount$" newsletter, send your name and address on a postcard to: Free Copy, $avvy Discount$ Newsletter, P.O. Box 27-N, Smyrna, NC 28579. Or you can fill out a form at the $avvy Discount$ Web site at: http://www.clis.com/savvynews. Or you can send your address via E-mail to: savvynews@mail.clis.com.

### Web Sites

○ The Dollar Stretcher "Living Better . . . For Less" (Web address: www.stretcher.com). Updated weekly, this Web site contains zillions of tips for saving money in all areas of life; The Dollar Stretcher also comes in a monthly print version. If you'd like a sample issue, send $1 along with your name and address to: The Dollar Stretcher, P.O. Box 23785, Fort Lauderdale, FL 33307.

○ Savvy Student Survival Guide (Web address: www. savvystudent.com). Web site listing tons of ideas for saving money for high school and college students.

○ Beat the Car Salesman—Your Online Resource for Your Car-

Buying Adventure (Web address: www.beat-the.com/beat-the-car-salesman/). Web site is a spin-off from author Michael Royce's successful book with the same title.

  ○ Energy Savers—Tips on Saving Energy and Money at Home (Web address: www.eren.doe.gov/consumerinfo/energy-savers). Web site created by U.S. Department of Energy; lists many tips for saving energy and money at home, including an appliance-buying guide.

  ○ Frugal Corner (Web address: www.best.com/~piner/frugal.html). Tons of links to other Web sites that provide money-saving ideas for a frugal lifestyle! Purpose of site is to help people know about all of the informative resources out there that are about saving money.

  ○ How to Live Better on Less with a Tightwad/Frugal Lifestyle, by Doris O'Connell, a.k.a. Tighwadmama (Web address: http://pages.prodigy.com/frugal_tightwad/index.html). Links for seniors, as well as information and links in most every area of saving money; also good for freebie links. There is a truly vast amount of information on this site!

  ○ Other terrific Web sites to check out:
    www.bargaindog.com
    www.salescircular.com
    www.coolsavings.com
    www.mercata.com
    www.priceline.com
    www.bluefly.com
    www.buy.com
    www.consumerworld.com
    www.bottomdollar.com
    www.dealtime.com

## Books

  ○ *Saving Money Any Way You Can: How to Become a Frugal Family*, by Mike Yorkey (Vine Books, 1994). Practical ideas to stretch the family paycheck. Suggestions are sensible and easy to do.

  ○ *The Frugal Mind: 1,483 Money-Saving Tips for Surviving the New Millennium*, by Charlotte Gorman (Nottingham Books, 1998). This book is a must-have handbook for saving money!

○ *The Best of Living Cheap News: Practical Advice on Saving Money and Living Well*, by Larry Roth (NTC/Contemporary Publishing, 1996). A collection of the very best money-saving articles, tips, and advice from the "Living Cheap News" newsletter.

○ *Living on a Shoestring: The Tightwad Twins*, by Ann Fox Chodakowski and Susan Fox Wood (DTP, 1998). Penny-pinchers to the maximum degree, these ladies offer tips to the extreme as well as practical tips for everyday consumers.

○ *Wealth on Minimal Wage*, by James W. Steamer (Dearborn Trade, 1998). This book offers the reader hundreds of money-saving tips and a lesson about having a healthy attitude toward money.

○ *How to Pinch a Penny Till It Screams: Stretching Your Dollar$ in the 90s*, by Rochelle Lamotte McDonald (Avery Publishing Group, 1994). Cut expenses in every facet of your life! Valuable lists of organizations that can help you save money.

○ *The Tightwad Gazette: Promoting Thrift as a Viable Alternative Lifestyle*, by Amy Dacyczyn (Random House, 1993). This is the first in a series of three books and is a great resource and a big hit with consumers. This book offers a wealth of wisdom for saving money.

# Senior Citizens

The retirement years are a time to explore new lifestyles, pursue different interests, and enjoy some well-earned leisure! If we plan wisely and use our accumulated experience and innate creativity to fashion a life that suits us, the second half of life can be immensely rewarding.

Retirement is the time to concentrate on maintaining good health, and we have some valuable tips on just how to do that! Maintaining energy and vitality can go a long way toward creating a sense of well-being and contentment. Your finances and legal documents can also surely benefit from careful planning and attention to detail.

Many people start a new career at this time in their lives, while others enjoy volunteering their time and energy in a wide variety of ways. Learning new skills, exploring new areas of knowledge, and developing long-neglected talents are all part of this second chapter. And don't forget to leave some time for travel plans! Whatever colors you choose to paint your new life, we have the information you need to help you get started.

## Opportunities

o Interaction is an association of international nonprofit organizations that publishes a directory of volunteer, fellowship, and intern programs for people up to age seventy-five. For more information, write: Interaction, 1717 Massachusetts Avenue NW, Suite 801, Washington, DC 20036, or call 1-202-667-8227.

o Listening to a shortwave radio can be a fascinating hobby. There are hundreds of English-language stations around the world, providing programs on many different subjects. You may want to tune in to Eastern Europe, China, or even Australia. The North American Shortwave Association can provide more information;

write to them at: 45 Wildflower Road, Levittown, PA 19057. Program guides to stations around the world are available from Grove Enterprises, 1-704-837-9200.

○ The American Association of Retired Persons, or AARP, is a wonderful resource for those fifty and older. Membership benefits include discounts on hotels and car rentals, as well as workshops and programs that help with finances, income tax returns, and employment. Access their Web site at www.aarp.org for more information or to enroll online. You can also write to them at AARP Membership Center, P.O. Box 199, Long Beach, CA 90801.

○ History buffs will enjoy archeological excursions where you can be actively involved or simply an interested observer. The Archeological Institute of America (AIA) publishes an annual listing of worldwide excavations, field schools, and other special programs called the Archeological Fieldwork Opportunities Bulletin. Call Kendall Hunt Publishing at 1-800-228-0810 for purchase information.

○ SeniorNet is an organization that provides a wide variety of ways to learn and stay active. Try the step-by-step lessons for acquiring basic computer skills and then move on to electronic classes on many different subjects through SeniorNet Online. For more information, access their Web site at www.seniornet.org.

○ Elderhostel's Learning through Service program gives seniors the opportunity to tutor special-needs children in U.S. summer camps. There are many other volunteer programs administered by Elderhostel. For a free quarterly catalog, write: Elderhostel, 75 Federal Street, Boston, MA 02110-1941.

○ Older job seekers should take advantage of a service provided by the American Association of Retired Persons. AARP WORKS sponsors nationwide seminars on how to approach job hunting for mature adults. The seminars also address self-esteem and help with evaluation of marketable skills.

○ If you're dying to write that novel, but need a little encouragement, you might want to take a writing workshop. In its May issue every year, the magazine *Writer's Digest* publishes a comprehensive list of conferences, seminars, and retreats. Many are held at colleges or universities and may include manuscript evaluation along with classes in fiction, playwriting, short story, poetry, and mystery writing.

○ Retired businessmen will enjoy sharing their accumulated knowledge with budding entrepreneurs. To find out how you can pass on your wealth of experience, call the Service Corps of Retired Executives at 1-800-634-0245. This organization has 386 chapters nationwide and can also be accessed online at www.score.org.

○ There are many individuals who cannot use regular textbooks or reference books because of physical disability. You can feel the satisfaction of helping these people access information by volunteering with Recording for the Blind. Anyone with a clear speaking voice and good reading skills can volunteer to record at local studios. For more information, call Recording for the Blind at 1-609-452-0606.

○ Why not volunteer your time to read on radio programs for the blind? Call the National Association of Radio Reading Services at 1-800-280-5325.

○ If gardening is your thing, you might enjoy volunteering to plant and maintain trees in your area. Contact the National Tree Trust at 1120 G Street NW, Suite 770, Washington, DC 20005, or call 1-800-846-8733.

○ Many universities offer free or reduced-rate classes for adults over fifty-five. Take advantage of this wonderful opportunity to increase your knowledge or learn a new skill.

○ Now you can have the fun of taking a class together with your grandchild! The Disney Institute near Orlando, Florida, offers classes for adults and children, age ten and up, on subjects ranging from rock climbing to cooking. Call 1-800-496-6337, or check www.DisneyWorld.com.

○ Constructing a family tree is a fascinating project and a unique legacy to pass on to your children. For more information on how to get started, call the National Genealogical Society at 1-800-473-0060.

## Health

o The Arthritis Foundation provides more than 100 free booklets with information on types, treatments, and coping skills for people who suffer from arthritis. The foundation also provides physician referrals, as well as classes on topics such as medication, water exercise, energy conservation, and joint preservation. Their bimonthly magazine *Arthritis Today* covers new treatments and articles about people coping with the disease. Call 1-800-283-7800 for more information.

o If you spend a lot of time in front of the computer, you may experience some eyestrain. To prevent this, try exchanging your current multifocal lenses for occupational lenses that have wider bands for viewing at computer-screen distance.

o Headaches that increase in severity and frequency may be a symptom of a disease called arteritis, which primarily affects people over fifty and involves inflammation of arteries in the head. Check it out with your doctor.

o Dental infections can have serious side effects, according to a study reported in *Stroke*, a journal published by the American Heart Association. Chronic or acute infections are linked to a thickening of arterial walls, which can result in a heart attack or stroke.

o It's a good idea to review all your current medications with your primary care doctor once in a while to determine whether you really need them all and to make sure there is no chance for harmful drug interaction.

o The American Podiatric Medical Association publishes free informative pamphlets on keeping your feet in good shape. You can also ask for referrals to podiatrists practicing in your area. Call the association at 1-800-366-8227.

o Consider taking a tai chi class to improve your balance and reduce the risk of falls.

o The National Institute on Aging offers a free booklet that can help you take medication more safely. To receive a copy of "A Safe Use of Medicines by Older People," call the agency at 1-800-222-2225.

## Money Matters

According to Adrian Grant of the accounting firm of Aarons, Grant, & Habif P.C.:

○ If your taxable estate is worth more than $600,000 (this amount will be gradually increased to $1 million over the next ten years), you can reduce the taxable amount by using the $10,000 annual gift-tax exclusion to make gifts to family members or others. If you are married, the gift-tax exclusion is doubled.

○ Financial software products like Quicken and Managing Your Money will organize your finances and give you a much clearer idea of where your money is going and how to save more.

○ When you draw money out of your IRA account before the age of 59½, you have to pay a 10 percent penalty on the amount withdrawn. The penalty is waived, however, if the money is used to make health insurance payments after twelve months of unemployment, or to buy a principal residence for yourself, your spouse, or your child, grandchild, or older relative. Higher-education expenses for a child or grandchild are also penalty-free, as are medical expenses.

○ If you are self-employed and earning more than $15,500 per year, you should consider an alternative to an IRA that may allow you more deductions. Ask your accountant about starting your own Simplified Employer Pension (SEP).

○ Savings bonds will stop paying interest after forty years, and the deferred income will become taxable. In order to keep the tax deferment, these savings bonds should be rolled over into Series HH savings bonds.

○ To reap maximum benefits, you should increase the amount you put into your 401(k) or other retirement plan every time you get a raise.

○ It makes good sense to consolidate your debts in one low-interest account. Moving $5,000 from an account charging 14 percent to one charging 7 percent would save you $350 per year. You might want to consider a home equity loan, which would have the effect of making the interest deductible.

○ If you need to reduce your capital gains tax on sales of

appreciated assets, use charitable remainder trusts and charitable gift annuities.

## Uncommon Sense

o Consider an elder-law specialist for help with legal matters relating to family, social, and medical matters. Contact the National Academy of Elder Law Attorneys (1-520-881-4005) for a free booklet on how to find an elder-law attorney.

o If you are over sixty-five and already receiving Social Security benefits, you will be automatically enrolled in Medicare. If this is not the case, you will need to apply for Medicare at any Social Security Administration office. Be sure to apply during the seven-month enrollment period that starts three months before your birthday; otherwise you will have to wait until the general enrollment period, which is between January 1 and March 31 of each year.

o You can make sure that your estate is handled efficiently by checking to see that you have named a beneficiary on IRAs or other retirement accounts, and by creating a living trust, which allows you to control all your assets and make changes whenever you see fit.

o Be aware of the dangers of joint tenancy, which gives each co-owner an interest in the property. If one co-owner dies, the property is automatically inherited by the survivor, even if a will or prenuptial agreement contradicts this. Thus, if you want your will or living trust to control the distribution of your property, you should avoid joint tenancy.

o When you retire, check with your local Social Security office to make sure all information and records are correct. This includes length of employment, past employers, and amount contributed.

o Review your life insurance policy from time to time; as you accumulate more assets, you may find that you are able to reduce your coverage.

o Are you claiming all the exemptions and deductions you're entitled to? Check up on this important tax matter by consulting "Protecting Older Americans Against Overpayment of Income Taxes," a pamphlet distributed by the Special Committee on Aging. To receive your free copy, call 1-202-224-5364.

o You can get a free up-to-date fact sheet on your Social Security account by asking for a personal Earnings and Benefit Estimate Statement. Once you fill it out and return it, you will get an estimate of your benefit rate when you retire. Call the Social Security Administration at 1-800-SSA-1213 for more information.

o Always notify your investment broker when you move. The state may end up getting your money if a financial institution cannot locate you.

o If your marital status changes, be sure to update your designated beneficiaries for pension plans, IRAs, and life insurance.

## Resources

o Call the National Institute on Aging Information Center at 1-800-222-2225 for a free copy of the "Resource Directory for Older People," a listing of agencies dealing with the issues and concerns of the over-fifty population.

o The Health Insurance Association of America has a toll-free hot line that offers help on a wide range of health insurance issues such as Medicare supplements and long-term care insurance. Contact them at 1-800-942-4242.

o To obtain additional information about someone you are trying to find, other resources to consider checking include the Bureau of Vital Statistics, the Department of Motor Vehicles, the U.S. Post Office, or through the Registrar of Voters.

o Protect yourself from con men by visiting the Web site of the National Fraud Information Center's Internet Fraud Watch at www.fraud.org.

o The Administration on Aging has a Web page with information on programs and services for seniors. Access it at http://www.aoa.dhhs.gov.

o You can get up-to-date news on Medicaid, Medicare, and other programs by accessing the Web site of the federal Department of Health and Human Services at www.hhs.gov.

**Books**

o *Unbelievably Good Deals and Great Adventures That You Absolutely Can't Get Unless You're Over 50* (10th Ed.), by Joan Rattner Heilman. This invaluable book is jam-packed with all kinds of information on saving money and having fun while you're at it. From reduced car rentals to tax and insurance breaks, from trips and clubs to programs and perks, this book will show you the way!

o *365 Ways . . . Retirees' Resource Guide for Productive Lifestyles*, by Helen K. Kerschner and John E. Hansan, editors. An easy-to-use guide with suggestions for becoming involved in hobbies, politics, environmental issues, education, and many other areas. There is an index of the contact organizations as well as a key-word index.

o *Successful Aging*, by Robert L. Kahn and John W. Rowe. The authors, who are both members of the MacArthur Foundation Research Network, debunk the myth that aging has to be both painful and debilitating. The ten years of research cited in *Successful Aging* reveal some little-known facts about health in later life. Rowe and Kahn also give advice on nutrition and the influence of creativity and social connections on well-being.

# Time Management

---

When was the last time you wished for an extra hour or two in the day? If time were for sale, I bet every one of us would buy some! Since time is such a commodity and we all run out of it daily, the idea of saving time becomes quite an exciting possibility. While there are no magic formulas for saving time, spending it more wisely definitely produces more efficient ways of doing things. This in itself can offer us more time for other things. Streamlining your life and getting your surroundings and environment organized is a key to saving and managing time. So be sure to read up on getting organized.

There is one secret that you probably know about saving time, but I bet you haven't taken it as seriously as you need to. The key to saving time is to plan ahead. According to time management expert Betsy Wilkowsky, "If you take ten minutes each evening to plan your next day, you will get that ten minutes back plus an additional ten to twenty minutes more. Clear off your desk and be sure your to-do list is complete before you leave at the end of the day. You won't forget things if you write them down, and you'll sleep better, too."

The following tips might be somewhat obvious, but applying them requires a commitment from you. And talk about bets, I bet you'll be totally surprised how much time you can save if you just make a conscious effort to work smarter. Not only will you save your energy, but you'll be able to save some time all for yourself!

## Time-Saving Tips

o Make an appointment with yourself to accommodate tasks. Make at least one a week and keep the appointment.

o Underschedule one day a week and stick to this rule. When you're short on time, you'll always know you've saved some on that designated day. Not only will this help you find time for things that pop up when you need it, but you'll also feel less overwhelmed when your week is jam-packed and you need a little extra leeway.

○ Increase your resources when it comes to professionals or individuals who are available to you to help get a job done. Keep an extensive file of resourceful names and numbers, from baby-sitters to dry cleaners who pick up and deliver, just in case you're short on time. I like to keep these numbers in clear file folders that are easy to find.

○ Delegate the job. If someone can do a job at least 80 percent as well as you can do it, then let the person do it. You'll find hidden talents in other people and they'll feel empowered with their new abilities. This works well with the entire family, your employees, or anyone else who is available to assist you daily in your efforts. With my permission, of course, our twelve-year-old helps me write out checks for her school activities when a check is due. Of course, I sign all checks, but she loves helping and she's very good at managing small amounts of money and keeping records.

## Time-Saving Telephone Tips

○ Post important numbers or numbers you call often on the back of the cabinet door next to the telephone. This can also be accomplished by keeping a list in a drawer, but if you call a number even once a day or once a month, make sure you can instantly find the number within seconds of needing it.

○ Group your phone calls. Make a batch of these calls in the morning, block out uninterrupted time for work, and then make another block of calls in the afternoon.

○ If your phone rings a lot and you are frequently unavailable, you might want to change your voicemail message daily. Let callers know when you'll be available to take and receive calls. Ask callers to leave a specific message about when they can talk, and you'll reduce phone tag.

○ Make a mini-agenda for your phone calls. The average business phone call lasts ten minutes. Using an agenda for that same conversation can shave up to five minutes off that call. Think about how many calls you make in a given day, multiply by five minutes, and look how much time you found!

○ If you don't have time to talk, tell someone that up front and how much time you have. This way you won't feel bad when you have to quickly hang up and your caller won't take it personally.

○ When you have to end a call, tell someone you can't wait to talk to them again, but you're out of time.

○ When you come home or back to the office and there's a stack of telephone messages, learn to prioritize and respond to the important messages first. Make a second stack of calls that aren't as urgent. If a secretary takes your messages, encourage her to help you identify which calls seem the most urgent.

○ Update your Rolodex or contact manager daily and keep it current. Keep Rolodex cards or a pad of self-sticking notes right next to every telephone and at your desk. Make it a rule to immediately make a card every time you wish to save a number.

○ If you find yourself constantly calling someone and the person doesn't return your call, leave a message that you have great news! The individual is bound to call you back quickly. (If your news isn't great, be sure to say it's urgent or very important that he or she call you back.)

○ If you call someone and it's urgent, ask the operator to page them or give them a note to call you ASAP.

## Saving Time at Home

○ Remember your ABCs! Alphabetize objects for easy use. For example, alphabetize your spices and you'll save time when looking for one.

○ Move things closer to where they are actually used. Place scissors in drawers near where you do a lot of gift wrapping. Place a pad and pen by every telephone for messages.

○ Always put your things in specific places. For example, you won't lose keys and spend time looking for them if you always put them on the kitchen counter in the same place every day. Or you'll never lose your glasses if you keep them only in a case by your bedside.

○ If you need items and don't have an extra drawer or space for them, purchase a small rolling cart that holds files or has baskets for drawers. These can slide under a desk for easy storage and access.

o Save time by keeping things off the floor. Have fewer objects everywhere and you'll save time cleaning.

o I save time on making beds by using comforters. Decorative duvet covers are beautiful. Add a little fluffing and they look absolutely perfect.

o Use the backs of cabinet doors to display business cards you call frequently or post self-sticking notes with information you use often. You can also put a corkboard on the back of the door for an instant bulletin board that's out of sight but comes in handy.

o Keep hand towels that you use often in a small basket or container right by the sink for easy use.

o Call Stamp Fulfillment Services of the U.S. Postal Service at 1-800-Stamp-24 and save time by purchasing a supply of stamps and personalized stamped envelopes over the telephone. Order a catalog for future use.

## Saving Time on the Go

o Consider the things you do daily, like putting on makeup or picking out your clothes. Have all the makeup you use on a daily basis sitting out in a basket or container next to the sink in your bathroom. If all of the containers are closed and you must open them to see what's inside, number them in the order you use them to save time thinking what goes next.

o Select what you are going to wear the night before to save time. You've probably heard this a million times, but the easiest way to do this is to have a few key coordinated outfits to choose from. A basic wardrobe that can be changed with shirts or accessories saves time and money. Have one standby outfit that you know is ready and waiting if you don't have time and can't decide!

o There are numerous times in your day when you spend time waiting for a service or someone. From getting gas to meeting with your doctor, learn to use waiting time productively. Even a few minutes can go a long way.

o If you have an errand to do, like dropping off the dry cleaning or taking something to be fixed, put it in your car that morning so you won't forget it. You could even keep a shopping bag in your car designated for errands.

○ If you notice you need to do an errand such as take your shoes to the shoemaker, check all of your shoes before going just in case another pair needs attention, too.

○ Carry paperwork with you. If someone keeps you waiting, you can use that time.

○ When you file your mail, keep a "read later" file nearby and put papers, magazines, articles, and other things you wish to read later in this file. It's a fabulous way to store things of interest you receive but don't have time to immediately read or review. Take the file with you when you're going to have some extra time to go through it.

○ Make your own standardized shopping list with regular items your family wants weekly. Photocopy the list and then add to it as time goes on. List the ingredients for favorite recipes, and you'll have everything you need to go shopping and save time.

○ Designate a certain day for specific activities so that everyone knows when you're going to the grocery, the dry cleaners, and so on. This way your family will know what to expect and be able to request items they need and help you budget and save time.

○ Save time at the grocery by knowing which brands you and your family prefer. Save time by deciding once and for all which brands are the best quality and buy overall.

## Saving Meeting Time

Call meetings only when they are necessary. Could you accomplish the same results with a phone call or E-mail? If you do need a face-to-face meeting, be clear about the purpose. Create an agenda and stick to it. Start the meeting promptly and end on time. Save the last five minutes for wrap-up to ensure that participants are clear about their postmeeting assignments.

## Saving Time with the Kids

○ Make a clipboard for each of your children and keep his or her important papers, calendars, and information on the board. Keep the clipboards in an easy-to-locate drawer and go through them weekly.

○ Every time you have a deadline or appointment for a child, draw a star or a special symbol to remind you of this event and put the date at the top of the page in large letters. You can also circle the information to help you stay focused and reminded.

○ Involve your children in grocery shopping and let them tell you two things they want for breakfast that week. Menu planning really does save time, and when children are involved and express their likes and dislikes in a positive way, they are more likely to enjoy the meal.

○ Instead of asking your child what he or she wants for breakfast, save time and give a choice between two things. Narrow the selections and save time!

○ When cooking pancakes, waffles, French toast, or something that requires more time since it is made with fresh ingredients, cook a second helping for the next morning.

○ Have a space and a place for everything from book bags to jackets, and just watch how easy it is to get out of the door in the morning. It also helps to have a bench or hooks by the door your children exit through to hold these items. Anything that helps them grab it and go saves time along the way.

○ Mornings can be a hectic time for families, so consider how you can prevent problems ahead of time. Have your children lay out what they are wearing the next day the night before and you're bound to save time.

○ If you involve your children in helping to prepare dinner, they'll be more likely to eat it. For example, younger children can tear lettuce, snap green beans, and help you set the table. There are many jobs kids can do that they will enjoy and that will really save you time!

○ Reinforcers often help save time. Here's one that really works. Have a routine habit be followed by a positive event, such as once a child brushes her teeth, have her get in bed, and then read her a bedtime story. When the story is over, time's up and it's bedtime.

○ Keep a few important things in your car that your children need often, such as tissue, napkins, Band-Aids, a nail file, a bottle of water, a snack, a hairbrush, and so on. Having little necessities on board will save you time and energy later from having to go back home because she forgot her ponytail holder or you broke a nail!

# Travel

Travel can be a very rewarding experience, but as we all know, it can also be frustrating and exhausting. The modern traveler is confronted with a staggering amount of information, which can be intimidating, if not overwhelming! A good travel agent is almost essential, unless one is prepared to master the intricacies of flight schedules, special fares, rail passes, and so on.

Unfortunately, things can and do go wrong, and we are often faced with unexpected delays, medical emergencies, and other problems. Experienced travelers know how to take these situations in stride and make the best of them. They have learned, usually through personal experience, how to deal with the inevitable small problems that arise.

Taking the trouble to be reasonably well informed and prepared often makes the difference between a pleasant experience and a disaster. With this in mind, I have gathered together some of the most helpful information available to make your travel enjoyable and hassle-free.

## Traveling by Airplane

○ Whenever possible, check to see that all of your baggage has been logged in on the right flight. Check to see that it's put on the conveyor belt and be sure you have all of your tickets and baggage claim receipts before heading to the gate.

○ When checking your bags for flying, be sure to place your name and address on the outside of each bag and also slip one address tag (available at the check-in counter) inside the bag with your destination right on top. If your exterior tag becomes detached or lost, the information inside will help locate you. Travel experts advise using a business address instead of your home.

○ Do not pack essential medicine or traveler's checks—carry them with you.

○ Be sure to lock your suitcases when possible. It might not prevent someone from breaking into your luggage, but it would prevent your suitcase from opening accidentally.

○ When given assigned seating on an airplane, always check to see if there are better seats available. If you discuss your options, you might find seats where no one else is sitting next to you, more legroom, or even seats in a favorite part of the airplane that weren't available at the time of booking. You have nothing to lose by asking!

○ Busy airports often mean long lines for taxicabs. You can solve this problem by exiting through departures instead of arrivals. You will have no trouble finding an empty taxi, since passengers have just been dropped off.

○ Often you can get a terrific deal with a fixed price from a limousine company for transportation to or from an airport. Check out your options and book a good rate. You'll be surprised at the deals and curbside service that are available if you schedule your transportation ahead of time.

○ You can minimize jet lag by using light therapy to get your body clock adjusted to a new time zone. If you are due to land in the morning, sleep as much as possible during the flight. If your arrival time is in the evening, keep the overhead light turned on and try not to sleep. Also, drink water before and during a long flight. It will keep you hydrated and you will feel much better.

○ Most print film will not be damaged by airport security X rays, but video cameras should not be held while walking through the security doorway. Always place your camera on the conveyer belt or have it hand-inspected to avoid damage.

○ Some airlines offer special meal options and are able to cater to passengers with special dietary needs, so be sure to check out your options when booking your ticket. If the airline is serving a meal, or sometimes even a snack, you can often make a special request. You'll be surprised at how many choices are available, including a kid's meal, low-fat, vegetarian, a fruit plate, kosher, and more.

○ If your child is age two or under, he or she can travel free on your lap on most domestic flights. But for older children, discounts are usually available only in conjunction with special promotions. Some airlines will offer a lower fare when asked about special rates or family discounts, so it's worth asking. International airlines are a little more generous when it comes to kids. They generally charge a nominal rate for small infants, and give discounts of 25 to 50 percent for children ages two to eleven.

○ When traveling on an airline with a child, check with your pediatrician for advice on dealing with air pressure and flying with young children.

○ If you are a premium member of one airline, you may be able to get similar status on another just for the asking. Many airlines will be happy to do this to get your business.

○ Check out the best times to visit a destination so that you can save on airfares. There are many times when it is cheaper to fly off-season. European vacations, for example, can be very costly during the summer when most people have time to travel, but late fall through winter months can offer a huge savings in airfare and other rates. However, be sure to check the weather and what will be occurring when you get there. Sometimes saving money on flights is not always the best deal if when you arrive you're stuck in a hurricane or monsoon season. Get the facts and check out your options.

○ A trip to a distant country that includes several stops may be cheaper if you buy a round-the-world ticket rather than a regular fare. These tickets often include multiple stops with unlimited stays at each stop.

○ It can be confusing to sort out the rules of various frequent flier programs. Now you can refer to the *Official Frequent Flier Guidebook* (1-800-487-8893), which lists all the major airlines as well as their partners and awards requirements. You can also access the Insideflyer.com Web site for help with tracking mileage and for information about promotions. Consider joining a few frequent flier programs, since many of them have special deals or discounts that might save you money.

○ Give yourself a good chance of sleeping on an international flight by booking a less popular flight time and requesting a seat in the middle section at the back of the plane. You will more than likely end up with three seats to stretch out on.

○ Often a flight will be sold out and overbooked. If you offer up your seat, you can usually get a voucher for a complimentary airline ticket to be used during the year, but be sure you know when the next flight is and that you will be guaranteed a seat. Check out the facts before you give up your seat too soon and make sure you find out about your free ride. If the next flight to your destination is at 5 A.M., the deal might not be so attractive.

○ Susan Lurie, CTC, and travel agent at the Sophisticated Traveler, advises, "When any minor under eighteen travels from the United States to Mexico, he or she must have the following: a notarized letter signed by one or both parents authorizing the child to travel to Mexico. You must also have a notarized copy of the death certificate of the passenger's other parent or a notarized copy of the divorce papers showing that the parent who signed the authorization letter has custody of the minor. Notarized means it must have a raised seal and stamp on the document. For U.S. citizens, these documents are in addition to proof of citizenship, which means a valid passport or a certified birth certificate with a raised seal, and a state-issued valid photo I.D."

○ When dealing with a problem with your flight, be sure to get the agent's name. It helps to know who said what. A gate agent can be your best asset when a problem arises, so know who's who and also be very courteous—they are important!

○ If you're flying with your pet, freeze a water bottle so that the pet can lick moisture from it when necessary. This eliminates a water dish, which may spill during flight.

○ In the event that your plane is delayed and you're stuck at the airport, talk to the gate agent and discuss what your options are. Sometimes you can get on another flight, but if that's not possible request a meal voucher and complimentary long-distance calls. If an overnight is required, request a hotel voucher.

○ Once your flight has landed, go directly to baggage claim. This helps reduce the possibility that your luggage could be accidentally taken or even stolen. Also consider tying a bright-colored ribbon or adding a large sticker to your luggage if it isn't distinctive-looking.

## What-Ifs:

○ If your flight is delayed or canceled, rather than standing in line at the gate to book your new flight, get a jump on your fellow travelers. Proceed to a pay phone and call your airline's toll-free number or your travel agent, whose phone line is more likely to be clear.

○ If your baggage is lost on a flight, do not leave the airport without filing a claim. Be as specific as possible and find out exactly what you can expect and who you should call to check on the status.

○ If you're worried about protecting your investment for your trip, consider travel insurance, especially when going to destinations that have severe weather. Travel insurance can be one of the best investments you make with your vacation, so be sure to check it out and find out how it might help you. In the event of an unexpected cancellation especially due to illness, you'll never regret this purchase.

○ If your vacation pictures are grainy and strangely colored, here's some helpful advice. This sometimes happens when film has been in your camera for too long. Unused film in its original case can last for six months past the expiration date, but loaded film may lose sensitivity over time, especially if it's been exposed to high heat or humidity. To avoid this, shoot film within a few months and have it processed as soon as possible.

○ If you're traveling and lose your contact lenses or they are lost with your luggage, here's a tip for getting an extra pair. If you are unable to find your particular brand, you can now call Lens Express at 1-800-872-5367 and have replacements (if in stock) delivered within two days. Carry your prescription information with you or your doctor's name and telephone number and this company will do all the work.

○ If you're enjoying a superb bouillabaisse at a small café in Paris and you somehow manage to spill a good-size spoonful of it on your new blouse, here's a quick traveling cleanup tip. Many a garment has been rescued from ruin by the swift application of plain white vinegar. It serves as a good emergency remover for food stains such as coffee, tomato sauce, or fruit juices. Be sure to test your fabric first.

**Resources**

&#9675; The Department of Transportation issues a quarterly news report that lists average airfares for most domestic flights. While this won't let you know which airline has the best fare to your destination, it does give you a base price that you can use as a comparison. For a free copy of the Domestic Airline Fares Report, call 1-202-366-1053. And better yet, every day thousands of fare changes take place, so it's best to call a travel agent and have them check current available fares.

&#9675; For cheap, same-day performance seats for New York theater, try the TKTS booths located in Times Square and at the World Trade Center. You can also call them at 1-212-768-1818 for information and location of booths. Another strategy is to call the theater box office on the day of the performance. Some theaters have discounted "rush" tickets that they sell about an hour before show time.

&#9675; Traveling vegetarians often have a hard time finding restaurants that cater to their food preferences. Help is available in the form of a comprehensive guide called the *Vegetarian Journal's Guide to Natural Foods Restaurants in the United States and Canada*. This is available through the Vegetarian Resource Group at 1-410-366-VEGE. There is also a Web site that lists vegetarian restaurants by country, state, and city (www.veg.org/veg/Guide/). For overseas travel you can consult the *European Vegetarian Guide: Restaurants and Hotels*, also available from the VRG.

&#9675; Consular information sheets and current travel advisories are available from the U.S. State Department's Office of Overseas Citizen Services (1-202-647-5225) or from its Web site (www.travel.state.gov).

&#9675; A good travel agent is someone no one should be without! To check on a possible prospect, contact the Better Business Bureau for that area and ask how long the company has been in business and whether it is a member of an industry association such as the

American Society of Travel Agents. It's also a good idea to get references from customers. Make sure your travel agent is a member of the Airline Reporting Corp., or IATAN, the International Airlines Travel Agent Network. If they aren't, a red flag should go up. Beware also if the agency requests large fees immediately or if they decline to accept credit cards.

○ When choosing a travel agent, inquire what they are best at. Many travel agents (even within a particular agency) specialize in specific types of trips. Some focus on luxury trips, while others are well known for being cost-conscious. Make sure you are matching yourself up properly and keep in mind that a really good travel agent can save you time, money, and lots of aggravation. The Sophisticated Traveler recommends, "you look for the 'C.T.C.' designation behind a travel agent's name. This represents completion of a two-year advanced course of study in the travel business and is the travel industry's highest award."

○ When purchasing travel, be sure to use a credit card. This way you are protected in the event that the company goes out of business or you are sold something that doesn't exist.

○ When leaf season rolls around again, you can find out exactly where fall color is at its finest by calling Tauck Tours' Fall Foliage Hot Line at 1-800-214-8209. The service covers the continental United States and Canada. Leaf reports are updated every week during September and October.

○ When you're traveling and unexpectedly need the services of a doctor, dentist, optometrist, or chiropractor, it's comforting to know you can call Hoteldocs at 1-800-468-3537.

○ An economical way to vacation in another country is to exchange houses with someone interested in doing the same thing. You can find interested parties through a directory published by Intervac in San Francisco (1-800-756-HOME).

○ Before traveling to a new city, call the concierge at the hotel where you are staying for expert advice and helpful assistance. A concierge can save you time, money, and lots of energy by helping you plan ahead. Check to see if the concierge has any discount coupons for sight-seeing tours and entertainment venues, as well as suggestions for recommended restaurants. Make sure to find out if any reservations must be made prior to your arrival. When you arrive at your destination, also inquire with your cabdrivers if they have any suggestions or discount coupons for specific shows or sights you shouldn't miss. You'll be surprised what you discover and learn if you just ask!

## Money Matters

○ ATM machines provide easy access to your funds in many parts of the world, as well as allowing you to take advantage of favorable exchange rates. The surcharge for withdrawals is usually comparable to, or less than, the commission charged to cash a traveler's check. An additional advantage is that you only withdraw the amount of cash you need.

○ Save money by planning ahead. Cruise lines reward early birds with discounts of up to 35 percent off the advertised rate. Note that "early" means six months before departure! You will also get a better choice of cabin, better deals on hotels, and a chance to upgrade later.

○ Banks get a special rate for currency conversions so you will benefit by paying with credit cards whenever you can. You will pay from 2 to 10 percent less than it would cost to change money and pay cash.

○ Don't be intimidated into buying the collision damage waiver when renting a car. If you have auto insurance or a credit card, it is possible that you are already covered for theft or collision while driving the rental. Call your credit card company for details before you rent a car, and check your insurance policy as well.

○ Save money with European telephone cards, which generally offer rates that are up to 40 percent cheaper than U.S. phone cards. The cards can be purchased at most convenience stores or post offices.

○ Air travel within Europe is very expensive and car rentals also cost a lot more than in the United States. A good alternative is to travel by train. Train service is efficient and relatively inexpensive. Buying a rail pass may save you some money and allow you to prepay excursions.

○ Tourist cards are available in all major European cities and can be useful time and money savers. The cards usually include unlimited use of the mass transit system for a specified number of days, also discounts for dining, shopping, and museum visits. The cards are sold at hotels, shops, train stations, and tourist offices and can often be purchased in advance in the United States.

○ If you want to do your own research online for both domestic and international travel, check out your specific airline, which will have its own Web site, or investigate other travel clubs and services such as www.bestfares.com, www.1800airfare.com, www.previewtravel.com, or www.travelocity.com.

## Packing

○ When flying, be sure to carry on all valuables, medications, important documents, passports, papers, medical information, and items that you can't live without should they be lost or delayed. Travel experts recommend packing less and carrying on all your important items. Choose luggage on wheels and with a handle for easy access.

○ Trips to out-of-the-way places can mean dealing with questionable drinking water. It's a good idea to pack a supply of water-purification tablets that will make any water potable. The tablets are readily available at camping or sporting goods stores.

○ When packing medical supplies for travel, be sure to check with your physician about medications that are suitable for you that might be helpful for potential problems along the way. Discuss common concerns and be prepared.

○ Secure your luggage with a combination lock rather than a simple key. Keys tend to get lost, and most manufacturers use one key for all similar bags, making these cases easy targets for thieves.

○ If you're traveling outside of North America or Western Europe, you might try bringing American perfume, soaps, lotions, and bath products to give as gifts. These items are highly prized in countries where they are in short supply.

○ When packing, group like items together in clear plastic bags for easy unpacking and use later on during a trip. Clear plastic sweater bags work particularly well and are inexpensive.

○ Bring along a large plastic trash bag or dirty-clothes bag to store dirty clothes in during travel. It helps to keep them separated from your clean clothing. When you get home from your trip, grab the bag and go. This also works well if you have two suitcases. Fill one bag with your clean items that will be unpacked, but the other suitcase goes straight to the cleaners.

○ Wrinkle-free packing depends on how carefully you stow your items. Wrinkles are caused when clothing shifts and moves around during travel. Some experts recommend packing each item in the dry cleaner's bags or layering tissue between items. Other wrinkle-free tips include rolling T-shirts and items like ties into neat packages to make more room for additional items.

○ Don't forget to pack the necessary travel aids when traveling to a foreign country, such as a converter, transformer, or adapter, depending on what appliances or electrical items you are bringing. Get expert advice so these items will work efficiently.

## Hotels

○ Book early when possible. You often get better rates when doing so.

○ When you book a hotel, always be sure to get a confirmation number. This is critical, especially if you have a problem. This number shows that you in fact did book a room at a specific rate. You can even ask the hotel to fax you a copy of your reservation. Check it for errors.

○ When booking your room, request an earlier check-in time or a later checkout time. Most hotels will hold your baggage until check-in time, but it's a good idea to see if you can check in earlier for no additional charge if you are arriving before the approved time.

○ Always inquire if there is a better rate when booking any hotel room. Ask if they have business rates, specials, discounts, or weekend deals. Look like a savvy shopper and you'll get smarter deals.

o When booking a hotel room, ask to speak to the manager of the hotel. Sometimes you'll get a better deal than from calling their reservation line.

o There are many travel clubs that offer rooms at a discount. Some charge you a fee to belong, while others are free. Check out these services carefully and compare them to your travel agent's recommendations. Consider using them only when you feel you are saving so much that it pays to give up the assistance and attention you receive from a travel agent.

o If something doesn't work at your hotel—for example, the hot water—ask to speak to the manager and request a reduction in the price of the room if it's not fixed within an acceptable time limit. If you don't receive all the services included with your room, why should you be billed for them?

o Use a cell phone or a pay phone to avoid costly hotel service charges and high rates on long-distance calls. Once you learn how much a minute costs, you'll see how even one call can add up quickly. Plus, some hotels charge for every local call you make as well, so get the facts.

o Some hotels charge you a service charge if you cancel less than 24 hours in advance or check out earlier than you had planned. Inform the hotel of any change of plans as soon as it is possible.

o Be sure to check your hotel bill carefully when checking out. You'll discover what you are really paying for and learn a lot about what hotel services actually cost. A cup of coffee delivered by room service might not look so appealing once you discover the final cost, which includes the service charge, tax, and a tip.

## Health and Safety

o Getting sick in a strange country is no fun, and can sometimes be quite frightening. However, if there's a U.S. embassy in the city, you're in luck! In addition to their normal functions, U.S. embassies will often provide recommendations for local doctors.

o Cruise ships that dock in the United States receive regular inspections to monitor food and water quality as well as other aspects of hygiene. A score of 86 is considered reasonable. The

Centers for Disease Control, which carries out the inspections, maintains a Web site that has links to the inspection program (www.cdc.gov/travel/). You can also obtain a current report by writing to: Chief, Vessel Sanitation Program, National Center for Environmental Health, 1015 N. American Way, Room 107, Miami, FL 33132.

○ Travelers who are prone to motion sickness and don't enjoy the drowsiness that many antinausea drugs cause can try the following remedies: avoid food high in fat before traveling, and nibble on crystallized or pickled ginger, which has a calming effect on the stomach.

○ If you're staying in a big city, request that your room not be on the first or second floor, as this is where burglaries are most likely to occur. Ask for a room that is clearly visible from the elevator and not at the end of a long passageway. Leave the TV on when you go out and hang the "Do Not Disturb" sign on the door as an extra precaution.

○ Hepatitis A is spread by contamination of food and water, and the risk of contracting it is therefore highest in countries where the general standard of hygiene is poor. Stay away from seafood, salad greens, fruits that cannot be peeled, and tap water and ice. The best way to protect yourself is by being immunized with the new, longer-lasting vaccine. Eleven out of twelve travelers fail to do this, and some pay the price with fever, abdominal pain, jaundice, and general malaise. There is a 2 percent chance of the disease progressing to liver failure, and the death rate is one in 250. Check this out with your physician.

○ It pays to be aware that your prescription will not automatically be filled when you are away from home. Even if your prescription is on file with a nationwide pharmacy company, certain states have strict regulations. Call ahead to make sure that your prescription will be recognized.

○ What to do when that crown on your molar comes off while you're enjoying a second honeymoon in Maine? No need to panic; simply call 1-800-DENTIST (1-800-336-8478) for a free referral.

○ Young children and the elderly might be advised to refrain from eating some soft cheeses in Europe. Check with your physician and travel agent, since some of these cheeses are often made from unpasteurized cow or goat's milk and may harbor organisms that can cause fever and body aches in susceptible individuals.

○ Bees and other insects are attracted to bright colors, so if you're vacationing in the tropics, try to wear light-colored clothing. Avoid loose, flowing garments that can trap insects in the folds.

○ Be sure to travel with your own over-the-counter pain, nausea, or cold medications. Although planes are often stocked with these items, airlines are reluctant to give them out to passengers because of the threat of potential lawsuits.

## A Change of Pace

○ You've always yearned to spend a night in the slammer, and now you can! The town of Preston in Minnesota has a room for you at the Jail House Inn. The converted prison gives you a taste of life behind bars softened by a breakfast fit for a king. For more information, call the inn at 1-507-765-2181.

○ View Paris at a leisurely pace from the vantage point of a bicycle. Faster than walking, but still slow enough to enjoy the sights, bicycling may be the ideal way to see the city. A 50-kilometer network of bicycle lanes makes the sport both safe and enjoyable. You can rent a bicycle from various outlets in the Bois de Boulogne for a day or a full week.

○ The original Orient Express made its last run in 1977, disappointing many who had hoped to ride on it. If you are one of those die-hard romantics, you will be glad to hear that a re-creation of that famous train is now running the rails. The new train, called the Venice Simplon-Orient Express, travels between London and Venice and into Istanbul via Zurich, Paris, St. Anton, Innsbruck, and Verona. For tickets and schedules, call your travel agent or 1-800-524-2420.

○ You can experience the extravagant elegance of steam travel on Rovos, the most luxurious train in the world, which is a unique safari through the heart of the African bush. These beautifully restored Edwardian trains offer accommodations of the highest standard, combining the opulence of prewar travel with subtle modern innovations. There are several different itineraries taking you from Cape Town, the Victoria Falls, and even to Dar es Salaam. For more details contact Mushinda, 1-800-522-8093.

## Travel Tips

○ When making a hotel reservation, be sure to ask whether any special packages are available. Many hotels offer special deals during the holiday season, which may include free dinners, shopping vouchers, theater tickets, and room upgrades.

○ If you are concerned about loss or theft of important documents when traveling, take the following precautions: Make a copy of your driver's license, the first page of your passport, your airline tickets, and your first and last traveler's checks, and keep this information in a separate place from where the originals are kept, and leave a copy at home with someone you trust, just in case.

○ For winter travel, pack a pair of fleece socks, which hold in the heat and dry in no time at all.

○ To get a little extra legroom when flying, request a bulkhead or exit row. Also, make sure that your seat is not in the last row, because these seats do not recline. On some planes, the seats in the exit row don't recline, either; check it out. Another strategy is to ask for an aisle seat, center section; because the middle seats in a wide-body jet are assigned last, you could end up with an empty seat next to you.

○ Now you can get state vacation guides on the Internet. Although the guides do not feature the colorful photos of the paper editions, the information is available immediately instead of having to wait for a hard copy to be mailed to you. The Internet address is based on each state's postal code, so the address for Georgia, for instance, would be http://www.state.ga.us/.

○ Ask for electronic ticketing when making your next airline reservation and eliminate the hassle of lost or stolen tickets.

○ New York City now offers a unique free service to first-time visitors. The Big Apple Greeter has more than 500 volunteers who will take you on walking tours, introduce you to the subway, and give you general information about the Big Apple. The tours take about four hours and reservations should be made at least a week in advance. Call 1-212-669-2896.

○ Instead of getting stuck in a traffic jam, you might want to do your viewing of fall color from the relaxed comfort of a ship. Holland America's *Westerdam* offers a foliage-viewing trip that travels from New York up to Canada and down the St. Lawrence River to Quebec City and Montreal. For more information, call your travel agent or 1-800-323-5893.

○ Take advantage of Amtrak's 15 percent seniors' discount to enjoy a train ride with your grandchildren. Children ages two to fifteen travel for half off the regular fare.

○ Many youth hostels now provide adult quarters in private rooms. Although these rooms cost more than the regular dormitory accommodations, they are still a bargain, rarely costing more than $20 per person. Members of Hostelling International-American Youth Hostels (1-202-783-6161) pay less and can stay at some hostels that are not open to nonmembers.

## Resources

○ Contact www.travelocity.com, which is a travel site where you can find an extensive list of flight and fare information, list of current travel sales, vacation packages, and destination information. You can then actually book flights and make rental car and hotel reservations.

○ Look into www.mapquest.com, which gives you personalized walking or driving maps for both domestic and international cities. You can plan trips using information on lodging, dining, attractions, and weather. They list travel times as well.

○ Check out www.trip.com, which offers reviews of hotels, restaurants, flight listings and reservations, and airport layouts to get you acquainted. It also offers a low-fare notification service.

○ Looking for a weather forecast anywhere in the world? Log onto www.weather.com for your weekly forecast, driving conditions, flight delays, and travel reservations for flights, cars, and hotels. See www.accuweather.com and get the scoop on Mother Nature in the city you are traveling to, including five-day forecast and current conditions.

o Other terrific travel Web sites to check out:
www.frommers.com
www.fodors.com
www.zagat.com
www.previewtravel.com
www.expedia.com
www.priceline.com

# Web Sites

With thousands and thousands of Web sites filling cyberspace, the Bet You Didn't Knows are endless! In fact, every day I go online I find new and exciting Web sites jam-packed with helpful information. In the spirit of saving you time and energy, this chapter lists a wide variety that relate to the topics in this book. What amazed me most was the really useful information you can find on the Web. Once you take a step into the Internet, you too will become addicted like the rest of us.

Like Internet sites, information on any given topic is rapidly changing. Use your search engines to check out a variety of sites and compare the advice and information you discover. Happy surfing!

## Appliances

○ www.aham.org: At the Web site of the Association of Home Appliance Manufacturers, you can get all the appliance-related information you need. Simply fill out an Internet form including what kind of appliance you are interested in, your price range, when you are going to purchase, your interest in current Internet promotions, links to local dealers, and general information and tips on buying an appliance, building a home, buying a new home, or remodeling a home, and they will provide you with lots of information on both major and portable appliances.

## Beauty Products

○ www.kleinman.com/cosmetic: This Web site, called the Cosmetic Connection, offers a complete source for no-nonsense cosmetic information and advice. You can get reviews of all the top products by all the top manufacturers. There is a page of telephone numbers where you can contact the manufacturers to find out if your shade of lipstick is discontinued or who carries your brand. You can also use the search engine to seek out reviews on products you use or are interested in trying.

## Cars

o www.cartalk.com: Based on an NPR syndicated show called *Car Talk* by Tom and Ray Magliozzi, this Web site provides information on mechanics, car reports from information from the NHTSA, a car-trip planner, repair-cost estimator, current loan rates, buying vs. leasing information, how to buy a car, safety information, car reviews, and a loan calculator to find out what your monthly payments will be.

o www.edmund.com: Edmund's Web site provides consumer information on new and used cars and trucks, including prices and reviews, safety information, incentives, rebates, leases, and buyers' advice. Also including the latest news and views, it is a must-see for anyone considering a vehicle purchase.

## Careers

o www.monster.com: Monster.com is the leading global online network for careers, connecting the most progressive companies with the most qualified career-minded individuals. Designed for both job seekers and employers, this Web site is terrific for anyone searching for a job or looking for qualified candidates to hire. With the help of Monster.com, you can track jobs, store your résumé and cover letters, and connect with their growing career community. Plus, employers will discover cost-effective and efficient recruiting solutions.

## Child Safety

o www.nhtsa.dot.gov: The National Highway Traffic Safety Administration's Web site, besides offering great information on cars and car safety, provides a comprehensive list of child safety seats including a registration form, installation information, and a list of those that have been recalled since 1988. You can also call their auto safety hot line at 1-888-327-4236.

○ www.safekids.org: This Web site provides information on swimming, bike helmets, car seats, and playgrounds, and a great list of frequently asked questions about child safety. There are also checklists and fact sheets with crucial information you need to know to keep your child safe.

## Cleaning

○ www.sdahq.org: This Web site, operated by the Soap and Detergent Association, offers information about cleaning products, including history, chemistry, safety, ingredients, and manufacturing. It also includes useful tips and information on laundry, household cleaning, and dishwashing. Environmental topics are included as well as cleaning health and safety issues.

## College

○ www.finaid.org: This financial aid information Web site comprehensively covers all avenues a person can use to seek assistance. It includes a scam alert, guide to free documents, phone numbers, and common myths. It provides an overview of sources of funds, loans, vendors, services, and government and school financial programs. It also has a special-interest section providing information on aid for certain groups including disabled, older, female, minority, and gay and lesbian students, as well as sports and athletics, veteran and military aid, graduate school, medical school, law school, business school, and private high school.

○ www.fastweb.com: Check out this Web site and discover the Internet's largest scholarship database. Answer questions and build a profile to receive a list of awards for which you may qualify.

○ www.collegeboard.org: This Web site offers comprehensive information on college for both students and parents. There is information on financial aid, guidance and counseling, placement and advising, college searches, online applications, online SAT registration, and much more! Any college-bound student or parent should check this out.

## Consumer Tips

○ www.pirg.org: The State Public Interest Research Groups is a nonprofit organization that serves as a watchdog for the nation's citizens and environment. This Web site includes information such as how you can fight back against rising bank fees, how to protect your privacy and personal information from theft of identity crises, and product hazards.

○ www.cpsc.gov: For important consumer information, check out the CPSC, the U.S. Consumer Product Safety Commission's Web site, which is an agency that is dedicated to saving lives and keeping families safe. CPSC is an independent federal regulatory agency created in 1972 by Congress with the Consumer Product Safety Act. In that law, Congress directed the commission to "protect the public against unreasonable risks of injuries and deaths associated with consumer products." Its goal is to help keep American families safe by reducing the risk of injury or death from consumer products. This is a valuable resource, and you can report any unsafe or hazardous products to them and also get important consumer updates.

## Cooking

○ www.reluctantgourmet.com: This Web site is a culinary guide for the novice cook, featuring tips on what to keep in your pantry, a glossary of cooking terms, great tools for cooks, basic techniques, and a collection of other cooking tips. This site serves up a wealth of information for all those nonprofessionals in the kitchen.

## Decorating

○ www.homeideas.com: This Web site includes information on almost all areas of home improvement and decorating. It includes a library, links to free brochures, a home talk discussion area, and additional information on buying furniture, furniture care, wood, and bed safety.

## Entertaining

○ www.moviefone.com: This Web site provides up-to-the-minute show times for theaters in most major U.S. cities. Many offer the ability to buy advance tickets. It also features information on the movies as well as a featured movie. You can search the site by theater, movie title, star, type, and time.

## Food Safety

○ www.foodpres.com: Written by two Ph.D.s specializing in food safety and preservation issues, this site full of scientifically based information will help you determine whether the food in your house is safe to consume or should be discarded. It includes information on preventing foodborne illness, canning, emergency foods, sack lunches, and specific groceries.

## Garage Sales

○ www.garagesale.nearu.com: This Web site is a great resource for advertising your garage sale and finding a garage sale near you. This free service will post your sale up to thirty days prior to the sale date and will automatically remove it after the sale date. Those looking to get good results and those looking for bargains cannot afford to miss this site.

## Gardening

○ www.garden.org: As the largest nonprofit gardening organization in the country, the National Gardening Association operates a Web site sharing its vast resources with the public. There are links and tips for all types of gardens. In the library section, you can type in a key word and get articles relating to your specific need.

## Health

o www.healthtouch.com: This Web site includes information about prescription and over-the-counter drugs, a search for pharmacies in your area that have Healthtouch in their stores, health information including wellness, diseases, and illnesses, and product data from the manufacturers.

o www.cdc.gov: This Web site, operated by the Centers for Disease Control and Prevention, includes information on diseases, injuries and disabilities, health risks, specific populations, and prevention guidelines and strategies. It also contains a section on travelers' health, with geographical guides to the precautions necessary for travel as well as a list of necessary vaccines for travel in certain areas.

o www.kidshealth.org: This comprehensive Web site includes information for parents on behavior, emotions, development, communication, feeding, growth, learning and play, medical care, movement, senses, sleep, childhood infections, emergencies and first aid, general health, nutrition, fitness, and safety.

o www.ama-assn.org: The American Medical Association's Web site offers great information on health issues and current medical news. The most fascinating feature of this site is the doctor finder. Not only can you search their database of over 650,000 MDs and DOs for a doctor in your area by name or specialty, but you can get a general map to show you where the office is located.

## Home Buying and Selling

o www.hud.gov: This Web site, operated by the U.S. Department of Housing and Urban Development, contains information on how to buy a home, find housing, keep your home, build a home, buy land, and make home improvements. It also contains a useful list of do's and don'ts for buying and selling your home.

o www.homefair.com: This Web site's mission is to provide interactive tools and useful information so that you can stay organized, make the right decisions, and keep more of your own money when buying a home, selling a home, or relocating.

## Information

o www.boardroom.com: This outstanding Web site connects you with up-to-date information from experts throughout the country on an endless amount of subjects. From health to wealth to consumer advice, you'll find every topic under the sun from the publishers of "Bottom Line/Personal," a fabulous newsletter that is jam-packed with timely tips and helpful insights.

o www.300Incredible.com: Want to be impressed, educated, or entertained on the Internet? If so, then check out www.300Incredible.com and order any of the books featured on this wonderful Web site. Based on a series of books that includes the award-winning *300 Incredible Things to Do on the Internet* by Ken Leebow, 300Incredible.com, LLS, Marietta, Georgia, this is your one-stop shop for Internet fun and is jam-packed with the best Web sites I've ever seen. The books, which range from 300 incredible things for kids to sports fans, to golfers, travelers, and more, present an informative, timesaving read that will help any Web surfer become an expert at Net navigation. Plus, be sure to sign up for Ken's free newsletter.

o www.ask.com: Ask Jeeves is a popular Web site designed to answer millions of your questions. That's right! Think of any question and then ask Jeeves, the ready and able resident genius on the Internet. You'll be amazed at all the topics and tidbits Jeeves knows. He's ready and waiting for your questions. All you have to do is log on and just ask!

## Insurance

o www.insure.com: This Web site, called the Consumer Insurance Guild, offers a comprehensive guide to auto, home, and life insurance. It pulls current insurance news articles of interest to consumers and explains how different kinds of insurance work in various situations. It also offers a guide to find out what is going on with insurance in your state.

o www.iiaa.org: This Web site, operated by the Independent

Insurance Agents of America, contains information on how to find an insurance agent in your area, what you need to know when shopping for insurance, current news and insurance industry information, and links to related state associations and other useful insurance information on the Internet.

## Kitchen Planning

○ www.nkba.org: This Web site by the National Kitchen and Bath Association includes consumer information on remodeling, examples of real projects, information on product manufacturers, tips from professionals, and a design-professional finder to help you locate someone in your area. Interesting tips on surfaces, cabinets, and design trends can also be found here.

## Legal

○ www.abanet.org: In their public information area, the American Bar Association provides a section on legal assistance, including lawyer referral and disciplinary agencies, a section on publications, a section on legal service plans, a section for students, and a section on additional resources including public services, public education, legal services, information on children and the disabled in the law, and discussion groups.

## Money Management

○ www.guidestar.org: This Web site provides a comprehensive guide to charities. It includes a Guide for the Responsible Donor to outline the steps you can take to ensure the effectiveness of your gifts. This is a useful tool for those including charitable donations in their money management plans.

○ www.credit.org: The Consumer Credit Counseling Service's mission is designed to help you get out of financial trouble. This nonprofit organization provides information on their services including debt management, homeowner help, and credit report review. It also offers tips on how to avoid scams. For those not online, the Consumer Credit Counseling Service can be reached at 1-888-462-2227.

## Moving

○ www.amconf.org: This Web site, operated by the American Moving and Storage Association, offers information on choosing a mover including a list of companies accessed by state and city. It also offers tips for before you move, relocation assistance, and evaluating the costs of moving. Additionally, it provides a list of terms you will need to know before you hire a mover.

○ www.moverquotes.com: This Web site contains the largest moving company database on the Internet, including over 15,000 pages covering full-service and do-it-yourself movers in every state. This database includes thousands of prices and statistics based on the size, distance, and timing of your particular move. It also provides weight calculators that let you accurately estimate your moving costs.

## New Moms

○ www.baby-care.com: Created by a practicing pediatrician, this Web site assists new and experienced parents with the important issues of newborn care. This site offers online infant care classes, lifesaving basics, up-to-date immunization schedules, product recalls, and other great information for moms, dads, and other caretakers.

## Organizing

○ www.123sortit.com: Did you know that a person loses an average of two years of his or her life searching for lost items? Well, this Web site provides comprehensive information on business and residential organizing. Covering everything from your office layout to your kids' rooms, the site will help you organize every aspect of your life.

○ www.napo.net: Check out the National Association of Professional Organizers Web site for helpful information on getting organized. This organization will help you find a professional organizer in your area who can educate you about getting organized.

## Painting

○ www.housenet.com: This Web site, besides being a great information source for decorating and home improvement, offers a unique feature in its calculation section. By using the paint calculator, you can plug in the dimensions of your room and determine how many gallons of paint you will need to purchase for the job. It also includes similar tools for wallpaper and drywall.

## Pets

○ www.apapets.com: This Web site by the American Pet Association is a must-see for all current and prospective pet owners. There are care tips, links to humane agencies, an "Ask the Vet" section, and a Vet Finder, where you type in your information and they will search their database of over 27,000 veterinarians for a vet near you.

## Saving Money

○ www.uGive.com: Want to save time, money, and give the perfect present? Log onto uGive.com, an innovative and interactive gift resource designed to make gift giving a cinch for even the gift-giving impaired. This fabulous Web site instantly helps you create a GiftFolio™ that contains up to twenty individual gift items hand selected for your gift recipient in the budget of your choice. On the date you select, they will send your GiftFolio™ by E-mail to your recipient along with your personal message. Rest assured you have given the perfect gift, because they get to choose from the twenty gifts. They also have a reminder service that sends you an E-mail when an event is coming up. From trendy and unique to the tried, true, and traditional, uGive.com makes gift giving a pleasure for everyone, especially you!

○ www.couponcentral.com: This Web site allows you to enter your zip code to search for coupons near your home, or you can choose national and Internet coupons. This great selection of coupons can be printed directly from your browser, with no special plug-ins needed.

○ www.stretcher.com: This Web site provides a weekly resource for simple living with innovative ways to save money. The newsletter contains topics such as grocery savings, dental care, comparison shopping, new carpet, and many others. Including past issues, the site contains over 600 free articles on how to improve your life. You can also subscribe to their free, weekly E-mail newsletter or order the print version of the newsletter by sending $2.00 along with your name and address to Sample Newsletter, P.O. Box 23785, Fort Lauderdale, FL 33307.

○ www.teleworth.com: This Web site helps you to determine the best calling plan for your business or residence. By entering the first six digits of your phone number of the state and city you want to rate calls from, the Web site will provide you with comparative information that will save you 20 to 50 percent on long distance. Those not on the Internet can call 1-888-353-6978 for the same service.

○ www.usps.gov/ncsc: This Web site is a 24-hour U.S. Post Office, including a store where you can find zip codes, purchase stamps, find an online change-of-address form, postage rate calculator, and Express Mail tracker. A great way to save on gas and make the post office quick and easy from the comfort of your home!

## Senior Citizens

○ www.aarp.org: This Web site, operated by the American Association of Retired Persons, offers information on care giving, healthy living, managed care, exercise, nursing homes, reverse mortgages, jobs, money management, welfare, wills, driving, grandparenting, and funerals, and a database full of resources for older adults. There is also information on AARP, the benefits of membership, and the community programs offered by this organization.

## Time Management

○ www.mindtools.com: This Web site offers wonderful information on time management skills. It tells you how to get the most for your time and gives specific time management tools. It also provides useful sections on stress reduction and goal setting, which can help you to organize your time.

## Travel

○ www.historytravel.com: This Web site, operated by the History Channel, tells you how to add a little history to your next vacation. It provides information on historic hotels, special History Channel tours, and a regional map to click on to see what historical sites are in that area. Other than the history, this Web site provides tips on air travel, traveling with seniors, family travel, traveling with kids, traveling with pets, and driving tips.

○ www.festivals.com: Calling all festival lovers: Here's a Web site designed to help you get valuable and up-to-date information on which festivals and events are happening in a city you might be traveling to or considering. From art festivals to food fairs to Mardi Gras, you'll be in the know before you go!

○ www.gorp.com: Whether traveling or looking for a fun outdoor activity, the Great Outdoor Recreation Pages offer tips on where to go and how to do it. With a complete guide covering everything from walking and hiking to city escapes, this is the place to go to learn how you can take full advantage of the outdoors near and far. For more information, check out their Web site or call 1-800-784-9325.

○ www.mapquest.com: Explore the world with a fabulous consumer travel site. This site also gives you an interactive atlas with maps and TripQuest, with detailed driving directions that you can print out immediately. We used their map on a recent trip to North Carolina and found the map to be very clear.

## Weddings

o www.theknot.com: This Web site provides you with every-thing you want to know about tying the knot, from engagement to honeymoon. You can search through pictures of over 8,000 gowns or get advice on wedding etiquette. Grooms can use this site, too, with information on proposals, rings, best men, bachelor parties, and great honeymoon deals. There is even a bridal registry!

o www.theweddingchannel.com: With a wedding planner, gift registry and shopping, tips on fashion and beauty, ideas for honey-moons, and a section for grooms, the Wedding Channel offers a comprehensive resource for those planning or attending a wedding. A local business guide is provided to help the intended couple lo-cate vendors in their area, as well as a section for newlyweds and how to cope with living together for the first time.

## Working at Home

o www.workathomesuccess.com: This Web site offers an on-line newsletter featuring profiles of successful work-at-homers, com-panies that hire home workers, home business basics on how to start and run a home business, and links to other useful sites. You are sure to find the latest details on the work-at-home world.

# Weddings

Planning a wedding? This should be one of the happiest times in your life, but so often wedding plans turn into major problems that are both costly and emotionally wrenching. There are dozens of bridal do's and don'ts, and the best advice comes from the experts who specialize in this area.

According to Sue Winner, the author of *The Complete Idiot's Guide to Budgeting Your Wedding* (Alpha Books, New York, NY, 1999) and a Master Bridal Consultant, which is the highest level of training offered by the Association of Bridal Consultants, an international organization of wedding professionals—"the key to a successful wedding is having a realistic budget based on a realistic estimation of guests. The number of people and the number of dollars are connected in a way that most brides do not realize. The biggest problem is that the bride has a specific budget and then must invite a certain number of people. What goes wrong? The more people you invite, the more you need of everything—more food, more pieces in the band, more tables, chairs, more centerpieces."

It's no wonder many parents offer their children a tidy sum of money to talk them out of a big wedding. Some bridal bribes could even be a down payment for a house! But having the wedding of your dreams is a special moment, and if you're indulging yourself it should live up to your every expectation.

It seems most weddings have at least one catastrophic moment, even if just a scare. From wedding cakes falling off tables to hotels losing electricity, things can and do go wrong. But why are so many weddings plagued with problems? The sad truth is that many of these problems could have been prevented. While my wedding on a Sunday in July was picture-perfect, we certainly had our share of problems during the weekend. In fact, my relatives threw us a beautiful Friday-night dinner for out-of-towners that made the 11 o'clock news. Ten of our guests (and close college friends) were walking on the street coming to the party, and they were robbed! All their jewelry and wallets were taken. Talk about a nightmare—I'll never forget the migraine headache I had for twenty-four hours before we got married. The lesson, you ask? Weddings need security and a policeman monitoring traffic. Take it from me!

On a more positive note, when planning a wedding, the one thing you also have to consider is that you are entertaining each and every guest. That should be the fun part. To help you consider all the details, be sure to also refer to the chapter on entertaining for super suggestions, including an entire section about working with a caterer. The same rules apply, with the motto being, "Get smart and get the facts!" Never choose a caterer, or anyone else for that matter, by cost. You need to weigh what you're getting for your money and make sure your expectations are being met.

The following suggestions will help you manage your wedding details and navigate the best possible experience along the way. It is hoped that everything will run as smoothly as silk.

## Bridal Tips

o  Create a budget and consider how much you can really afford. This should be a perfect day, but striving for perfection might cause a great deal of financial stress. So consider your budget and plan accordingly. Sue Winner suggests, "Keep in mind, this is a five-hour event; how much can you realistically spend and cover the details?"

o  After you have decided upon a budget, divide it to determine how many people you can have. Don't start with a guest list and think you can stuff them into a budget.

o  Consider hiring a professional bridal consultant. A professional has completed a series of educational courses offered by the Association of Bridal Consultants. He or she has also been working in the field and has experience in many types of weddings. Bridal consultants can be hired for a flat fee, hourly rate, or percentage (15 percent) of a wedding. Which you choose depends on your situation. Check out your options.

o  A professional bridal consultant is important because this expert can save you time and money and is your advocate. Get references and talk to other couples who used that consultant. Since weddings are not repeat business for most vendors, brides and grooms are often taken advantage of. However, the bridal consultant is a repeat customer. Vendors are less likely to take advantage if a consultant is involved.

○ A bridal consultant is present on the day of your wedding and coordinates the ceremony, runs the rehearsal, and directs the processional, recessional, and reception. This consultant also knows all the answers to your questions on etiquette.

○ Before hiring anyone for your wedding, it's best to put the person on a tentative hold and check references. Ask for a first right of refusal while you are doing your checking and never book anyone without checking the person out.

○ Sue Winner suggests, "Staff in a community can change, since you book them so far in advance. It's a good idea to travel with a tablet and carbon paper. Every time you speak to the vendor, take careful notes. Always give the wedding professional a copy of everything you discussed. Keep a copy so you know everything that was promised. This will make it possible for you to easily reference what has been discussed and what has not. It also gives you a record of items they might forget they said later on."

○ Request a contract from every vendor you deal with, including the limousine driver. Put every detail in writing, making sure the time, place, and any special requests are included.

○ Read and reread every contract carefully. Have your consultant read them, too, to make sure you agree and understand every detail. These contractual details control what will happen at your wedding and ultimately will result in either the most organized wedding on earth or the most disastrous!

○ Make all your deposits using a credit card. This way you'll have some recourse in the event that something goes wrong and you must resolve a disagreement. Your credit card doesn't guarantee that the person will show up, but if you don't get the service, you have a record of the payment.

○ It's important to know what each vendor's refund policy is. Some vendors will apply the deposit toward next time! Others will refund it if they book the date again.

o Every gown is considered made to order. Your dress will probably need alterations, and you must allow time for those details. Plan to order the dress six months before the wedding. If you're buying a sample or purchasing a style that's been discontinued, take it home with you that day unless they are altering it.

o Check out the store's insurance coverage for your dress while it is being altered!

o In the event that your wedding is called off, you do have to return all the gifts, so don't use them before the wedding.

o Do not plan your bachelorette or bachelor party for the night before the wedding. It's best to schedule parties a week or a few days ahead of time. This way you'll enjoy your wedding and won't be too tired.

## Details Every Bride and Groom Should Know

### The Location

o Experts agree that one of the most difficult things to secure is the location. Either it's already booked or you just aren't sure where you want to get married. Getting a date on hold is the toughest part, so begin lining up the location as soon as possible.

o Check it out! Many brides and grooms book a location and then all of a sudden discover hidden costs. Get the facts at first, have them put in writing, and don't rely on anyone's promises.

o Get educated. Some locations are outrageous when it comes to bar services, so be sure you know what you are getting into. Is parking extra? Can you bring in your own wedding cake or must you use the caterer's? Investigate the additional charges—I can guarantee you there will be some you didn't expect.

o Check to see if an engineer is included and is on-site during your wedding. If the air-conditioning or the electricity goes out, you need an expert ready to help! Candlelight is romantic, but how will they cook your dinner?

o Negotiate the extras. They will cost more later on, so if you want a room for the bride and groom included with the hotel reception for no additional charge or a hospitality suite for out-of-towners, now's the time to speak up! If you don't ask, you definitely won't get it.

o If you're having the wedding at home or in a private hall, request that each vendor supply a certificate of insurance and show that they also have workers' compensation. If an employee of the caterer falls on the carpet in your living room, you could be liable!

o Plan for bad weather. Murphy's Law usually applies during most major events when you want everything to go right. Be flexible and prepared for emergencies with a plan B (tent, umbrellas, etc.) ready to be implemented.

o "The biggest problem I see," says Sue Winner, "is brides' choosing locations that are not accustomed to doing weddings. You don't want them to learn on your big day."

o Avoid putting too many people in a space. Limit the number of guests to make sure there's no problem.

## Invitation and Ceremony Etiquette

o There are many situations where etiquette becomes a concern when addressing an invitation. What's correct for a wedding might differ from what's correct for another occasion. In the case of addressing a wedding invitation, if both guests are doctors you should put The Doctors Patricia and Daniel Smith. Ladies are always first.

o However, if the female is the doctor and the husband is not, the invitation should read Dr. Joan Simpson on the first line and Mr. Michael Simpson on the next line.

o If a couple is not married but living together, list the lady first and the next name on a separate line.

o If the bride's or groom's parents are divorced, the mother of the bride sits in the first row with her immediate family (grandparents only). The father then is in the second row with his family. Everyone else follows in the third row and beyond.

o If someone single you invited to the wedding responds that he or she would like to bring a guest or escort, Sue Winner advises that the bride should call and say, "We had to cut our list to those people who are most dear to us. I wish I could include your guest, but I simply cannot. I hope you will join us anyway."

## The Music

○ Meet with your musicians and discuss the music that will be played at your wedding. You should specify the first song, the song you'll dance to, and the last song, as well as the style of music and special requests. It's crucial to make a list of these selections to ensure they are played.

○ When you hire your musicians, inquire if they are the exact ones that will be playing at your wedding. Sometimes the musicians you hear are not the regulars. Also, decide if you want a female vocalist, a male vocalist, or both. Will the manager be there? Who will be your contact if something goes wrong or you have a question? Get the facts!

○ Discuss what the band members will wear at your wedding. Make sure you know how they plan to dress and they know your expectations.

○ Bands take and need breaks, and it's important to know how often and when. Discuss with your band how often they break and request that music be played during the breaks so the room is not silent. When and how they break should be outlined in the musicians' contract.

○ Talk to your bandleader about the music selections and make sure you like their version of your requested songs, especially the first dance. Their rendition of "The Wedding Song" might be rhythm and blues instead of traditional.

○ Discuss with your band if they need a place to break. Consider that you are running a show and must know where they go when they take five. Sometimes your wedding facility has a special room the band can go to.

○ Make sure your band is prepared to play until the end of the wedding. They might contract for four hours and anything additional is overtime. Contract your band for the longest period possible and plan for an hour over the time you think it will end. Many weddings go on longer than the bride and groom could ever imagine, and you don't want to have to pay more.

## Tips for Hiring a Florist

○ Make sure when you hire a florist you see an example of what you will be getting. Make sure there are no substitutions or changes; should substitutions be necessary, add to your contract that they are with your approval. At my wedding, the white lilies that we ordered didn't come in and the florist substituted gardenias, which have a very strong smell. Guess who was allergic to the flowers?

○ Discuss with the florist what will happen to the centerpieces when the evening is over. Does the florist take back the containers? Make sure you know what's yours to reuse or keep.

○ Make sure your florist can transfer your flowers from the religious institution to the reception. Someone has to be ready to load the flowers; they don't magically appear.

○ Valentine's Day is one of the most expensive times for flowers. The price could be 40 percent higher. People also don't want to work on Christmas!

○ If your numbers shrink, call the florist. You'll save money on the centerpieces.

## Tips for Hiring a Videographer and Photographer

○ Make sure you meet with each and record in writing the exact photographs you want to have taken at what time. Some photographers suggest taking pictures ahead while others prefer candid shots. Get the scoop.

○ Decide if you want to have videos of the wedding ceremony as well as the party. Most brides and grooms want to have the wedding ceremony taped and put at the beginning of the entire videotape. Make sure your videographer includes this and any editing you might want after seeing the tape.

○ Photographers charge by the event or by the hour. Compare the difference!

○ Make sure if you are talking about a package deal; make sure you know how much the additional photographs are.

○ Discuss with your videographer and photographer how much they charge for reprints, enlargements, or duplicates. Negotiate that fee up front for the best savings.

○ Ask your photographer if he will be the one doing your wedding. Make sure you get the specific person you expect, rather than a substitute. Put in your contract that he will be the one doing the photography.

○ Find out how long the photographer and videographer keep your wedding negatives and film on file. This is a good thing to know, lest you be disappointed later on when you call for a picture that was lost or damaged. Some photographers keep an archive for many years. Find out what your professional does. You'll be glad you did!

### Gifts

○ Register for all kinds of things in all price ranges, but each item in only one place. Otherwise, you'll get duplicates that have to be returned. You can spread things around, but keep your good dishes at one store. Always register for open stock—things that are available year-round and for many years. Avoid seasonal patterns that are available only at certain times of the year.

○ According to Sue Winner, "The best way to keep your gifts organized is to have them removed as quickly as possible from the ceremony and put in a safe place. If possible, advise guests to send your gifts ahead of time."

○ Traditionally speaking, guests have up to one year to give a wedding gift. The bride has up to thirty days to write a thank-you note. The bride's note should arrive before the person receives the charge card bill! A smart bride will condition herself. Write the note, and have it addressed and ready to go.

○ Check out uGive.com, a fabulous Web site that will save you time and help you give a perfect gift to newlyweds or anyone on any occasion. This unique and innovative gift-giving site instantly helps you create a GiftFolio™ that contains up to twenty individual gift items hand-selected for your gift recipient in the budget of your choice. On the date you select, they will send your GiftFolio™ by E-mail to your recipient along with your personal message. The best part of the gift is that they get to choose what they want from the twenty gifts. Brides and grooms will love this gift, since they get to choose!

o Check out my book *The Perfect Present: The Ultimate Gift Guide for Every Occasion* (Crown, 1998), for a comprehensive resource filled with great suggestions for year-round gift giving and wedding gifts that the bride and groom will forever treasure. Click on www.RobynSpizman.com for more information.

## Just in Case!

o According to Barbara Roos, owner of Event Design Group, a total production and event company that has designed and produced thousands of outstanding weddings and events, "Whether an event is big or small, there should be no surprises. How to avoid surprises is by being well prepared. For example, if the weather is hot, perishable flowers should be delivered in a cool truck. This means the truck's refrigerated and the climate can be controlled. What if the truck breaks down? What if the weather is bad? Our motto is 'no excuses . . . no matter what!' "

o Roos adds, "Always have a backup plan. For example, if it's April, the weather is getting warmer and you are giving a tent party, make sure you have a generator so you can cool or heat the interior of the tent. Or if it's raining, you must make sure the guests aren't going to get wet. If a bus is delivering the guests, can it pull under the overhang? Check to see if a full-size bus can actually pull up the driveway or if you need minibuses. Or, will the props fit in the elevators or do you need to hire ten more strong men to carry them up the steps? Check and double-check every detail, and know your backup plan just in case."

o "Another important rule of thumb is to be prepared for the what-ifs. When you rent linens for an event, always order a few extra in case of a spill or a problem. Also, make sure that the vendors or company you use have proper insurance coverage, and that there is enough electrical power for your event. From the coffeepots to the band, you'd be surprised how much additional electricity some events require. By hiring a professional with a successful track record, you can avoid these and many other problems that can pop up," recommends Roos.

o Check out the advantages of wedding insurance. While this

insurance doesn't cover the bride or groom's getting cold feet, it just might be a good idea, since it will pay for nonrefundable costs that are incurred in the event that things are postponed or canceled owing to illness, weather, or loss and damage.

○ If you are having a wedding at home, make sure your plumbing can handle the number of people you have invited. From the toilet to the disposal, you wouldn't want a backup of any kind on this occasion.

○ Check out trip-cancellation insurance. This is a very good idea, especially if your trip is nonrefundable. Before you purchase it, check with your tour company or travel agent and see what options you have in the event of an emergency. Purchase this insurance from a different company than the one you bought your travel from and get the facts.

# What-Ifs

We've all certainly experienced the "What-ifs . . ." You know, as in, "What if I had only read the contract?" "What if I hadn't listened to that too-good-to-be-true pitch on the phone?" or "What if I had known about tax extensions? I wouldn't be in this jam now." We've all found ourselves in unfortunate positions at one time or another, and somehow we survive.

That's why I've created several hypothetical "what-ifs . . ." This chapter will help you get the jump on a bad situation before it's too late. While I couldn't possibly get to every imaginable "what-if" on earth, the following are some common ones. If you can avoid problems in advance—or know how to effectively deal with them when they occur—you can eliminate some sleepless nights or hefty fines. Life is complicated and full of surprises, after all, so we can never be too savvy, too prepared, or too smart!

### What if I'm Stopped by a Policeman?

It's best to get out of the car and stand where your hands can be seen, recommends Atlanta criminal defense attorney Bruce H. Morris of Finestone & Morris. That way you appear to be nonthreatening and cooperative. He adds that while you always want to comply with a police officer's request—providing proof of insurance and a driver's license, for instance—you don't have to say anything or answer any questions at that time. And you don't have to give permission for your car to be searched.

For some passengers, particularly women, who are concerned about reports about criminals posing as police officers, it's advisable to ask to see an officer's badge (through the window) before getting out of the car. Since most police officers also carry a portable radio, ask to hear their connection with a police switchboard. If you have a car phone, you can also call the police station to verify a badge number.

What if they want to arrest me and impound my car? You need to comply with the police officer's requests, but again, you don't need to answer any questions at this time. When you arrive at the station, you can call your attorney to be present, if you feel that's necessary. As for your car, there is another option if you have a passenger in the car with a valid driver's license. Often police will allow that driver to take your car home, which avoids the hassle and expense of an impounded car, notes Morris.

### What If My House Is Broken Into?

Morris recommends, "Don't enter the house yourself. Go next door to call the police, and let them be the first ones to enter and search the house." If the intruder entered with a spare or stolen key, you'll want to call a locksmith immediately. Incidentally, experienced burglars know to check the usual hiding places for keys (under planters, on top of a door frame), so you're better off leaving a spare key with a neighbor.

### What If I Want to Shop Online? How Can I Be Sure It's Safe?

Most "virtual stores" (commercial opportunities you find on the Internet) are as safe to buy from as any other medium, counsels Edward Smith, president of the Atlanta Better Business Bureau. If you're unsure about the reliability of an establishment, however, get its physical (not Internet) address and phone number and check it out with the Better Business Bureau in that city—or with other consumer agencies. In fact, sometimes you can order merchandise you see on the Internet by phone, as in a catalog. If you become a virtual store's "member" or some such procedure that requires you to create a password, don't choose obvious ones such as your birthday or telephone number, and never tell anyone your password. Beware having to give out your Social Security number or banking info; that's a red flag to rethink the transaction. "Common sense should always prevail," Smith adds.

### What If I Need to Return the Item?

Your rights should be the same as with any other catalog purchase, particularly if done by credit card (always preferable to cash). Always read the fine print about returns before undertaking any online purchase.

### What If I Want to Reduce My Banking Fees?

Shop around, since banking fees can vary widely. You might find that a smaller, neighborhood bank has more competitive rates, for instance. Ask if your rates might be reduced if you use direct deposit, or if you keep a minimum amount in checking or savings. Also determine how many checks you use per month, and if that can be reduced with programs that automatically deduct expenses (such as mortgages) from your checking each month. Some people have discovered online banking, which allows people to do business with virtually any bank in the system, to find the best banking deals possible. Don't feel that you have to do all your banking transactions at one company, by the way; you can have checking at one place, savings at another, and certificates of deposit at yet another place.

### What If My Checking Account Statement Charges Me for All Sorts of Miscellaneous Fees?

Find an account that doesn't charge monthly per-check fees, usually because you keep a minimum balance in checking or savings accounts. (Make sure you don't go below that balance.) If you're charged by transaction, make fewer withdrawals of larger amounts rather than a lot of small withdrawals. Learn the rules regarding teller use and ATM use. Most banks don't charge for their own ATMs (automated teller machines), but there is a surcharge—or two—for using another bank's. Some banks charge for a real-life teller, which can be avoided if you can use the bank's ATM machine.

### What If the Bank Issues Me a Debit Card?

Remember that a debit card is not a credit card or charge card, but functions essentially like writing a check, so that the transaction amount is deducted from your account within a day or so. Some banks charge a fee per debit card use, so weigh the advantages of checks versus a debit card in that regard. Consider setting up a checking overdraft account that will cover any accidental "bounced" checks or debit card transactions. As with any banking matter, keep good records, and remember that you might not have the same protection, legally, with a debit card purchase as you would buying with a credit card. What if I'm sent a credit card I didn't apply for? Am I legally obligated to send it back or pay for any charges I didn't make? You're not responsible for any credit cards sent to you in the mail that you didn't apply for. Any cards you receive in the mail that you don't want should be cut in half, and keep the information in your records. It's often a good idea to call or write the bank and tell them you are *not* interested in the credit card and to remove your name from their list.

### What If My Checks Are Stolen?

As soon as possible, get a police report on the crime and notify your bank to close your account. You'll need a notarized letter from your bank indicating that your checks were stolen to help you deal with potential creditors. The nightmare is that someone could steal your checks from your mailbox, for instance, and incur a lot of debt on your checking account, and you might not even know it, especially if you didn't know when your checks were mailed to you. (A way to avoid this hassle is to always order checks through your bank and request that they be delivered to your bank, rather than your home.) Don't let your bank or check-printing company reissue checks with the same numbers as the stolen ones; that could cause a lot of potential headaches. Do keep a file of all correspondence regarding the stolen checks so that you can always document your innocence in the matter. It's always a good idea to contact credit bureaus to let them know not to blemish your credit record with any bounced checks from the crime.

### What If I Can't File My Income Taxes by April 15?

You can get an extension by filing Form 4868 before April 15. By filing this, you may avoid a late filing penalty, but you will be charged interest on any taxes owed to the IRS but not paid by April 15. Therefore, some people estimate the money owed and attach a check to their extension form. For more information, you can visit the IRS's Web site at www.irs.gov.

### What If I Can't Pay All My Taxes That Are Owed?

You can ask to make monthly installment payments, but be warned that you'll be charged interest and a late-payment fee. Consider alternative sources to obtain the tax money owed, such as borrowing from others or a bank.

### What If Someone Calls with a Great Deal on Some Real Estate or Gold?

Always be skeptical of unsolicited calls to sell you anything, particularly high-ticket items such as rare coins, precious metals, stocks, and land deals. (Similarly, beware of too-good-to-be-true deals that pop up on the Internet.) You shouldn't be pressured to buy anything on the spot. Before buying anything over the phone, ask for written materials, such as a prospectus, and review with your attorney or financial consultant. Check out companies soliciting your investment with state organizations and your local Better Business Bureau. Beware of companies that involve your calling 900 numbers (although there are other telephone prefixes that also charge), where you might be charged by the minute for so-called information on real estate or job listings.

### What If I'm Told I've Won a Sweepstakes?

Listen carefully (or read carefully) the details involved with the so-called prizes. A good rule of thumb is never to pay more than the cost of a stamp for any sweepstakes. Legitimate sweepstakes operate with a "no purchase necessary" motto. Frequently with telemarketing scams, the caller says you've "won" a week's vacation in Florida, but later asks for your credit card to cover some incidental "costs" involved in the trip. Never provide a credit card or checking account number to such a caller. When in doubt, ask for information on the company to check with the proper authorities. You can also ask to be placed on the company's "do not call" list.

### What If I'm Approached to Contribute Money to a Charity on the Phone?

Ask if the charity is licensed by the appropriate state and local authorities, and if a donation is considered tax deductible. It's always best to get the caller and charity identified and first call the Better Business Bureau or other such organization for verification that they're legitimate. Don't be pressured into immediate decisions. Ask them to mail you information (if you're planning a sizable donation, ask for their annual report from the previous year). Always pay charitable donations by check, not cash, and never make the check out to an individual rather than the charity.

### What If My Business Gets a Call from an Office-Supply Company Offering a Once-in-a-Lifetime Price on Toner?

This is just one common office scam, whereby an accomplice calls ahead of time and finds out the office equipment in a particular business, then later calls back wanting to "restock" the items, often with faulty merchandise. Another common office marketing scam is to receive a phony invoice, such as for a renewal on a business ad. The Federal Trade Commission estimates that telemarketing artists take in billions of dollars each year. To avoid such ripoffs, train your employees to double-check all sales calls that come in—and never give out information about office equipment over the phone. Insist on written purchase orders, and make sure one person (and one person only) in the company makes purchasing decisions. Don't accept any COD shipments, and never deal with a new company until it has been checked out first.

### What If I Want to Work from Home—Should I Trust One of the Companies Advertised in the Back of Magazines?

The Better Business Bureau ranks work-at-home opportunities as one of their highest categories for inquiries. The problem is that many of the companies that advertise "work from home, no experience necessary" require an up-front fee for "materials," which is often a photocopied list of instructions on how to set up a business, with no materials to speak of included. Few respondents ever earn the amounts of income that are promised, so be cautious about spending money on such enterprises. For more information, visit the Better Business Bureau Web site at www.bbb.org.

### What If My House Is Struck by Lightning or Damaged by a Tornado?

Check your homeowner's insurance policy, because most cover such damage. Report your loss to your agent as soon as possible after the damage. They will file a claim and get an insurance adjuster assigned, who may or may not come look at the damage, depending on the severity. Be wary of hiring someone too soon to fix any damage. Charlatans prey on accident victims, unfortunately, so it's wise to check references and get quotes from others.

### What If I Lock Myself Out of the House?

Go to a neighbor's house and call a nearby locksmith. They should be able to come out within an hour or so and open the door for you, but be warned: You must have proof that you live there or they won't help you. Often, if you have proof inside, you can arrange for services anyway.

### What If I Join a Health Club and Then Decide the Next Day That I've Made a Mistake?

Every state is different, advises Edward Smith with the Atlanta Better Business Bureau, but some states may allow you to rescind the contract, so check the fine print of your contract and find out about the law in your area. You may be able to get out of the contract, but owe the health club some money as a penalty. Also, depending on the laws in your state, a health club contract might fall under the category of a "three-day cooling period," which allows consumers a few days' grace period when purchasing some items.

### What If I Receive an E-mail and Don't Know Where It Came From? How Can I Protect Myself from Harmful Computer Viruses?

According to Ed Hansen, public relations manager of MindSpring Internet Services, "Computer viruses are a very real threat, but can be dealt with effectively by remembering a few simple rules. First, the threat isn't always real. Internet users frequently E-mail warnings against opening a particularly titled E-mail that supposedly contains a virus. Most of these have been hoaxes or 'urban legends,' but every computer user should be prepared to deal with a virus because almost every computer will be exposed to one eventually."

Hansen adds, "Most viruses arrive in one of two forms, and always as an 'attached file,' which means the sender has embedded a document, such as a word processor, spreadsheet, database, or graphics file, in the E-mail. Opening the E-mail won't cause any problems, but opening the attached file can. E-mail programs should also be configured *not* to automatically launch attached files. The first kind is a 'macro virus.' Macros are small formatting routines that run within a specific file, which is a good thing, but a virus disguised as a macro can result in a correctable problem. Opening a file containing a macro virus will infect the base program, but most macro viruses won't cause a computer crash or any permanent loss of data. Macro viruses tend to be more mischievous than malevolent.

"The other type of virus is contained in an executable file, which is any file that can run by itself. They are frequently disguised as games or animations, but can be embedded in any program you receive. Again, most are prankish, but others can completely wipe out the contents of your hard drive in a matter of seconds. It is also possible that future viruses may be imbedded into Web pages, using Java or other common scripting languages, but we haven't seen any of these, yet," he adds.

"Understanding computer viruses is only half the battle; the other half is being prepared for them. At MindSpring, we recommend that antivirus software be installed on every computer, and the owner obtain a subscription to allow continuous upgrades as new viruses are identified. Of course, the surest way to avoid computer viruses is to never share information with another computer; don't use the Internet, and don't exchange floppy disks, which is exactly the opposite of what people do in this information age. If you suspect a file might contain a virus, either because you don't know or don't trust where it came from, just delete it without opening it.

"Finally, if you run a file and your computer starts behaving strangely, turn it off, immediately! The keyboard and mouse will be disabled by the virus. Turn off the power switch or power bar. Remember, a virus will override your control of the computer and can wipe out your hard drive before you realize what is happening. The best way to stop it in its tracks is to kill the electricity to the computer. Don't start the computer again, but call a computer service professional and ask their advice. You'll need to be able to describe how the computer was behaving and what action you took."

# Working at Home

Every year, more of us are opting to drop out of the corporate culture to try our hand at running a home-based business. The dream is to use inherent talents and abilities to build an enterprise that bears the stamp of our unique personality. Working at home presents many challenges, including added responsibility, long hours, and the need to be versatile and self-motivated. It also can present new difficulties filled with potential isolation, cash flow problems, and a balancing act with clients.

These realities are offset by a newfound freedom and flexibility, as well as increased job satisfaction and the opportunity for financial success. The prospect of making the leap from the relative security of a job to an uncertain future can, however, be daunting, so keep reading for loads of helpful tips on how to get started.

## Setting Up

o A separate room is an ideal location for a home office, because by having a dedicated office space you create a physical and mental transition from home to work. Try to select a room that is large enough to accommodate a small meeting or conference area where you can meet with clients. A ground-floor room eliminates the problem of customers' having to walk through your personal space.

o Make sure you have adequate ventilation in the space you have chosen to serve as an office. Also check for noise volume, number of electrical outlets, and lighting.

o Search used–office furniture stores for good prices on chairs and desks. A hollow-core door on top of two filing cabinets makes an inexpensive, yet practical, desk.

o The ideal computer desk should be 26 inches high, so that

your elbows remain at right angles when you type. If your desk is higher, you can modify it by adding a keyboard tray that slides out underneath.

○ Your desk chair is probably the single most important piece of furniture you will buy. It should have arms, a cushioned seat, a five-pronged rolling wheel base, an adjustable back, and a height adjustment. A badly designed chair will cut your productivity and could cause backache.

○ A lightweight telephone headset is a good idea if you spend a lot of time on the telephone and computer. It prevents cramping in neck and shoulders and leaves your hands free to type.

○ When buying a computer, choose your software first. By doing this you won't make the mistake of purchasing a computer that can't run the software you need or that can't run it fast enough.

○ Plenty of good light, both natural and artificial, will cut down on eyestrain. Full-spectrum bulbs are a good choice for overhead lights because they produce a warm pink glow that is easy on the eyes. Use incandescent or halogen bulbs for more specific task lighting.

○ Don't try to save money on printing your own business cards and stationery. A flimsy, badly printed card is an instant tip-off to potential customers that you are just starting out or that quality is not high on your list of priorities.

○ Consider purchasing a conference option on your phone line. This useful feature allows you to connect independent callers for a conference call.

## Protecting Yourself

According to Christopher Owens, CIC, and Jeff McCart, CPCU, ARM, of McCart Insurance and Risk Management, you need to take the following basic steps to ensure that your business is adequately protected:

○ Arrange for workers' compensation coverage, which is mandatory in most states. A few states require that you have this coverage only if you have three or more employees, but we recommend that you secure coverage even with one employee because you, as the employer, can be held responsible for medical expenses incurred as a result of a workplace accident.

o Don't assume that your homeowner's insurance will cover your home-based business. Most homeowner's policies exclude any business activities in the home, from both a property and a liability standpoint. Some policies do provide limited coverage, but they usually do not include business liability. Talk to your insurance agent about special small-business packages called BOPs (business owner policies), which cover equipment, fixtures and fittings, contents, loss of income, valuable papers, and premises liability (which covers accidents that may occur while your clients come and go from your office). Also, a nonowned auto liability endorsement can be added to your business policy to protect you from claims resulting from a car accident where an employee causes injury to another party while on company time.

o A simple way to protect your equipment from power surges, lightning strikes, or power outages is to buy a surge protector for every outlet in your home office. Available at hardware or office supply stores everywhere, these simple attachments are an inexpensive way to practice risk management.

o Minimize the chance of losing valuable data by doing a daily, weekly, and monthly backup and storing the monthly backups in a safety-deposit box off the premises. In the event of a tornado, fire, or other disaster, preparation will drastically limit your loss of data.

o At what point should you take out a policy to insure your business? Our experts recommend that you purchase a policy from day one if you are deriving income from your business, as opposed to being a telecommuter, who simply works at home.

## Where to Get Free Business Advice

o Small-business development centers. These centers are partly funded by the Small Business Administration and are usually located in local community colleges. They offer courses as well as individual counseling on topics such as researching your market, drafting a business plan, and obtaining financing. To find an SBDC in your area, call the SBA hot line (1-800-8ASK-SBA).

o Business schools. You may be able to get your local university or college to work with you on formulating a business plan. You get the benefit of their expertise while they gain experience with real-life business problems.

o National Business Incubation Association. This organization offers locations where small businesses can rent inexpensive space while they are getting up and running. The centers also offer training and networking opportunities. Most of the incubators will provide the same services for home-based businesses. To find a center near you, send an SASE to NBIA, 20 Circle Drive, Suite 190, Athens, OH 45701, or access their Web site at www.nbia.org.

o Association for Enterprise Opportunity. This nonprofit organization provides low-cost training and counseling to economically disadvantaged small-business owners. For more information, call 312-357-0177.

## Financial Matters

o Discuss your financial needs with your banker after you decide how much money you will need to get up and running. Banks typically like to make large loans for short periods of time, like two to five years, so that they can earn the most interest with the least risk.

o Banks are becoming more open to making loans to home-based businesses, but still want some form of collateral, such as real estate or equipment, to back up the loan.

o Give yourself the best chance of getting a loan by drawing up a well-researched business plan. Be prepared to explain your marketing and advertising plan and how you will manage cash flow.

o If you're a homeowner with sufficient equity in your home, you can take out a home equity loan for up to 80 percent of the value of your house. Interest rates are reasonable because your home is viewed as reliable collateral. An added bonus is that the interest is tax deductible on amounts up to $100,000.

○ The Small Business Administration has a variety of loan programs for small businesses. The SBA does not actually lend the money; it simply guarantees your loan at the bank. Most banks are approved SBA lenders. The SBA's rules for lending are a little less stringent than a bank's, and they are generally more willing to take risks and to grant long-term loans without a second form of collateral.

○ To qualify for an SBA loan, you must operate for profit, not be a speculative business, and you must meet the definition of "small" for your field.

○ Microloans, up to $25,000, are also available from the SBA. These loans are administered by local nonprofit organizations rather than banks and can be for amounts as small as $450.

○ If you are interested in knowing which banks are the most active SBA lenders, call your local SBA office and ask for a Preferred and Certified Lenders List.

○ For more information on SBA loans, call the Small Business Answer Desk at 1-800-827-5722 or access their Web site at www.sba.gov.

○ To have the best chance of getting a loan from the SBA, you will have to show your commitment by contributing 30 to 35 percent of your own cash to the start-up capital for your new business. A well-thought-out and logical business plan will also strengthen your position.

○ If you need less than $100,000, the SBA offers what are called LowDoc (low documentation) loans, which are fairly easy to apply for. The application form is just one page and approval takes from two to three days. Most loans are granted for 5.5 years, but you can apply for a longer loan. If the loan is for over seven years, the maximum interest the bank can charge is prime plus 2.25 percent.

## Marketing

○ Build a list of potential customers. A good source of prospects is a conference directory that contains names and addresses of all attendees. If your potential customers belong to a certain professional organization, you might want to pay for a copy of the organization's mailing list. Be sure to test the list first by buying a small number of names and checking your response rate.

○ Social and business networking is an important marketing tool. People like to do business with people they know and like.

○ Constantly reevaluate your business by being aware of what's working or not, as the case may be. Be ready to make changes.

○ Promote yourself. Every week, ask yourself what you have done to reach new customers. Make it a rule to do one new thing each week to increase your visibility. For example, offer your advice to the media with an educational slant and watch the free publicity you can attract. Check out your neighborhood newspapers and local magazines for additional advertising opportunities. Some publications will consider printing your ad for a reduced fee if they have leftover ad space to use up. Have a small ad prepared and discuss the opportunity with a variety of publications that would reach your target market.

○ Time is becoming the most important commodity for today's consumer. Find a way to save your customers time and you have something valuable to offer. Use that as a unique selling proposition to promote your services.

○ Once you have a list, you can use direct mail as one way of reaching prospects. The most personal-looking envelopes are the ones least likely to end up in the trash, so use a stamp rather than a postage meter and choose a computer font that looks like handwriting.

○ Offer discounts, coupons, or other incentives for repeat business. Ask for referrals.

○ Share direct mail, a trade-show booth, or promotion with other noncompeting, complementary businesses.

○ Use technology to build your business and to free up more time to devote to those all-important customer relationships.

392 • Bet You Didn't Know

○ Trade shows are a good place to display goods, give out samples, and meet suppliers, manufacturers, retailers, and end users.

○ Classified ads offer the advantage of being relatively inexpensive and targeting customers who are already looking for products or services. Use active verbs in your ad and play up exclusivity and the benefits you are offering that your competitors don't.

○ Marketing also involves creating a positive perception of your company. Sponsoring community events, participating in your chamber of commerce, and giving free seminars are all ways of getting free publicity and generating a favorable image.

○ To get free publicity in newspapers or magazines, you must have an angle on your product or service that makes it newsworthy or interesting to readers. If you find it difficult to come up with a new trend in your industry, you could try offering your services as a consultant or expert in your field.

○ Regular direct mail can become pricey, with envelopes, letters, and first-class postage. You can cut costs by opting for a postcard campaign instead, or combine efforts with another noncompetitive but related business. Postcards are inexpensive to print and the postage is one-third that of a no. 10 envelope. With no folding, stuffing, or sealing involved, you'll also save time.

○ You may be able to get a free or reduced-price ad placed in a publication by offering to write an article on your area of expertise. This is a very effective way to promote your business, because an article is perceived as being objective, plus you have the added benefit of double exposure.

## Working Parents

○ Set boundaries and enforce them and try not to allow "work" time to run into "family" time. Let both your family and clients know what your working hours are. By doing this, you will have accomplished the first step toward avoiding resentful children and frustrated clients.

○ Kids want your undivided attention at least some of the time. Many work-at-home parents have found that kids will respect your need for quiet and privacy if you give them predictable quality time at intervals throughout the day. This technique buys a lot more uninterrupted work time than just ignoring your child's pleas for attention.

○ Make kids feel like a part of your business by allowing them to help in whatever way they can. Stuffing and sealing envelopes is one example. For younger kids, keep a basket of "office stuff" for them to play with. Pads, pencils, markers, paper clips, and old checkbooks make the child feel part of your world. Add new items occasionally to keep them interested. A great boredom buster is to save simple tasks you know they'll enjoy doing in a special file for a rainy day. From sorting to categorizing or searching for items in newspaper clippings, there are many things children can do that will make them feel special.

○ Involve the kids in planning what they can expect during your workweek. Even younger kids enjoy being a part of what's going on and will like coming up with solutions to problems as well as consequences for those who fail to follow the rules! And don't forget that kids can bring up problems, too. Be flexible and creative in approaching solutions, and don't be discouraged if you have to make changes every couple of weeks to run things more smoothly.

○ A dedicated business line (and fax line) will help to separate work from family life. This also sets a professional tone by ensuring that the phone will not be answered by your spouse or kids. Another tip to avoid younger kids' answering the phone: Make sure the business phone is out of reach.

○ Use a portable phone so you can remove yourself from any commotion when answering a call.

○ Purchase a phone with a mute button so that when your client is talking he can't hear Junior screaming in the background.

○ Treat kids who are helping with small office chores with the same respect you would any employee. Praise them for a job well done and don't yell when they make a mistake. Make them feel that they're an important part of your business enterprise.

## Resources

### Web Sites

There are many Web sites that cater to home-based businesses, and these are excellent sources of information, articles, and newsletters.

○ Working Solo Inc. is a company that develops seminars, tapes, and books on working at home. Their Web site features a newsletter with articles on marketing, finances, and other related topics. Access at www.workingsolo.com.

○ American Home Business Association provides an array of services as well as a newsletter. Visit their site at www.homebusiness.com.

○ For parents, there is the Work at Home Parent's Cafe (www.workathomeparents.com), which has message boards, chat rooms, and an E-mail discussion list.

○ Dads can check out the At-Home Dad Web site (www.athomedad.com) that features plenty of resources plus a newsletter.

○ www.staples.com is an excellent source for all businesses. Save time and money with three ways to shop: in-store, catalog, and online.

### Books

○ *Launching Your Home-Based Business: How to Successfully Plan, Finance, and Grow Your New Venture,* by David H. Bangs Jr. and Andi Axman (Dearborn Trade, 1997). This book offers detailed information for setting up your new business. The authors provide dozens of worksheets to help determine start-up costs, identify customers, and develop a marketing plan.

○ *On Your Own: A Guide to Working Happily, Productively & Successfully from Home,* by Lionel L. Fisher (Prentice-Hall, 1994). While most business books deal with the nuts and bolts of setting up a business, this one targets the mental and motivational problems of going solo.

○ *Home But Not Alone: The Parent's Work-at-Home Parents' Handbook,* by Katherine Murray (Jist Works, 1997). A comprehensive reference for parents with numerous questionnaires, planning guides, and helpful tips.

o *Getting Business to Come to You: A Complete Do-It-Yourself Guide to Attracting All the Business You Can Enjoy*, by Paul and Sarah Edwards and Laura Clampitt Douglas (Putnam Publishing Group, 1998). Filled with excellent ideas for advertising, marketing, and publicity.

# Index

If you have a Bet You Didn't Know tip and would like to submit it for forthcoming books, please send your name, address, telephone number, and suggestion to:

Bet You Didn't Know
PMB 118
6300 Powers Ferry Road, Suite 600
Atlanta, GA 30339

## ABOUT THE AUTHOR

ROBYN FREEDMAN SPIZMAN is a consumer advocate with more than sixteen years of experience, having reported as "The Super Shopper" on NBC affiliate WXIA-TV's *Noonday*. Well-known nationally for her consumer advice, Spizman's lively, high-energy segments have been featured extensively in the media, including appearances on *CNN Headline News*, *Talk Back Live*, *The Discovery Channel*, CNBC, *CNN FN*, *Roseanne*, *Good Day New York*, *ABC Radio Network*, and *National Public Radio*. A contributing writer for *Woman's Day*, Spizman is also an accomplished speaker and author, with over sixty award-winning educational, parenting, and self-help publications to her credit. She lives in Atlanta, Georgia, with her husband and two children.

www.robynspizman.com